To George,
Sincerely,
Tom   Jan 22, 2003

RAPE ᴏꜰ MIDIAN:

ᴛʜᴇ SAGA ᴏꜰ ZIPPORAH ᴀɴᴅ MOSES

BY

THOMAS B. HARGRAVE JR.

ISBN: 0-7596-5366-6 (Dust Jacket)
ISBN: 0-7596-5365-8 (Soft Cover)

Library of Congress Control No. 2001118635

This book is printed on acid free paper.

Printed in the United States of America
Bloomington, IN

1stBooks – rev. 02/15/02

DEDICATION

For my daughters,
ANNA
whose probing questions
inspired me to write this novel.
And for
BARBARA and TERRI
with love.

I hope you enjoy the book as much as I do.

Anna Hargrove

ACKNOWLEDGMENTS

When I began work on my historical novel, *The Rape of Midian: The Saga of Zipporah and Moses,* several of my friends and relatives asked what motivated me to write a story about the exodus from the perspective of Zipporah, the Midianite wife of Moses. The simple answer is that from my research I discovered in the Bible's books of Exodus and Numbers traces of an interfaith love story that was compromised by political intrigue, murder, and ethnic conflicts. It concerned me that for more than two thousand years the vast majority of religious leaders have effectively censored the story by their silence. I felt the time had come to bring this story out of the closet and, as the African-American spiritual says, "go tell it on the mountain."

I am grateful for friends who helped me with their editing, critical questions and comments. Among them I want to thank:

My daughter, Anna, whose inquiring mind and probing questions inspired me to write this novel. My wife, Meredith, who supported me during the three years it took to write the many drafts, and my sister, Yolande Adelson, for her probing comments, suggestions and encouragement.

The members of the writer's mentor group who, for a period of two years, gave me valued comments on each chapter: Carol Hoover, Eric Glick, Eugene Jeffers, Hope Marindin, and Chris Lambert.

Special thanks to Leslie Murray Rollins, my graphic artist and editor; Christine Toll and Ellen Alderton, my proofreaders, and volunteers, Kathleen Shahan and Jerry Jellison who gave me valuable feedback.

I am grateful to All Souls Church, Unitarian, which has nourished and encouraged my spiritual quest for truth for the past quarter century. I am also indebted to Robert Funk and the Fellows of the Westar Institute, who have devoted themselves to the cause of Biblical literacy.

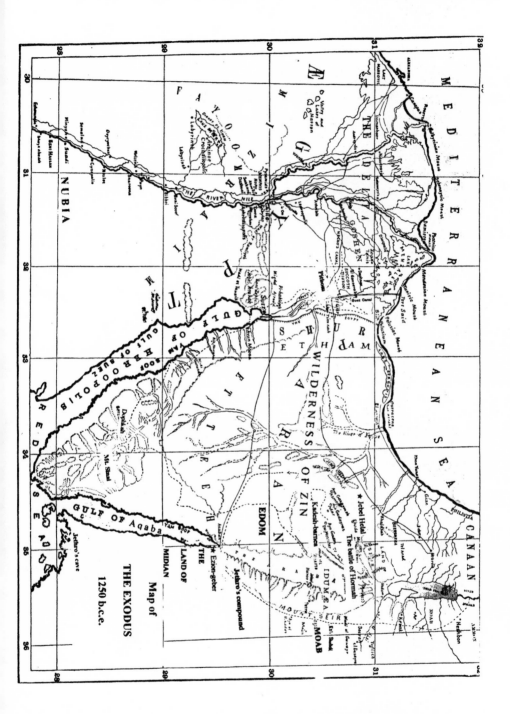

Map of
THE EXODUS
1250 b.c.e.

CHAPTER 1

I am the nostrils of the Lord of the winds who maketh all men to live on the day when the eye of the sun becometh full of Annu. Sin is an abomination to me.

Egyptian Book of the Dead

The young woman shaded her eyes as she looked for signs of movement among the craggy boulders that lined the mountain trail. She motioned to her companion, a girl of ten years, not to follow her to a jagged sandstone boulder three times her size. After placing her staff on the ground, she pulled herself to the first ledge, then strained and clawed her way to the top of its flat surface. She stood and balanced herself, trying to see through the blowing sand as she searched the rocky terrain for a missing sheep. A gust of wind obscured her vision, making it difficult to maintain her balance. The grains of windswept sand that struck her face felt like hundreds of needle pricks.

"Do you see her?" the girl shouted.

"No. She can't be that far. She was at the head of the flock when we entered the pass," the young woman replied.

"Do you think the laughing dogs got her?" the girl asked, looking in both directions.

"Not the ones we chased away yesterday. They would never follow us through this mountain." She carefully lowered herself and jumped to the path. Retrieving her staff, she walked over to the girl and placed both hands on her shoulders.

"Timna, go to our sisters. Tell them to take the flock to the wells. The young lambs must have water before nightfall. I will remain here and search for Ga," she said, pointing to the trail they had been traveling since noon.

"I want to stay with you, Zipporah. Father told us to always stay in pairs. What if you get hurt?"

"Do not worry for me. I have traveled this trail often," Zipporah said, rubbing her eye to remove a speck of dust. "Ga may be having her lamb at this very moment. Both will die of thirst if they are lost among these rocks."

"No matter. Please let me stay with you."

"Do as I say. Ga has been my friend for nine seasons. I could never leave her alone."

The sisters covered their heads with their shawls as a sudden gust of wind forced them backwards several steps. They knelt with their backs to the wind,

1

and wrapped their arms around their black ankle-length skirts until the wind subsided.

"We should stay together," Timna protested, shaking dust from her skirt. "Our father cares for you more than Ga."

"If I were a son, I might believe it," Zipporah said, laughing. "His sheep are his greatest treasure, no matter what he says to the congregation."

"Not so," Timna replied. "Our father loves our God above all else. And he cares for us more than any of his sheep and goats."

"You are the youngest daughter," Zipporah said, pulling Timna's braid. "He spoils you."

As the winds slowed, Zipporah wiped the powdery dust from her face and brushed the sand from her skirt.

"Go now, before dark comes. Our sisters need you to help guide the flock. If these winds grow worse, others in the flock may wander off. If I do not return before dark, tell Leah I will come at first light," Zipporah said. Timna's eyes watered as Zipporah placed dried dates and figs in her leather pouch.

"Eat this when you get hungry, little sister. Now don't worry. I will be fine. Remember the wolf I killed last spring?" Zipporah said, holding up her bow and shaking it.

Timna hugged Zipporah then ran down the trail. Zipporah watched until she was out of sight, then she gathered her staff, bow, and the water pouch with its narrow gourd neck and goat's bladder lining. She backtracked along the trail, calling at the top of her voice, "Ga, call to me. Where are you?"

All she heard was her echo off the jagged mountains, returning its broken refrain, "Ga, call- me, me- you." At this elevation the night air, with its gale-force wind, would soon blow bitter cold. She needed to find shelter. She spied a narrow slit along the outcropping of rocks. The opening was low to the ground, with just enough room for her to slide under. Experience had taught her that other creatures might be using it. She knelt and stared into the opening. In the dim light she could see it was no deeper than the length of her staff. She removed her six-inch knife from the leather sheath she carried on her side. With her left hand, she stuck the shepherd's staff into the opening and raked along the stone floor ever so carefully. Her hand tightened on the knife as she felt something strike the staff. When she probed again, a snake with colors like the reddish sandstone cliffs, lunged at her face from the shallow opening. With equal swiftness, her blade found its mark, leaving the snake's head in the dust. She watched as its body twisted and thrashed about wildly, as though searching for its missing part. Zipporah gingerly picked up the head of the snake, looked into its eyes and whispered, "I pray you a safe journey to the spirit world." Reverently, she placed the head and severed body under a pile of stones, then returned and made one final inspection with her staff. Seeing a fracture in the stone, she slid her knife along the tenebrous crannies, causing several scorpions to exit, only to be squashed under the heel of her sandal.

Satisfied it was safe to enter, she crawled under the ledge, placed her knapsack under her head and waited for the winds to cease. As she rested, she remembered the night her father took her to the stall. She was eleven when her father blessed the sheep that was in labor and told her that he would place its newborn lamb in her care. She had watched the ewe struggle to push the lamb from her swollen belly, and stared in wonder as it freed itself from the afterbirth and shortly stood on wobbly legs. The ewe had nuzzled her lamb and made a soft grunting noise that sounded to Zipporah like "Ga." She told her sisters that the lamb's name was Ga because that is what her mother called it. As the lamb grew to maturity, a special bond developed between them.

At eighteen, and the oldest of seven daughters, Zipporah was proud that only one of her father's sheep had been lost during her watch. It was killed by a pack of hyenas, which were rarely seen in the land of Midian.

As she rested, the wind moaned as though it somehow shared her loss. In that period between awareness and sleep a familiar sound caused her to bolt up, striking her head on the stone ceiling. She crawled to the edge of the outcropping and listened. Above the whispering wind, the cry of a sheep in distress sounded a second time. Yet, it was more than a cry. It was the sound of grieving.

"Ga, I'm here!" Zipporah shouted in both directions, as she stumbled from the shelter and sought the path. "Call to me." She paused and listened, but heard only the wind whistling like twin flutes between two boulders. It was useless to search in the darkness, so she sat on the ground, crossed her legs and waited for the first rays of light. Time seemed to drag. She cursed the darkness, certain it was the longest night of her life.

Light finally reflected on the tips of the rugged mountain peaks. Able to see the trail, she placed her bow and quiver on her back, tightened her belt around her waist, and with staff in hand, retraced her steps. When she heard a bleating sound she knew it was Ga. The sound came from a narrow opening between two waist-high boulders.

"Ga, call to me," she shouted. She pumped her fist when she heard the familiar braying response close by. Squeezing through the boulders, she found herself in a clearing a few yards from the face of the stone mountain. Her smile quickly faded when she saw Ga resting beside the bloodied body of her lamb. She knelt, only to discover it had been split open, its heart and liver removed. No animal had done so diabolical an act. The ewe seemed unaware of Zipporah's presence and did not greet her with the nuzzling and short snorts that signaled the bond between them. It stared at the rock formation behind her.

Zipporah sprang to her feet, thinking some wild beast was nearby. Instead, she saw a man dressed in a goatskin vest and trousers, seated on a flat rock watching her. His coarse black hair formed a crown above his head. His beard and the front of his vest were caked with dried blood, and his face was thickly coated with dust. Before he could speak, Zipporah flung her water pouch aside, balanced her staff, and lunged at him. He threw himself to one side, avoiding the thrust. To her surprise she found herself pinned to his chest. When she kneed his crotch, he gasped. Free of his grip, she crouched in a battle stance and circled him looking for an opening. He backed away, clearly impressed by her strength and cunning.

"I beg you, put your staff away. I will not harm you." He spoke in a gentle voice.

"You killed my lamb," Zipporah screamed. The pounding of her heart energized her. She twirled the staff, faking moves to throw him off balance. He stood still and made no further effort to defend himself.

"Allow me to pay you," the stranger said. He cautiously reached in his pocket, removed a leather pouch and poured its contents into his hand. Not taking his eyes off her, he tossed a gold coin at her feet. "For days I have traveled in the desert of the Sinai. The blood and heart of your lamb have restored my strength."

Zipporah glanced down quickly, but made no effort to retrieve the coin and kept her distance. She stood erect and took several deep breaths. It surprised her that the rage she felt moments before was subsiding. Something in his speech and bearing forced her to lower her guard, despite herself. He seemed so taciturn and downcast and the sadness in his eyes fascinated her.

"Where do you come from?" she asked.

"Egypt. I journey to the land of Midian, for I am no longer welcome in my own land," he said quietly.

"You are in Midian," Zipporah said, observing that he was tall, thickset and square-shouldered.

To her surprise, his eyes watered. He dropped to his knees and raised his arms toward the sun, its rays highlighting the tears that flowed into his blood-caked beard.

"I have been delivered from a hostile land," he cried. "Ra has guided me safely to the land of my kinsmen."

"You speak to Ra, the sun god. Here in Midian we worship Elohim," Zipporah said, being familiar with the religions of many traders. "Who are you?"

He licked his parched lips, staring at her water pouch. She saw in his eyes a plea for understanding.

"I thirst." He stumbled to a shaded rock and motioned for her to put her staff aside. Sensing no threat from him, she picked up her water pouch and threw it at his feet. He drank deeply then smiled.

"Pray, rest here beside me," he said, patting the flat stone.

4

"Why should I trust you? You may be one of the tribesmen from the Wilderness of Zin who enters our land to steal sheep."

"Would such tribesmen have offered to pay for your lamb in gold?" he asked.

She felt him staring at her with a lingering appraisal that was all too familiar. The shepherd boys who once raced with her across her father's meadows, now gawked when they saw her coming. Her oval face, with its smooth, unblemished complexion and dark brooding eyes, fascinated them. Her mother had warned her that the time for games with boys was over, for she now was a woman.

"I don't want your money," she said, kicking the coin back with the toe of her sandal.

"Tell me your name," he asked.

She adjusted the sheath that held an ivory-handled knife, then stared at him proudly. "I am Zipporah, first daughter of Jethro, the Priest of Midian. And by what name shall I call you?"

He paused to clear his dehydrated throat. "Moses," he replied.

CHAPTER 2

Now the priest of Midian had seven daughters and they came and
drew water, and filled the troughs to water their father's flocks.
                                                    Exodus 2:16

Timna emerged from the mountain pass and felt relieved when she saw her
father's sheep grazing on sparse vegetation. With late afternoon shadows
covering the meadow, she feared her sisters might have moved the flock to the
wells at Ezon. The water table in their families' wells was extremely low, and
their father had instructed his seven daughters to take the flock to the Ezon oasis
on the other side of a mountain. It meant driving the sixty sheep over a mountain
pass, a trip they usually made twice a year during the dry season. Timna waved
her scarf when she saw her sisters, Leah and Reuel, cooking over an open fire.

"Leah, what's cooking?" she shouted. Adjusting her backpack, she raced
across the rocky field, carefully avoiding the thorny scrub bushes in her path.
Leah, the older of the two, pushed the locks of her black hair to one side and
waved. She placed her cooking utensil on a rock and hurried to meet Timna. An
excited black and white sheep dog raced past her and leapt into Timna's arms,
knocking her down.

"Tro, go to the sheep," Leah shouted, pulling Timna to her feet. "Where is
Zipporah?"

"She's searching for Ga. I did not want to leave without her, but she made
me come. She said if she is not here soon, we should take the sheep to the
wells."

"Ah, she should have come with you. Are you hungry?"

"Yes, I finished the last of my fruit and I'm starving."

"You are just in time, little sister," Leah said. She cupped her hands to her
mouth and called to a third sister who was guarding the flock. "Anah, Timna's
back. Come eat with us."

Timna sniffed the air. "Something smells good."

"Reuel killed two hares with her sling," Leah said. "I found a beehive and
smoked the bees away. We have honey for our bread, but I have two stings to
show for it." Leah held up her swollen left hand.

"I passed through a swarm of locusts and stuffed my pouch full of them. If
the ashes are still hot, we can roast them." Timna opened her pouch and
removed a handful of suffocated insects.

"The ashes are hot," Leah replied, quickening their pace to the stone fire pit. "I'm glad Zipporah sent you ahead. We need your help if we are to reach the wells before dark."

"I'm worried about Zipporah. Shouldn't we wait for her?"

"Worried about Zipporah? By all the gods, no. I pity the man or beast that crosses her path. If she doesn't arrive soon, we must move the sheep to the wells ourselves."

Timna went to the fire pit and dumped the locusts into the hot ashes. Reuel removed the baked rabbits from a stake and placed them on a flat stone to cool. Timna stood on tiptoe, searching the area. "Where are Naomi and Katurah?" she asked, as she plaited her hair into twin braids.

"They culled out the sheep with lambs and have gone ahead. Here, eat quickly for the afternoon shadows are growing longer." Reuel handed Timna a slice of cheese and a well-charred rabbit's thigh. Timna used a stick to scrape the locusts from the ashes. She kept a lookout for Zipporah while portioning out the roasted insects.

After they finished eating, Timna put out the fire and covered the pit with dirt and stones. All knew the danger a brush fire would pose if winds began gusting suddenly. With the pit secured, she joined her sisters who had positioned themselves around the flock. An older sheep named Rab took the lead, being familiar with the trail. The sisters whistled and shouted as the flock moved toward the oasis. Tro barked excitedly, nipping at the heels of stragglers.

It was dusk when they reached the oasis. Leah stopped abruptly when she saw sheep standing nearby, nursing their lambs. The cries of the thirsty sheep could be heard protesting the lack of water.

"Something is wrong. Why aren't the sheep at the water troughs?" Leah said, shading her eyes as she searched the area.

"Naomi, Katurah, we've come," Reuel shouted. They saw movement in a cluster of tall grass. From the evening shadows a young woman sprinted in their direction. The sisters stood petrified when they heard their seventeen-year-old sister, Katurah, screaming hysterically. Leah ran to meet her.

"What's the matter?" Leah shouted, shaking her sister to calm her. "Where is Naomi?"

Katurah bent over, taking several deep breaths and pointed in the direction of the wells. "Amalekites," she said, gasping for breath. "Amalekite shepherds came upon us while we were watering the sheep. They drove the sheep away and kept Naomi. One of them grabbed me but I bit his hand and got away. He chased me, but I escaped and hid in the tall grass."

"Amalekites!" Leah hissed. "How many?"

"Six, maybe seven. They brought goats and sheep with them and their leader is an ugly, one-eyed man. What shall we do?"

"Amalekites from the wilderness of Zin! Their wells must have run dry for them to come this far into our country," Leah cried.

"If only Zipporah were here," Timna cried, wiping her tears on the sleeve of her blouse.

"You are the second daughter, Katurah," Leah said, handing her the pouch containing the last of their water. "You must decide for us."

"We must drive the sheep back to the pass and wait for Zipporah."

"But what about Naomi?" Leah asked. "We can't leave her."

"What chance do we have against seven armed men?" Katurah replied. "Quick, gather what sheep we can and let us make haste from here. Zipporah will know what to do." The sisters raced to head off the flock. Four men emerged form the shadows of the trees and headed in their direction. A fifth man followed behind them, dragging their screaming sister by her hair.

"It's Naomi. Look what he's doing to her!" Timna screamed. Leah tried to restrain her.

A muscular man, with graying black hair and a patch over his left eye, raised his staff and shouted in the Amalikite language, "Infidels, come no further with your flock." His sleeveless wool jacket was open, exposing the course black hair that covered his chest.

With their father's compound located on a major trade route, the girls understood his language. Katurah stood her ground and answered in his tongue, "You are in the land of Midian. Our fathers have watered their flocks here for thousands of seasons." Bolstered by her courage, the sisters held their ground. The man laughed and shoved Naomi toward them. The terrified girl stumbled as she fell into Katurah's arms. Anah and Leah tried to help her to her feet, only to realize she had fainted. They were horrified when they saw blood soaking through her skirt.

Katurah stared at the shepherds in disbelief. "What have you done?" she screamed. The men burst into raucous laughter.

"Bring your sheep to these wells and we will take all of you, especially the young one," the one-eyed man roared, licking his lips. He placed his hand between his thighs and lifted his crotch. Timna panicked and tried to run away. Leah grabbed her arm and held her.

"Our father is Jethro, Priest of all Midian. He will call on our God to strike you dead for defiling our sister," Katurah shouted. The man's single eye widened, for he had heard of this priest and the power of his God. He stepped toward Katurah and slapped her face, knocking her to the ground. Tro growled and sprang forth, sinking his teeth into the attacker's leg. The one-eyed man cursed as an arrow pierced the dog's heart. The sisters screamed when he kicked its body aside and congratulated his son who had shot it.

8

He grabbed Katurah up by her hair, pulling her closer. "I feel heat rising in me again," he said, running his finger along her lips. She recoiled from the stench of his breath. "Be gone or I take you also." He released her and motioned for his followers to return to the well.

Anah knelt beside Katurah and wiped blood from her lip. Naomi regained consciousness and began shaking uncontrollably, her head on Leah's lap. Timna sat beside Tro trying to remove the arrow.

"Tro is dead, Timna. Help us with Naomi," Katurah cried, exasperated.

"We can't leave Tro here," Timna sobbed as she tried to lift the dog's body.

"You must help us keep the sheep moving. I do not want any weeping from you, do you hear?" Katurah shouted, pulling Timna to her feet. "We must stay strong."

"Can you walk?" Leah asked Naomi, looking nervously over her shoulder. She half expected the men to return for all of them.

Naomi held her hand over her abdomen. "I'll try," she said. Leah placed a shawl around her shoulders. "If they come for us, I will kill myself before I-" She covered her face with her hands and wept.

Until that moment the sisters had been too frightened to fully comprehend the horror their sister had endured. None of them had ever known a man. They gathered around Naomi and helped her to her feet. Reuel and Katurah armed their bows and stood guard as Timna, Leah and Anah gathered the scattered flock.

The sisters were silent as the return trek to the mountain pass began. Only the pitiful cries of the sheep filled the night air.

CHAPTER 3

And the shepherds drove them away, but Moses stood up and helped them, and watered their flock.

Exodus 2:17

Zipporah rested in the shadow of a boulder, keeping a suspicious eye on this stranger who called himself Moses. As he ate the dried figs she shared with him she studied his facial features. He had washed layers of dust and blood from his face with some of the water she had offered him. His face and arms were cracked and peeling due to the long exposure to the desert sun. She sensed by the alertness in his brooding eyes that he was intelligent, and his patrician features were not unattractive. In fact, if he bathed and trimmed his beard he might even be handsome. Still apprehensive, she kept her distance.

He cleared his throat and said, "I am grateful for the water and food you offered me."

"By your tongue I know you are well educated," Zipporah said, carefully retrieving her water pouch and placing it over her shoulder. What was it about this man that cooled her anger so quickly?

"My education has not served me well," Moses said, brushing at flies attracted to the moisture on his face. "Do many of my fellow citizens travel this way?"

"Yes, the main caravan route passes through our valley. Many Egyptians and other travelers stop at my father's compound to rest and water their flocks. Tell me about yourself. Why do you travel alone in the desert? Traveling with a caravan is difficult enough." Zipporah asked. She removed her scarf and shook her head, allowing her wavy black hair to fall loose to her waist. By the way he stared at her she knew he found her attractive.

"Forgive me for staring at you. I am weary from my days in the sun. The desert has sapped my strength," Moses said. "I slew your lamb and yet you put aside your anger and shared your water and food. Because of your kindness, my strength will soon return."

"But why did you leave your country?"

"I seek sanctuary, but do not ask why just now. But if I may ask, why are you here alone?"

"I go to join my sisters. We are taking our father's flock to the oasis at Ezon, as our wells are low." Zipporah gave a guarded smile. "You look like you have not eaten a good meal or bathed for months. Come help us water our flock and I will take you to our father's house to rest." She saw his eyes light up at the prospect of food.

"If you are ready to trust me, I will gladly assist you," Moses said smiling. He placed his few clothes and hunting knife into his leather backpack. "Be assured I will rest at your home for only a short time, for I will not be a burden on your father's house."

"I trust you," she said, surprised by her own words. "And you will not be a burden."

When Moses stood erect and came closer, Zipporah noticed he was a head taller than she. She watched as he walked over to Ga and tried to pat her. The sheep lowered its head and backed away.

"I'm afraid Ga may never forgive you," she said, stroking the sheep's head.

"What matters most is that you overcame your anger," Moses said as he strapped on his backpack. "In time, this sheep will know that the spirit of her lamb lives in the pastures of the god, Osiris."

Zipporah found comfort in his words. Feeling totally at ease with him, she placed a rope around Ga's neck. As they prepared to leave, the sun's rays cast a pink glow that illuminated the highest peak of the mountain.

Moses dropped to his knees, lifted his arms and began chanting. His deep baritone voice echoed off the cliffs, "Homage to you, in your rising, O Ra, in your crown of beauty. You rise, you shineth and sheddeth light into the darkness. O Ra, who comes from the east at dawn, I greet you." He rose to his feet then turned to Zipporah. "I'm ready now."

"You paid homage to Ra, the sun god," she said quietly. "My father knows the text you recited."

"I received my religious training in the house of a royal family of Egypt. The mother who adopted me taught me to worship and keep Ra's commandments. Only recently did I learn that I am Hebrew by birth. Before I left Egypt, my people gave me scrolls that speak of a God that spoke to our ancestor, Abraham. During my travels I began learning of him for the first time."

"At my father's table you will learn more of him because we worship the same God," Zipporah said proudly. "We call his name, Elohim. The Hebrews call him Yahweh." It dawned on her that if God had guided this stranger to Midian, he must have had a special purpose. Was it accidental that she was the one who found him? Would she be linked to that purpose? Her heart beat rapidly as she strapped her satchel on her back and motioned for Moses to follow her. With Ga behind them, both set a fast pace toward the semi-arid valley.

Where the trail ended, Zipporah felt apprehensive when she saw several sheep searching for vegetation. As they drew nearer the thirsty cries of young lambs could be heard. She spotted Leah running toward them. Her sister stopped abruptly when she saw the stranger.

"Leah, what has happened? The flock should be at the wells by now," Zipporah called out to her.

"Who is this stranger who walks with you?" Leah asked. She reached over her shoulder and removed an arrow from its quiver.

"Put your bow aside, Leah," Zipporah commanded. "He is an Egyptian and he comes to Midian seeking refuge. Now why are you not at the wells?"

"How do you know you can trust him?" Leah screamed. Her shouting brought the sisters, Katurah and Anah, running to her side. They cautiously approached Zipporah, all keeping their distance. Timna crawled from under a scrub bush and ran to join them.

"Sisters, we have nothing to fear from him. This man has come to help us. Now why are you not at the wells?" Zipporah shouted as she rushed to Leah and snatched the bow from her hand.

"Amalekite shepherds came and drove us away, but not before they took Naomi and defiled her, all of them," Leah screamed, her voice quivering. "There were seven. They warned us not to return."

"That evil man beat Katurah and they killed our Tro," Timna screamed.

"Where is Naomi?" Zipporah rose on her tiptoes to see beyond them.

"She rests in the shade of that bush," Timna cried, pointing to a cluster of bushes where they had hidden her. "Poor Tro. We did not have time to bury him."

Zipporah pushed Timna aside. "Forget that dog," she shouted frantically. "Take me to our sister."

"I'm glad you've come," Leah said. "We feared those men would return and take all of us."

Moses stepped forward and stood among them. "Listen to me all of you. Gather your sheep and return to the wells now." The sisters were stunned by his commanding voice.

Zipporah saw the rage in his eyes. With hope restored, she ordered the sisters to gather the flock. Timna led her to the bush where Naomi was lying.

When Naomi saw her, she turned away whimpering, "Let me die here."

Zipporah lifted her into a sitting position, cradling her in her arms. "Do not speak of dying, sister. Can you return to the well?"

"There is no life in me," she whispered. "The pain is great."

Moses knelt beside her. When he placed his hand on her shoulder she cringed and turned away. "He won't harm you, Naomi," Zipporah said, squeezing her hand. "He's here to help us."

Reluctantly, Naomi glanced at Moses. "Don't let them hurt me again."

"No one will hurt you." While holding her trembling hand Moses realized she was in no condition to make the return trip to the well. "Zipporah, two of

12

your sisters should remain with her until we return." When Zipporah hesitated, he placed his hand on her shoulder. "We will return for her, trust me."

The sisters huddled around Naomi and agreed that Timna and Leah should stay with her. Moses was impressed that the sisters accepted his suggestion without protest.

Moses and Zipporah walked briskly at the head of the flock and within the hour the grove of palm trees at the Ezon oasis came into view.

Zipporah glanced at Moses but his eyes were fixed on movement among the trees. His pace quickened with every step, forcing her to run to keep up with him. The flock, now crazed by thirst, began stampeding toward the wells. Their incessant cries echoed as they neared the water troughs.

Two shepherds sitting in the grove jumped to their feet and shouted for the others. The one-eyed man appeared holding a staff and a hunting knife.

Moses and Zipporah stood beside each other as the man and his band of six followers approached. Moses raised his staff. "I demand you leave this place now," he thundered.

The one-eyed man glanced over his shoulder, then slapped his chest. "I am Amalek, Prince of the Amalekites. Leave before I cut your throat and feed you to the hyenas," he growled.

"These wells are in the land of Midian. I give you fair warning. Leave now," Moses said, balancing his staff with both hands.

Zipporah doubted the one-eyed man would back down. She tightened her fingers on the taut string of her bow. Katurah stood to one side and carefully armed her sling with a stone.

"By your tongue I know you are Egyptian. Why is this your affair?" Amalek asked with growing agitation.

"I am Moses of the tribe of Levi. These women are descendants of Abraham. We are cousins," Moses said, advancing toward Amalek.

Amalek frowned, knowing this was now a matter of honor. "These women will not save you, Hebrew." Amalek nodded, signaling for his shepherds to fan out on both sides of Moses. He grunted and lunged at Moses. The sisters screamed as Moses blocked the thrust, throwing Amalek off balance. Moses jammed the edge of his staff into Amalek's groin causing him to howl and double over in pain. The swiftness of the blow left the Amalekites stunned as they fell back from their stricken leader.

Zipporah drew her bow and aimed the arrow at Amalek' s chest, but Moses pushed it aside and shouted, "Do him no harm. Guard him." He turned toward the shepherds. They cowered in fear as Moses walked toward them twirling his staff. The oldest son of Amalek stepped forward to challenge Moses only to be struck across the face as their staffs clashed.

"In the name of the gods, spare our father," the son shouted, falling to his knees before Moses. A stone from Katurah's sling struck the man's temple, knocking him unconscious.

"You pig," Katurah screamed. "You defiled my sister." When Moses waved the sisters back, Anah grabbed Katurah's arms and restrained her as she struggled to place another stone in her sling.

Zipporah jabbed the tip of her arrow at the black patch covering Amalek's left eye. He howled as she shouted, "Swine, be grateful I did not deprive you of your sight."

In the confusion the shepherds turned and ran, leaving Amalek kneeling in the dust holding his groin. Zipporah raked the point of her arrow across his cheek, drawing blood, then spat in his face. Amalek's single eye blazed as he stared at her. She knew he would never forget his humiliation at the hands of a woman. Moses rushed to her side and dragged Amalek to his feet.

"I should have killed him. He does not deserve to live," Zipporah screamed.

"There is a time to kill, and a time to refrain from killing." Moses pushed her weapon aside. "It is far better that we release him, but not before he pays for his crime."

"Pays! No amount can pay for what he has done to our sister."

Moses dragged Amalek by his goat-lined collar to the shade of a palm tree and forced him to kneel before Zipporah. "Son of swine, I spare your life," Moses said, slapping Amalek's face with the back of his hand. "Take your men and leave. If you return, I will slay you with these hands and leave your head for the vultures to feast upon. For abusing the woman, you will leave your spices and your sheep as tribute to the House of Jethro."

Amalek struggled to his feet, still holding his groin. Zipporah saw the humiliation in his eyes but it did not satisfy her. Had Amalek won, he and his men would have killed Moses slowly, then raped and made slaves of them.

Prince Amalek told his men to unload the spices from his camel. The sisters watched with admiration as Moses ordered the shepherds to mount their camels and head into the wilderness.

With the danger over, Moses returned to the bush where Naomi was resting. Timna and Leah hugged him when they learned that Amalek and his men had gone. He picked Naomi up and carried her back to the oasis. After resting, he helped the sisters draw water and fill the troughs, and watched as the sheep pushed and shoved to quench their thirst. Finally able to relax, Moses studied the striking similarities in all the sisters' features. Zipporah, Leah and Katurah possessed high cheeks, narrow eyes and full lips. Their smooth facial skin was the color of ground cinnamon, highlighted by thick black waist-length hair. All three had slender, hard, muscular bodies and firm upright breasts. He saw the family resemblance in Reuel and Anah; however, their faces were pocked with scars resulting from childhood diseases. Both were short waisted, but were not excessively stout. Moses guessed they loved eating. This was confirmed when Zipporah heated a pot of lamb stew left by the shepherds. Both sisters filled their bowls three times. Timna was thin, like a reed, and still developing. He was certain she would grow tall and beautiful, like Zipporah. Naomi cringed and kept her face covered whenever he approached her. Despite the terror in her eyes, and the cuts and bruises on her face and neck, he knew she was beautiful. He wondered how she, or any woman, could recover from such a brutal assault.

Zipporah portioned out food for herself and Moses. They sat together and ate with their fingers. In addition to the lamb stew, she shared with him the hard-boiled pigeon eggs and cheese she had brought with her.

"I'm glad you came to our land, Moses. I believe our God guided you to us in our time of trouble."

"I am pleased you held your anger and did not take Amalek's life. You could have started a war." Moses rose and searched the horizon, concerned the Amalekites might return in force. He saw only antelopes sprinting across the herbaceous landscape.

"I will never forget the face of that evil man as long as I live," Zipporah said as her jaw tightened.

"And I'm sure he will never forget you," Moses said with concern. "That's all the more reason that we make haste and leave this place. The Amalekites worship a god who loves blood sacrifices. I must make sure it is not ours."

CHAPTER 4

And when they came to their father they said, "An Egyptian delivered us out of the hands of the shepherd..."

Exodus 2:19

Zipporah and her sisters gathered around Naomi to give her privacy. Leah placed packs of spun wool between Naomi's thighs with the hope it would stop the bleeding. They soon realized she had lost too much blood to make the return trip on foot.

When Moses returned from rounding up the flock, Zipporah took him aside and whispered, "My sister will not be able to make the trip home. She cannot be moved. We must remain here another day."

"No. We have to leave now," Moses said, adamantly. He shielded his eyes and searched the distant landscape. "Amalek may return with more of his kind. Your king must be told that Amalekites have entered your country and violated your sister."

"Our sister may die if she tries to walk to our home. She is in no condition to travel," Zipporah said anxiously. "You should know we have no king in Midian. Our confederation is made up of seven tribes. The tribal chiefs choose one of their own who guides their council. He is Chief Kaleb of the tribe of Kish."

"I was told by my people that Ezion-geber is your capital. I was on the way there when I lost my way. How far is the capital from your father's compound?"

"A half day on horseback."

"Then your chiefs must be told what has happened here. I will make a yoke from cedar wood," Moses said, pointing to several timbers that had been discarded. "Take reeds from the pond and fashion two slings, one for your sister and another for an equal weight of Amalek's spices that I will take to your father. The remaining spices, divide among your sisters."

"I know your strength has returned, but some parts of the mountain trail are steep. Can you carry our sister and the spices that far?"

"Stay beside me and I will have all the strength I need," Moses said smiling. He reached out and touched her cheek.

The feel of his callused hand left Zipporah momentarily speechless. She went to the pond to gather reeds. As she sat weaving them, she felt excited, her face flushed and warm. It was no longer from fear or the sun's rays. When she finished, Leah helped her lift Naomi into the sling while their sisters spread out and drove the flock from the grove. They watched in astonishment as Moses tied the slings to the yoke and placed it upon his muscular shoulders. When he lifted it with ease, they cheered.

"When we reach the highest point on the mountain trail, you will see our valley," Zipporah said. "It is called the Valley of Arad. Unlike this place, our vineyards and pastures are lush with grasses, especially after the spring rains. This year the rains have come late."

"I have had enough of dry places," Moses replied. "I will welcome any green space that is like the rich lands along the Nile delta."

By late afternoon they reached the mountain's summit. From their vantage point Moses could see the green valley and beyond, the glittering waters of the Gulf of Aqaba. Moses released the weight of the yoke from his shoulders and paused to rest. Zipporah pointed out her father's grove of olive and date trees. The fertile fields were a stark contrast to the arid valley they had left behind.

Beyond the valley was a barren mountain range. "Do you see the highest peak on those mountains? When I was a child, our people told us that the god who lives there cursed the land we just left. He was angry because someone cut down one of his sacred trees and used it for firewood. That's why no crops grow there and it is worthless for grazing sheep and goats."

"Do you believe such a tale?"

"I don't know. Any god who would curse land and make it a desert has to be insane."

"You speak with courage, Zipporah." Moses said, hoping he would have an opportunity to know her better. In all his years he had never met a woman who was so beautiful and courageous.

During the rest period, Zipporah sensed her sisters' growing tension. Timna came to her and whispered, "Our sisters are upset with you. They say they are doing all the work of keeping the sheep moving while you talk to the Egyptian."

"Do I count you among them?" Zipporah responded, playfully pulling Timna's braid.

"No, but we need your help with the stragglers. Others might get lost. Our sheep obey you."

Zipporah took Timna's hand and walked to where her sisters rested. "I see by your silence you are displeased with me. The Egyptian carries a heavy load. I walk beside him to give comfort to Naomi."

"It is the Egyptian you give comfort to, not our sister," Leah replied sarcastically.

"Zipporah, you are needed in the rear, not up front with that stranger," Katurah said assertively.

Zipporah reflected for several moments. "You speak truthfully, Katurah. As second sister you may walk beside him and comfort Naomi. I will go to the rear and keep watch for strays."

Surprised by her response, the sisters all nodded their approval. When Zipporah returned to Moses and told him of the change in plans, he could not conceal his disappointment.

"Until now the weight I carry has seemed light," Moses whispered. He glanced at Katurah and took a deep breath. "If I grow weary, will you return?" he asked.

Jethro, the Priest of Midian, sat before his altar quietly meditating. His wife entered his mud brick temple, shouting, "Our daughters have returned. A terrible thing has happened." Jethro removed his prayer shawl and rushed outside. Timna ran to him and dropped to her knees sobbing. When he pulled her to his feet and held her, she blurted out the horrors they had endured.

"Calm yourself little daughter. What is this you speak? You say Naomi was harmed and a stranger from Egypt saved all of you from Amalekite shepherds?" Jethro asked with alarm.

"It is true, father. The Amalekites did unspeakable things to Naomi, all of them."

Jethro's sunburned face grew flushed as he looked skyward. "Elohim, God of our father, Abraham, why has this happened," he cried, rubbing his hands frantically.

He took his wife's hand and hurried toward Katurah when he saw her approaching at the head of the flock. "Of what madness does your sister speak?"

"She speaks the truth, father. Amalekites attacked us. You must send a message to the Council of Chiefs telling them what has happened."

"Where is this stranger of whom your sister speaks?"

"He walks with Zipporah at the rear of the flock. He is an Egyptian and his name is Moses. I fear he tired of my incessant talking," Katurah said sadly. "He has carried our sister in a yoke upon his shoulders all the way here."

"Daughter, go in haste and tell the stranger he is welcome in my house. Do not let him depart without my blessing," Jethro shouted.

As the sheep moved into the pasture, each of the daughters rushed to their father and kissed his hand. Zipporah arrived, walking beside Moses with Naomi balanced in the sling. Naomi lowered her head and was unable to look into her father's eyes. Moses and Zipporah removed her from the sling and placed her on a bench at the entrance of the temple door.

Moses stretched his tired back and looked around him. Near the temple were four tents that housed Jethro's family. In front of the building were five cedar trees that shaded a well and a stone fire pit.

"Father, this is Moses, the Egyptian. He fought Amalek, prince of the Amalekites, and punished him for the terrible things he and his sons did to our sister," Zipporah said. Jethro embraced Naomi and kissed her.

"All will be well, my child," Jethro said. Using the edge of his prayer shawl, he wiped the tears from Naomi's cheeks. She turned her head and looked to her mother. Jethro rose to his feet and placed his hand on Moses' shoulder.

"My daughters have told me all that happened. You are welcome into my home, Moses," Jethro said, as Ruth and Zipporah took Naomi to the tent of the sisters. "I am grateful that you delivered my daughters from the devil worshiping Amalekites and that our God protected you."

"The Amalekites have paid for their crimes. Your flock has increased and I bring you rare spices from the land of Kush," Moses said.

"Sheep and spices will never compensate for the shame my daughter has endured," Jethro said, wiping his eyes. "There is no price above virtue."

"I have heard the name Jethro spoken in Egypt. Your wisdom is known among my people."

"Come to my temple, as humble as it is." Jethro took Moses' arm and led him into the simple structure that he and his brothers had built. When Moses' eyes adjusted to the dim light, he saw a simple stone altar in the center of the room. Jethro motioned for Moses to sit on the wool carpet that covered the floor. Zipporah brought them a bowl of dates, cheese and cups of wine.

"I go to prepare a place for Moses," Zipporah said.

"Speak of yourself, Moses. Why do you journey to the land of Midian?" Jethro asked.

"I grew to manhood in the home of a royal family of Egypt. The woman I thought was a servant turned out to be my birth mother. From her I learned I am Hebrew and a member of the House of Levi."

"Why did you leave?"

"I saw a taskmaster abusing one of my people. I became angry and killed him. My people advised me to seek sanctuary in Midian, knowing of our ties to your people."

"Yours is a remarkable story," Jethro said, shaking his head in disbelief. "So you are of the tribe of Levi. Your ancestors left the land of Canaan during the great famine four centuries ago. We know how his brothers sold Joseph, the grandson of Abraham, and when he was taken into Egypt, how he interpreted the dreams of Pharaoh and saved the land during the seven years of famine that followed. His fame is sung throughout the lands of Midian, Edom, Moab and Ammon."

"I know of Edom, Moab and Ammon by name only."

"You must learn of them. Like Midian, the people of these nations have sprung from the seed of Terah, the father of Abraham and his brother, Haran. Abraham and his nephew, Lot, are the fathers of these four nations."

"I hope to learn more about the God of Abraham," Moses said, taking a deep breath. "Ra, and his son, Osiris, are the gods I worship and love above all other gods."

"Pray, stay with us and I will teach you. As you see, I have no sons to tend my sheep, only daughters. For years I prayed to the Lord to bless my wife's womb with sons, but she bore six daughters. I continued to pray for a son. Finally her womb conceived for the final time, and lo, I was blessed with my seventh daughter, Timna," Jethro said smiling. "But she is a special comfort to me."

"What of your daughter, Zipporah? I have seen her courage in the face of danger. She is a remarkable woman, and has the heart of a lion," Moses said boldly. "Her beauty is as a rose in the gardens at Lisht, and she is fair to look upon."

Jethro's eyes brightened as he reached across the table and patted Moses' hand. "Moses, I like you. I am certain the God of our fathers has brought you here for a divine purpose. If you have no place to rest your head, work for me as shepherd of my flock," he said, restraining his smile. "If you prove a faithful servant, other rewards will follow." Jethro held his breath, fearing he might have tipped his hand too soon.

"I gladly accept your offer and your hospitality."

"The Lord be praised. We will speak more after you rest. I will ask Zipporah to show you to the tent I reserve for my special guests. I leave you now, for I must go comfort Naomi."

Zipporah and Leah sat milking goats near their mother, Ruth. Ruth smiled ruefully at her daughters' whispering and giggling.

"Tell me, daughters. Is all this talk about the Egyptian you call Moses?" Ruth asked. "Although he now works for your father, I must warn you both. Do not trust men who are not of our faith."

"But mother, Moses is Hebrew. His people are our cousins," Zipporah protested. "In the weeks he has been with us he has shown us nothing but respect."

"Ah, cousins indeed. Many travelers come through our village. I heard him speak. He is a high born Egyptian who knows not the ways of our people, or the commandments of our God. Your father has been taken in with his smooth tongue. I'm not sure I believe his tale about his being adopted by a royal family of Egypt. It sounds like nonsense to me."

"It's true, mother. While we traveled, he told me how the Egyptians are mistreating his people. He became so angry he killed one of them. That is why he had to leave Egypt in order to save his life."

"He killed in anger?" Ruth asked, horrified by the revelation.

"Yes, and after what happened to us, I understand it. If Moses had not restrained me, I would have killed that pig, Amalek," Zipporah replied, remembering how close she had come to releasing her arrow into his eye that had sight.

"What nonsense is this you speak? You once cried after your father killed a duck," Ruth said throwing up her hands. "What more do you know about this stranger?"

"Not much, but I'm certain our God guided him out of Sinai to me," Zipporah said.

"You mean all of us, don't you?" Leah said sarcastically.

"What's this I am hearing from you two?" Ruth said. "Do I see that snake called jealousy sliding between you? Jealousy has no place in our home."

"There is no jealousy between us, mother," Zipporah said, as she milked the goat, pulling its teats with such rapid strokes the animal brayed in protest.

"Be careful, daughter. At the pace you are going there will be cheese in the goat's udder," Ruth said laughing. She playfully pulled Zipporah's plaits, then kissed the top of her head.

In the cool of the evening Zipporah led Moses to the pasture where Jethro's sheep were grazing. As they reached a vineyard, she paused under a broad Acacia tree.

"This is a fine vineyard. Does all this land belong to your father?" Moses asked.

"My father has five brothers. They live with their families in this valley, each in their own compound. We graze our sheep and goats together and tend the vines of this vineyard. Our compound is known for its fine wines. Many caravan leaders stop here so they can purchase it."

"Your valley has been blessed by the gods." Moses reached down, scooped up a handful of soil and smelled it. "I'm glad your father asked me to be the shepherd of his flock."

"I am pleased that you chose to remain with us," she said shyly.

"It will be lonely tending sheep with no one to keep me company."

She faced him, smiling mischievously. "You will not be lonely. There are the birds and the foxes to keep you company by day. And in the evenings my sisters and I will entertain you."

"And if I wish for only you to entertain me?"

"I would never think of depriving my sisters of your company," she said coyly. "Come, there is much to see." She took his hand and led him across the pasture to a grove of date trees. They approached one tree that was twice the height of Jethro's temple. She pointed to the clusters of dates hanging from stems below the branches.

"When I sailed with my family down the Nile river, I saw farmers climbing trees to harvest their dates." Moses said, surveying the tree. "Who does the harvesting for your father?"

"My sisters and I do," Zipporah said proudly. "There are twelve trees in this grove,"

"You and your sisters climb these trees?" Moses asked. "I would think your father would not risk so beautiful a neck as yours."

Zipporah smiled as she opened her satchel and removed a hemp rope wrapped with strips of wool cloth. "Just watch me."

Moses followed her to the tree where she looped the rope around its trunk. Standing a body length from the tree, she placed the two ends of the rope around her waist. Facing the tree with her back to him, she said, "Tie the ends tightly." She glanced back and saw the puzzled look on his face as he tied the two ends together. He tested it to make sure it would hold. She kicked off her sandals. With him standing close behind her, she could feel his warm breath on the back of her neck.

"You don't have to prove your skill for my sake," Moses said nervously.

"I do this every season," Zipporah replied, holding the two sides of the looped rope with both hands. After stepping closer to the base of the tree, she tossed the slackened rope up the trunk as high as it would go, then leaned back and held it tightly in place. With ease, she placed her feet against the trunk and scampered up the tree with the grace of a mountain cat. When she passed the point where the loop rested, she quickly flung the rope higher, leaned back and continued climbing. On the fourth toss of the rope, she reached the dates. With her feet firmly planted against the bark and her back resting on the taut rope, she cut the stems with her knife and tossed the fruit to Moses.

Moses shook his head with amazement as she lowered the rope and descended the same way. He held out his arms when she reached the base of the tree. With his arms around her waist, their eyes met momentarily. Her face felt flushed as she removed his hands. After they gathered the fruit and her sandals she turned to him and smiled. "My sisters and I can do the work of men, but we are glad you are the shepherd to our father's flock."

Zipporah held his arm and guided him beyond the grove to a shallow stream. "Sit here beside me," she said. They removed their sandals, sat on the bank and placed their feet in the cool water. "This is my favorite place. When I want to be alone and meditate, I come here."

"I hope some evenings we will meditate together," he said quietly.

"I would like that," she replied smiling, keeping her eyes focused on a single yellow leaf floating in the stream.

CHAPTER 5

Hail to thee, great god, the lord of Right and Truth. I have not committed murder, nor have I wronged the people. I have not committed fornication, nor have I defiled the wife of any man, nor have I defiled my body. I have done no murder.

The Egyptian Book of the Dead

Moses and Timna spent the early mornings guiding the sheep to the pasture. Without a trained dog to assist them, keeping the flock together proved to be exasperating. Timna brought her new dog but it playfully chased the stragglers in all directions. When the dog finally tired, Timna tied it to a tree and helped Moses round up the strays. When the sheep settled down, he sought the shade of an olive tree. Seated against the trunk, he took a scroll from his leather satchel. After removing the outer parchment, he unrolled a papyrus sheet. From his vantage point, he could read and still keep watch over the sheep.

With the dog securely fastened to a hemp rope, Timna walked it among sheep. After an hour she brought the dog to Moses. "I'll have her trained soon. She met all of our sheep today."

"Be patient with her. She's only six months old," Moses said, patting the dog's head. "Have you given her a name?"

"Yes, I've named her Trogee. But I still miss my Tro." Timna settled beside Moses.

"It's a fine name. This dog will soon win your heart."

"Moses, are you happy living with us?" Timna asked.

"Yes, why do you ask?" Moses said, gently restraining the dog that began licking his face.

"Well, Zipporah would be angry if I told you, but I think she likes you."

"And I like her and all of your sisters," Moses said. "I feel like a member of your family."

"You know what I mean," Timna said grinning. Pulling the dog by its rope, she ran back to the meadow and left Moses to his reading.

In the heat of the day Zipporah arrived carrying a basket of dates, hot bread and cheese. Deeply engrossed in his reading, Moses was surprised when her shadow fell across his sheet. He placed the sheet aside, stood up and smiled.

"I'm glad to see you. I have tended your father's flock with only Timna to keep me company. Where have you been for the last two days?" Moses asked.

"My cousins and I went to Ezion-geber to warn our chiefs about the Amalekites." Zipporah said, placing the basket beside him. "I'm surprised father did not tell you. We remained in the capital another day as the rains have finally come. The muddy roads slowed our return."

"Your father should have sent me to protect you."

"Protect me! You should know by now I can protect myself." Zipporah slapped the ivory handle of the curved knife attached to her belt, then sat beside him.

"Are your cousins women also?" Moses said, resisting the temptation to touch her hand.

"No, my uncle Eber has three sons. They live in the next valley." Zipporah leaned over and ran her finger along the figures painted on the sheet. "What are you reading?"

"This scroll is from the Egyptian's Book of Ani. It speaks of man's preparation for the afterlife."

"Speak to me about the Egyptian god you worship?" She could see her request caught Moses by surprise.

Moses spoke softly, having never spoken of his religious beliefs with a woman. "From my youth I have worshiped Ra, the father of all the gods. His spirit resides in the sun. His beloved son and scribe, the gentle Osiris, is also one of my favorite gods. In the sun's rising and setting I feel a special reverence for both of them," Moses said, stretching the papyrus scroll over her lap. "Until recently I knew little of the religion of my own ancestors. Your father is teaching me about the God who spoke to Abraham."

"The Book of Ani?" Zipporah said, quizzically, pointing to the scroll. "What do these figures say?"

"You are a woman. What is written is for the eyes and ears of men only," Moses said.

Zipporah's eyes narrowed. She drew back with her hands on her hips. "I am the first daughter of Jethro, Priest of Midian," she said, lifting her head proudly. "My father was not blessed with sons. He has taught me to read the scrolls he has written. I help him write his text."

"You write and are a scribe unto your father? Can this be so?" Moses asked skeptically.

"It is so. I also speak the tongues of the Canaanites, the Amalekites, and the Jebusites," Zipporah added boastfully. "As a child, my father was proud of my quickness, so he taught me to read our history. Do you know that our people descended from Abraham and his wife, Katurah?"

"I have never heard of Katurah. The Hebrew elders told me Abraham's wife was named Sarah."

"True. Sarah was his first wife. After her death Abraham married Katurah who bore him six sons. The son named Midian is the father of our nation," Zipporah said proudly.

"You speak with the knowledge of men," Moses said, looking into her mysterious eyes. "But you are the most beautiful of women."

Zipporah's face flushed. She pointed to a figure on the papyrus and tried to calm herself. "I know the meaning of only a few Egyptian figures, but not enough to read these words," she said, hoping to divert his attention. "Will you read it to me?" She could not conceal her pleasure as he unrolled more of the scroll and moved closer to her.

"It speaks of the rituals all spirits must perform before the gods after our earthly death. When a man dies, his spirit enters the great Hall of Double Right and Truth. The spirit must be purged of all the sins he has committed while living. Upon entering the hall, he first sings a hymn to Osiris, the god of death."

"Purged of his sins! How so?"

"Forty-three gods sitting in judgment will hear the spirit's confession. The universal God among them is Ra, the Lord of Right and Truth. All of the gods worship him." Moses hesitated, reminding himself that his conversation was with a woman. But what an exceptional woman.

"What sort of confession?" Zipporah asked as she studied the odd collection of figures.

"When the spirit stands before the gods he will say, 'I come unto you, and I bring before you Right and Truth,'" Moses said, gliding his finger across the sheet. "'I have come, my Lord, that I may look upon your beauties. I know you and I know the names of the forty-two gods who dwell with you in this Hall. Cast me not down to your knives of slaughter, and bring not my wickedness into the presence of the god whom you follow. Each day have I labored more than was required of me. I have not committed murder; nor have I ever hired any man to slay on my behalf. I have not stolen from the orchards; nor have I snatched the milk from the mouths of babes. I have not defiled the wife of any man, nor have I polluted myself; nor have I transgressed or caused terror,' And there is much more."

"But what if a man has done all these evil things during his earthly life?"

"Every man has done evil deeds. No one is perfect in the sight of Ra," Moses explained patiently, pointing to the scroll. "After the spirit has made his confession he will say, 'I pray you, declare me right and true in the presence of the universal God whom you follow.' If he is truly repentant, the gods will confer among themselves and his sins will be forgiven. If not, his spirit goes to the place of eternal darkness and is no more."

"I wish all men would abide by such commandments while they are living," Zipporah said, remembering the suffering that Naomi had endured.

"Maybe they will some day," Moses said as he dipped a gourd into a wooden bucket and poured water over his head.

"Of the forty-two gods, do you know all their names?" Zipporah said reflectively

"When I was young, the priest required me to learn them."

"Do you still remember them?"

"I was afraid you would ask," Moses said smiling. "I remember those I love and those I fear."

"Name a few." Zipporah inched closer to him, her face glowing with anticipation.

Her closeness left Moses momentarily speechless. He replied, "There is the god of the flame who comes from Het-Ptah-ka. We see his power in the fires of heaven, followed by the pounding of drums during a storm. He judges those who cause pain and suffering. And there is the god who comes from Pa-Amsu. He judges those who have polluted themselves with strong drink. And the god, Qerer, who comes from Amentet. He judges those who commit fornication and defile the wives of men."

"Qerer probably has more to judge than all others," Zipporah said smiling shyly. "Are any of them goddesses?"

"Yes, the goddess Maat and there is also the beautiful Isis, wife of Osiris."

Zipporah ran her finger along the papyrus, pausing at a figure shaped like a dripping male organ with testicles. "This figure looks like the organ on my father's bull when it is ready to mate," Zipporah said with contrived innocence. "What does it mean?" She was amused by his embarrassed expression.

"*An Nek-a hamt ta*," Moses replied. "The words say 'nor have I defiled the wife of a man.'"

"I did not ask for the whole meaning," Zipporah replied boldly. "The word for a sheep's organ in our language is 'ruk.' But that's not a sheep's organ, is it?"

The shrill shouting of Timna interrupted Moses before he could reply. Both sprang to their feet as Timna ran toward them waving an object over her head.

"Look what I found," Timna said breathlessly, tossing Zipporah a necklace made of shells, bones and bright beads. Zipporah examined the object and handed it to Moses.

"This belongs to an Amalekite. Amalek was wearing one like it when you drove them from the well. Do you think he has returned for his sheep?" Zipporah asked fearfully as Moses scanned the field. "We must warn our relatives. Timna, go to father and tell him of this thing. I will stay with Moses."

Moses picked up his staff and tightened his belt that held his short sword. "Zipporah, it is best you go with your sister. There may be danger."

"I go with you," Zipporah replied defiantly, as she pushed Timna toward the compound. Moses resigned himself, knowing it was useless to argue.

"If you insist, but stay close behind me," he said, placing his hand to her cheek. Their eyes met momentarily, then they raced toward the pasture where

26

they found the sheep grazing peacefully. Moses motioned for Zipporah to move to his left and searched the area.

"Look at this," Zipporah cried, pointing to footprints in the damp soil.

Moses examined the markings. "Three men passed this way. I see by these hoof marks they have taken several of your father's sheep." Moses stood erect and gazed at the nearby foothills. "They are heading toward that mountain."

"If we hurry, we may overtake them," Zipporah said. "I can tell by the marking that one of the sheep is about to deliver her lamb. It will slow them."

"Is there a trail over the mountain?"

"Yes. But we never go up there. Our father forbids us."

"What is he afraid of?" Moses asked as he hesitated a moment, eyeing the mountain.

"Yahweh Sabaoth lives there," Zipporah whispered.

"Yahweh Sabaoth? Is he a man or a god?"

"He is a god, but not just any god," Zipporah said, her voice trembling. "He is the god of volcanoes and the ruthless god of war."

"A god of war? I would like to meet such a god," Moses said, grinning.

She grabbed the sleeve of his jacket. "Moses, you must promise me never to go up there. Have you forgotten the story I told you on our return trip?"

"What if the Amalekites escape with your father's sheep?" he asked, removing her hand from his garment. "He has placed them in my care, and I intend to get them back."

"Leave them to Yahweh Sabaoth," Zipporah pleaded. "Father will understand."

"I can't do that. We will follow the tracks. Maybe we can overtake them before they reach the mountain."

Zipporah followed Moses cautiously as he read the tracks. Suddenly, she heard a swishing sound pass close to her ear. Moses pushed her into a clump of tall grass and threw himself on top of her. Zipporah struggled to remove his hand from over her mouth. "Don't speak," he whispered, pointing at an arrow protruding from the stump of a dead tree. "That arrow just missed you."

Three warriors charged from behind a clump of bushes, screaming and waving their spears and swords. Moses leaped up and knocked the lead runner's spear aside with his staff. As the warrior stumbled past him, Moses struck the back of the warrior's neck with his bare hand, breaking it.

From her prone position Zipporah removed her knife from its sheath and prepared to defend herself. The two men hesitated. When they saw it was a woman, they ignored her and moved to position themselves on either side of Moses. Guttural sounds escaped their lips as they jabbed their spears at him. Moses' short sword and staff proved no match for their longer spears. The taller of the Amalekites looked back at Zipporah and grinned. She knew what they intended to do if they killed Moses. He turned his back to her, only to gasp and fall forward on his face. An ivory handled knife protruded from his shoulder blade.

Zipporah ran to the fallen warrior, placed her foot on his back and removed her knife. She lifted his head and slit his throat with the same precision she had seen Jethro employ when he sacrificed a lamb on his altar. The lone attacker turned and ran up the trail with Moses in close pursuit. The foot race continued until they reached the base of the mountain. Zipporah screamed, "Let him go."

To Moses' surprise, Zipporah caught up with him and held onto the edge of his wool jacket. "You must not go up there," she pleaded.

Moses tried to remove her hands, but she held on tenaciously. He ceased resisting, knowing it was useless to argue. "We may regret this," he said as he placed his arms around her. They watched as the man escaped along the trail that led to the mountain. Moses held her closer when she began trembling. He had just witnessed her remarkable courage during the short-lived battle and realized it was the god of this mountain she feared above all else.

"We must leave this place," she said, removing his arms from around her waist.

Zipporah followed Moses to the place where the two bodies lay. They placed stones over them, then gathered their weapons and started searching for the sheep. A fast-moving storm forced them to take shelter under an outcropping of rocks. While they sat waiting for the rain to cease, a bolt of lightning struck a nearby tree causing it to split down the middle. Zipporah screamed and buried her head on Moses' chest.

"I hope you believe me now," she whispered. "See what Yahweh Sabaoth did to that tree?"

"What you saw was the god of flame that I spoke about earlier. Why he took out his anger on the tree we will never know." He recalled the story Zipporah had told him about the god who turned the valley into a wasteland because someone had cut down his tree.

Once the storm passed, they walked to the tree and discovered the carcass of a sheep that had taken shelter under its branches. Its wool was still smoldering. The other two sheep stood nearby, protecting a newborn lamb. Two jackals waited nearby for the intruders to leave. When darkness covered the valley, Moses took one last look at the mountain and paused when he saw a flickering light near its summit.

"The Amalekite must be camping for the night. I can see his campfire," Moses said.

Zipporah tugged at his arm. "That's not a campfire. We must hurry from this place."

CHAPTER 6

And Moses was content to dwell with the man; and Jethro gave Moses Zipporah his daughter.

Exodus 2:21

Zipporah entered the sheep stall where she found Moses setting the broken bone of a young lamb. She watched as he tightened the short loincloth that had slipped below his waist. His muscular bare chest glistened with sweat. She wondered what was causing this tingling sensation that spread throughout her body?

After applying the splint to the lamb's leg, Moses wiped his brow and sat beside her. "It pleases me you've come to keep me company," he said, swatting at flies. "I have only my scrolls to comfort me during my rest periods."

"I'm not here to keep you company. I come at the bidding of my father who wishes you to join him this evening. He wants to introduce you to his guests who are traders from the land of Moab. They have been in Egypt and are returning to their homes," Zipporah said. She reached for a gourd dipper and poured water over his head, then gently wiped his face with a cloth. Standing close to him, she sensed it was the nearness of her that caused his rapid breathing.

"Are they from the caravan that arrived last night?" Moses asked.

"Yes. The prince of Moab is among them."

"Before I left Egypt a Hebrew shaman told to me a tale about the birth of Moab," Moses said.

"Moab was the grandson of Lot, and the great-great nephew of Abraham."

"Grandson? In the shaman's story he spoke of Lot as being Moab's father," Moses said, having second thoughts if he should speak of it. "Your lovely ears might find the story offensive."

"I have read and heard tales told by both men and gods, the worst of which were by the gods themselves. So tell me," Zipporah said inquisitively.

"Then you know of the destruction of the cities, Sodom and Gomorrah?"

"Yes. It is said that Lot and his family once lived in Sodom."

"The shaman told me that before God destroyed those cities by turning them to salt, he sent Lot and his two daughters to the place called Zoar. Once there, they dwelled in a cave in the mountain." Moses paused and cleared his throat. "The oldest daughter told her sister that their father was old, and there were no men to marry them. They decided to get their father drunk on wine so they might sleep with him. Soon both daughters became pregnant and gave birth to sons. The son born to the eldest daughter was named Moab, who is the father of the

29

Moabites to this day. The son born to the youngest daughter was named Benammi, who is the father of the Ammonites to this day." By her smoldering stare, he knew he had made a mistake.

"How can such a contemptible tale be told from the lips of a shaman?" she said, astounded. "Shaman are entrusted to remember people's history accurately and not fill it with filthy lies."

"How can you be sure it didn't happen? Such things took place in days gone by, as they still do," Moses said, forgetting he was speaking to her as an equal.

She lifted her head defiantly. "I have often heard travelers telling such tales around their camp fires when they were full of wine. They often speak lies to discredit the tribes and nations they despise. The Hebrews have nothing but contempt for the Moabites and Ammonites. Why that is so I do not know. We are all related by blood."

She watched as Moses wiped perspiration from his face, and wondered what motivated him to tell her such an erotic tale. Did he hope to amuse her or what? She sensed that he had never stopped to question the motive of the shaman who spread the tale through his storytelling.

"I will speak of this no more," he said, reaching for her hand. She snatched it away and refused to look at him. "I did not mean to offend you."

"Never speak of daughters who have lain with their fathers," Zipporah said. "Or sons who have lain with their mothers. I find it disgusting. I will never understand men, not even our forefather, Abraham."

"Why do you say that?"

"Surely you know the story of how Pharaoh took Abraham's first wife to his bed? He did it because Abraham was a coward. He lied when he told the Egyptians his wife was his sister."

"Where did you hear such a tale?" Moses asked incensed.

"From Hebrew scrolls purchased by my father. It is just as loathsome to my ears as the tale of Lot and his daughters," Zipporah said, amused by his discomfort. "If you doubt me, read my father's copy. His library is filled with scrolls he has purchased from many countries. He draws his wisdom from all the worlds' religions."

Moses grinned sheepishly, knowing he had met his match. After placing the lamb in its stall, he dragged a ram by its horns to the center of the shed and began shearing it.

Zipporah watched as she reflected on his tale of Lot. It was the second time in her life she had a conversation with a man where the fascinating subject of sex was introduced. In her fourteenth year she met the teenaged son of a traveling merchant. Jethro told his family that these dark-skinned peoples called themselves Dravidians, and were from a powerful kingdom far to the east of

Midian. She had seen the youth watching her when she served wine to the guests. The contrast of his white teeth and shining black face had fascinated her.

When Zipporah and Leah went to the fields to tend the sheep, he had followed them carrying a small carpet under his arm. He wore a red turban and matching pants made of pure silk. His bare upper body was hard and lean. When he came to the shaded tree where they rested, he bowed and spoke a tongue they did not understand. Zipporah patted the ground, inviting him to sit beside them. Once seated, he unrolled the carpet and spread it across their laps. The green, pink and red silks enhanced the background of the pictorial scene. Zipporah giggled when she saw the head of an elephant attached to a nude male body, seated cross-legged. Its erect organ reminded her of bulls that were ready to mate. Two bare-breasted women in sheer skirts were seated next to the creature. One was holding the creature's organ while the other licked its enormous shaft.

Leah had covered her eyes and turned away, but Zipporah pulled the carpet closer to better study its elaborate details. The young man placed the palms of his hands together and bowed his head, indicating that this was the image of a god. She became so engrossed in the scene she did not notice that the youth was now sitting in front of them with his arms folded, legs crossed, and with his erect organ exposed. He pulled the foreskin back and gestured for them to reenact the scene. She recalled his cries when she jammed her staff between his legs and chased him away. He never returned for his carpet.

The protesting ram interrupted Zipporah's thoughts as Moses dragged it back to its stall. Then, without a word, he turned and placed his arms around her waist. She did not resist when he kissed her lips, but the probing of his tongue unnerved her. Why was she allowing him to open her blouse? She suddenly remembered Ruth's warning and reluctantly removed his hands.

"You must prepare to meet my father's guests," she whispered in a husky voice she did not recognize. She pushed him away and ran to the meadow where the smell of fresh-cut hay cleared her nostrils of the scent of him.

"Zipporah, what's the matter with you?" Leah asked, slowing her spinning wheel. "You have not said a word to any of us since you returned from the sheep stall."

"She had more than enough time to give Moses the message from our father," Katurah interposed sarcastically. "Tell us what happened."

"Nothing happened. Let me rest," Zipporah said, adjusting one of the blue wool pillows piled on the edge of the carpet. All seven sisters lived in one tent, and at times it proved to be exasperating for Zipporah. It was their afternoon rest period and she knew Ruth would soon be calling her to help serve their guests.

"We all know Moses wants you," Reuel said. "Every time you two are together, you can't take your eyes off each other. So why don't you tell us the truth."

"We just talked," Zipporah said. The sisters burst into laughter.

"You and Moses do more than talk, dear sister," Leah said. "Are you still a virgin?"

"You have no right to ask me that," Zipporah said, grateful that Timna had not yet arrived. "Let us end this conversation now."

"We know you take him to the stream where you say you go to meditate," Katurah said enviously. "Did you show him the carpet that you hid in the stall?" Zipporah refused to answer.

"When he went to the stream to bathe, Leah and I hid in the bushes and watched him," Anah said, taunting her. "We saw his *organ*. Did it hurt when he stuck it inside you?"

Naomi rose from her pillow, walked over to Anah and slapped her face. "You disgust me, all of you," she cried. The sisters sat stunned when Naomi collapsed in Zipporah's arms and wept.

It was dark by the time Moses arrived at the temple. Jethro invited him to join the eight men seated on the carpeted floor. From their turbans and colorful silk robes, Moses was certain these were not ordinary merchants; instead, members of a royal court. Jethro placed his arm around Moses' shoulders and escorted him to the center of the room. He saw Ruth and Zipporah standing in the doorway with wine jars and bowls of fruit.

"This is the Egyptian I have spoken to you about," Jethro said. "He is Moses of the House of Levi." The men acknowledged his presence with grunts and nods. Jethro motioned for Moses to sit beside him. "Moses, these are our cousins from the land of Moab. You will recall from my teachings that the Moabites are the descendants of Lot, the son of Haram. Haram was the brother of Abraham."

"I am honored by your presence," Moses said, as he bowed, then sat cross-legged in the circle. He noticed the man seated next to him was wearing a black velvet robe trimmed with elaborate gold borders. He was stroking his beard and watching Moses with a curious eye.

"I am Elam, Prince of Moab. My father is King Balak, the Magnificent. Speak to us of yourself, Moses. Your accent is not that of a Hebrew."

"I was raised by a royal Egyptian family. They were my adoptive parents. Only as a young man did I learn that I am of the House of Levi. Jethro is teaching me of the God who spoke to Abraham."

"You have the best instructor in all of Midian," Prince Elam said. "Are you aware that your people do not fare well in Egypt?"

"I know of their plight," Moses replied.

"The current Pharaoh no longer acknowledges the great works of your ancestor, Joseph. It was Joseph whose dreams saved Egypt during some great famine centuries ago. The Hebrews are no longer in favor. Have you asked yourself why this is so?" Elam asked. His arrogant smile puzzled Moses.

"I am aware that some tribes are no longer welcomed in Egypt, even those who have lived in the land for many generations."

"While we were there we spoke with the Hebrew elders. Shall I tell you what we learned from them?"

"I would welcome any news of my people," Moses replied with growing unease.

The prince sipped his wine, never taking his eyes off Moses. "I'm sure you know when Pharaoh made Joseph governor of Egypt four centuries ago, the families of Isaac abandoned the land of Canaan and prospered in the Egyptian region of Goshen. Your people multiplied and held great power and influence throughout the land."

Moses' throat felt dry as Prince Elam paused to sip his wine. The room grew quiet. "Long after the death of Joseph, the Hykos invaders swept out of Hauran, with their horses and chariots and their instruments of iron and steel. Such powerful weapons were unknown to the Egyptians and for one hundred years they ruled Egypt with steel fists."

"I know of what you speak," Moses said.

"Tell us, Moses, how did the Hebrews fare during the period of Hykos' rule?"

"They and all Egyptians suffered under the Hykos," Moses replied, wondering why he was being questioned. He suddenly felt as though he was on trial.

"Then why are your people singled out for special scorn?"

Moses did not respond as Prince Elam leaned forward. "I will tell you why. The Egyptians told us that the Hebrew merchants collaborated with the Hykos, Moses. Many grew rich during this period of Hykos rule, and at the expense of the Egyptians. That is why the High Priest and scribes of Egypt are clamoring for the removal of your people from their land."

"I repeat, my people are citizens of Egypt. They suffered under the yoke of the Hykos, as did all Egyptians," Moses said, struggling to control his temper. "Hebrew men served in the army of Pharaoh Ahmosis and many shed their blood to help drive the Hykos out of the land."

Prince Elam reached for his cup as he turned to Jethro. "Jethro, what have you taught this young man about my people?"

Jethro shrugged his shoulders. "I have yet to teach him of your history."

33

Prince Elam reached over and slapped Moses' back. "You must learn and visit us."

Before Moses could reply, Jethro interrupted by clearing his throat. "When the families of Abraham and his nephew, Lot, arrived in the land of Canaan there was strife between them over grazing lands. Abraham wanted to avoid strife between his herdsmen and those of Lot, so the two families agreed to part. Abraham and his family settled the coastal land of Canaan, and Lot and his family settled lands to the east. Now Lot's daughters presented him with two grandsons, Moab and Benammi. Moab is the father of the kingdom of Moab."

Moses took a quick glance at Zipporah. She placed her finger to her lips, cautioning him not to say anything stupid.

"Well spoken, Jethro," Prince Elam said.

"What of the kingdom of Edom that borders the land of Midian? Are its people also related to us?" Moses asked, hoping to shift the conversation away from his people.

"Yes, they are the children of Esau, the oldest son of Isaac and the twin brother of Jacob. But I did not bring you here to speak only of history," Jethro said, lifting his cup as he turned to his guests. "I have asked Moses to join us for I have a special announcement." Jethro stood and brushed crumbs from his robe. He extended his hand to Moses and pulled him to his feet. "This young man came to us out of the Sinai wilderness five months ago. He was half starved and yet he found the strength to come to the aid of my daughters after Amalekites drove them from the wells at Ezon. There were seven of them. They had ravaged one of my daughters." Jethro said as his voice quivered.

"How did one man stand up to so many?" Prince Elem asked.

"The power of our God was with him. As you know, I have only daughters. The Lord, in his infinite wisdom, did not bless me with sons, but he has now answered my prayers," Jethro said, as his graying eyebrows arched upward, covering the first line of wrinkles above his sunburned brow. He turned and placed his hand on Moses' shoulder. "Moses, I offer you my daughter, Zipporah, in marriage." The guests made grunting sounds as they nodded their approval and raised their cups.

"A fine choice, Jethro," Prince Elam said. He stood up and slapped Moses' back.

Before Moses could reply, Jethro patted his cheek, then turned to his guests. "I have seen the glow in his eyes from the days he first came to us. It will be a match blessed by Elohim, and all the lesser gods of heaven," Jethro said proudly.

Moses remained speechless as he walked to Zipporah, took her hand and escorted her to Jethro. Tears filled his eyes as he tried to contain his joy. "You have offered me the finest fruit of your vineyard," Moses said as he tightened his arms around Zipporah's waist. "I accept Zipporah and by doing so I will be a loyal son in the House of Jethro."

"Elohim will bless and keep you. I pray that soon you both will bless me with only grandsons," Jethro said, reaching out and embracing them.

"You will also be a loyal son of Midian. Never forget it," Prince Elam warned. Moses bit his lower lip, knowing he could never deny his Hebrew roots or forget the land of his birth.

Jethro raised his cup to make a toast. "Let us rejoice and be thankful for this day." As Moses drank the wine, he wondered why it left a bittersweet taste in his mouth.

Zipporah and Moses sat on the beach at the tip of the Gulf of Aqaba and watched as the setting sun cast its golden sheen across dark blue waters. As it dipped below the horizon, the sky flamed red, then faded into a purple haze. Seagulls flew over them, diving into the sea and flying off with fish in their beaks.

Jethro had married them in an elaborate outdoor ceremony. Guests from neighboring villages filled the compound and for two days and nights the feasting, drinking and dancing had continued without let up. As their need for privacy grew, Moses and Zipporah had slipped away in the early morning hours of the third day and pitched their tent in a secluded cove along the rocky shore of the gulf. A heat wave had sent temperatures soaring. Moses, clad in a light-blue loincloth that hung from his waist to his knees, spent the afternoon fishing. Zipporah kept herself cool by wading along the shore searching for clams. Moses returned holding a large fish with the hook embedded in its throat. He cut off its head, carefully avoiding its sharp teeth.

"Such fish grow larger than a man," he said, struggling to remove the hook. "Sailors and fishermen have been killed by them."

While preparing the fish, Zipporah stared at its eyes, having never seen such a fish. Its teeth reminded her of Amalek. After cooking over an open fire, they enjoyed their meal of fish, clams, goat cheese and figs topped off with the best wine from Jethro's vineyard.

When the air cooled, Zipporah wrapped herself in a white linen cloth that she knotted above her full breasts. She placed on her finger the silver Cobra ring with fangs holding a blue lapis-eye stone at its center. Moses had given it to her during the wedding ceremony. She felt a knot in the pit of her stomach, knowing that with the coming of cool sea breezes he would take her to their tent to consummate their wedding vows.

"Moses, do you still think of Egypt?" Zipporah said, hoping to ease her tension.

"Sometimes," he said barely audibly. "On evenings such as this I often watch Ra's golden face return to the underworld to spend time with his beloved son, Osiris. On such nights I recite a passage from the Nebseni holy text. Hear these words. 'I have pacified my god, for I have done his will. I have done no murder, I have not stolen, I have not caused pain, nor have I dealt deceitfully with others, nor have I defiled the wife of any man."

Zipporah searched his eyes. "I am pleased such beautiful words are spoken from your lips on such a night as this." She gently brushed the sand from his bare shoulder. "Turn your thoughts to the life we will share together and the sons I will give you."

"I am convinced that the commandments of Ra give life meaning while we live in this cruel world. They hold the keys to the after life."

"Yes, but it is the key to this life that I want to know." Zipporah reached for the wineskin and filled their cups. "Drink your wine and speak only of love, Moses."

Moses reached into his pouch and removed a silver armlet. "My adopted mother gave this to me on my twelfth birthday. She said if my bride wore it on our wedding night, it would bring us luck."

"It's beautiful. She must have loved you dearly," Zipporah said, sliding it up her arm.

"I broke her heart when I left Egypt after I killed the overseer. But I don't want to think about that now," Moses said. He leaned over and kissed Zipporah's lips.

After drinking two cups of wine, she felt lightheaded. She giggled as she removed two silver bells from her pouch and attached them to her skirt. With her hips swaying, she clapped her hands and danced around him. She laughed when she tripped and fell. Sensing his growing anticipation, she crawled beside him. There was a mystery about Moses that she was determined to understand. Her curiosity grew when she saw his loincloth protruding. She reached under his garment and felt the object, then quickly jerked her hand away. How could she tell him that it felt like the snake she had killed hours before they first met.

When he reached for her, Zipporah sprang to her feet and ran toward their tent. He gave chase but she remained a step ahead of him, sending a spray of sand into his face. They laughed as they dived through the tent's opening. She barely managed to remove her garment when she found herself pinned beneath him on the wool carpet. His heavy breathing and the pressure of his knee on her thighs frightened her. She instinctively grabbed the locks of his hair and yanked several times, letting him know she would not tolerate being rushed.

He paused, then removed his garment and gently took her in his arms. The tension she felt began to ease when his kisses explored her lips, her breasts and inner thighs. Sensations she had never experienced started pleasantly, then

36

flowed like liquid music through her veins. Her mother had definitely not spoken of this pleasure nodule where he quenched his thirst. She dug her fingers into his scalp and gasped at the intensity of a pleasure that caused a lapse of memory momentarily. Consciousness returned with the fullness of him pressing in on her. The wine she had consumed dulled the discomfort of it. With the tearing of her curtain, she felt the rhythm of his organ stretching and molding her secret channel. His high-pitched moan sent seagulls fleeing from their nesting places above the secluded cove.

They rested in each other's arms as they pondered the splendor of their first night together. Moses removed the goat skin flap so both could enjoy the night's broad canopy of starlight. He whispered in her ear, "Now, through the pillars of Shu, I have taken my beloved. Like honey, the sweet taste of her is on my lips. Through the gates of Sert, we have walked among the stars of heaven. Before the dawn the envious stars will center in her eyes. And with this pledge, I will love her forever."

"May you always find joy in my arms," Zipporah whispered. She smiled as she thought of Ruth and the simple advice she had given her the night before her wedding. Her mother would never understand the love ritual she experienced for the first time.

With the first light Zipporah was tempted to wake Moses but decided to let him sleep. As the sun rose higher she grew impatient. She slipped outside and found a twisted branch of driftwood. Carefully raising the covering of the tent she slid the stick beneath him. Moses sprang to his feet, pulling the stakes from the sand. As the tent collapsed over him, Zipporah laughed uproariously.

"Did that little snake frighten you, my love?" she purred. He pulled her into his arms and tickled her as they laughed and tussled in the sand.

"Not only have I married a beautiful woman but a trickster as well."

After he reset the tent, she sat beside him, gazing at his contented face. While he mended his net, she slipped into the full-length purple dress he had purchased from an Egyptian trader as a wedding gift. The straight linen garment, with its narrow pleated hem, reached from her bosom to her ankles. She decorated her arms with silver armlets and bracelets.

"How do you like it?" she said spinning around.

"You are far more beautiful than the goddess, Isis," Moses said, reaching to embrace her.

"Be careful what you speak. She may hear you," Zipporah said as she kissed his cheeks and lips. "I have heard of gods and goddesses who become jealous of us mortals." She removed the dress and came into his arms.

"Isis would never be jealous of earthly women. She has her beloved Osiris," Moses said. He ran his fingers over the shapely contours of her brown body to convince himself she was there and truly his.

37

"Did you sleep?" he asked.

Zipporah placed both hands over her abdomen. "How could I sleep?" she whispered. "All night I felt your seed taking root within me. Before the spring rains come I will give you a son."

"Was man created to know such joy? I slept late, fearing if I woke I would find it was only a dream," he said, tightening his arms around her.

"If we have a son what will you name him?"

"I must think on this," Moses said, as he gazed toward the western horizon.

Zipporah sensed his thoughts were now drifting to his Hebrew people and Egypt. She dismissed the thought, for if she could bring splendor to all his nights she felt certain he would soon forget Egypt and be content to remain with her for the rest of their lives.

CHAPTER 7

And Zipporah bore Moses a son, and he called his name *Gershom*,
for he said, "I have been a stranger in a strange land."

Exodus 2:22

Moses took cover in the sheep stall when a violent windstorm struck suddenly. After three hours everyone felt pushed to the edge of exhaustion as they coped with choking dust and stinging grains of sand. Only Jethro remained cheerful through it all. He had prayed twice a day that Zipporah would soon honor him with a grandson. When the winds calmed, Jethro entered the stall with a jug of wine, two bows and a quiver filled with a dozen arrows. Moses continued cleaning sand and dust from the oxen's harness.

"The winds have been kind to us after all, Moses. They have brought flocks of ducks into our fields and pond. Push aside your work and come hunt with me."

"Ruth told me Zipporah's time is nearing. I want to remain close by."

"Your wife is in good hands. I told Ruth we will be in the east fields where I saw the flocks heading," Jethro insisted. Moses followed Jethro to the pasture where they hid themselves in a clump of tall grass. He knew not to argue when Jethro had his mind set on anything.

"Zipporah tells me you've been teaching her to read the Egyptian way of writing. She read to me from one of the scrolls you brought from Egypt. She speaks kindly of this god, Osiris," Jethro whispered as he placed an arrow in his bow. "Do you think it wise to allow your wife to learn the commandments of lesser gods? The mind of a woman can be easily influenced."

"Allow her?" Moses whispered with amusement. "Who was it that taught her to read your sacred scrolls?"

Jethro lowered his eyes and looked chagrined. Moses gently slapped his father-in-law's shoulder. "Her thirst for knowledge matches my own, thanks to you."

"When she was a child, I punished her with the rod when I caught her trying to read. Later I found her hiding behind the curtains of my temple listening as I taught the village boys the sacred words of our God, Elohim," Jethro said with pride. "When I punished her the second time, she stood before me unflinching. With every stroke of the rod she gritted her teeth and shouted out the sacred passages. Mind you, she spoke each passage correctly."

"She is teaching me to sing the hymns you taught her."

39

"Having only daughters, I took pride in her quickness of mind. I confess I broke my own rules by tutoring her in my spare time. She became my star pupil."

"Be not concerned. The commandments of Osiris will not corrupt her mind."

"You must place your faith in Elohim, the God of Abraham. He alone must you love."

"Zipporah spoke of Abraham and of the time he came to the land of my birth."

"What did she tell you?"

"She spoke disrespectfully of him, saying he was a coward because he denied Sarah was his wife."

Jethro shrugged his shoulders. "She speaks of stories remembered by your people. In the days of Abraham, nobles of Egypt often took the daughters and wives of peasants for themselves, especially those who were fair. During a famine, Abraham brought his family to Egypt. He told everyone Sarah was his sister, fearing he might be killed because of her great beauty. Thinking she was his sister, Pharaoh took her to his bed. He was so pleased with her, he made Abraham a very wealthy man."

Jethro gestured to Moses not to speak when a flock of ducks flew into the pond near them. He imitated the sound of a hawk then let his arrow fly, hitting its mark. Moses watched with admiration when he returned with the duck on the tip of his arrow. "That bird will make a fine meal," Moses said. "Now I know who also taught my wife to use the bow so skillfully."

Jethro sat beside Moses and continued the tale. "The Hebrews say God punished Pharaoh for making Sarah his concubine. Pharaoh returned her to Abraham and drove him out of Egypt."

"The Pharaohs I know would have boiled him in oil," Moses said smiling. "You know that all Pharaohs are divine. As living gods they are only given high-born Egyptian girls who are virgins. There is no truth in the tale." He suddenly remembered how upset Zipporah became when they discussed the story of incest involving Lot and his daughters. As they waited for another flock, his thoughts drifted to the evening she told him about the black youth and the carpet with its image of a Elephant-headed god. It was during a period of foreplay when she spoke of it.

"He wanted Leah and me to suck his organ the way lambs suckle their mother's teats," she had said without the slightest hint of embarrassment. "After I hit him, he ran away and never returned for his carpet."

"What did you do with it?"

"We hid it in the sheep stall from our father. Would you like to see it?" Zipporah had not waited for a reply, but bounced off the bed, wrapped a cloth around her waist and rushed outside. She returned with the carpet tucked under

her arm and spread it across his lap. Poking her finger through a moth hole, she watched his expression.

"Now I understand why you did not want your father to see it."

"He would have burned it," she said gleefully. "All my sisters and our cousin, Rehob, have seen it." *She placed her finger to his chin and looked into his eyes. "Would Isis approve if I pleased you that way?"* *She slid her tongue across her upper lip.*

A sharp rap to the back of Moses' head rudely interrupted his daydream. He jumped to his feet when he saw Ruth staring down at him. For a moment he wondered if she knew his secret thoughts.

"I know how much you two enjoy scaring the birds, but Zipporah needs you," Ruth said urgently.

"Is anything wrong?" Moses asked.

"Your wife's hour has come. Go in haste, but do not stay long. I don't want either of you near the birthing tent until after that child is born."

Moses shouted as he raced across the field, scattering the sheep in all directions. Ruth restrained Jethro. "Let him go to his wife alone, dear husband. Have you forgotten the night Zipporah was born and the way we complained when our relatives stood jabbering outside our tent?"

"How can I forget it? Please understand my joy. I have prayed that God would give me a grandson these past nine months," Jethro said, his voice high-pitched with delight. "God spoke to me last night in a dream and told me Zipporah will have only sons,"

"Don't get your hopes too high. Seven times God told you I would have sons. And what happened? Seven times God was wrong."

Jethro's eyes widened as he clamped his hand over Ruth's mouth and looked in all directions.

"Hush woman!" he whispered. "He may hear you."

Moses entered Zipporah's tent and saw Naomi and Leah rubbing her back. Naomi avoided Moses' eyes as she brushed passed him and left the tent. Leah took him aside and whispered, "I know how much you love her. She needs us, so don't stay too long."

"Leah, you sound just like your mother," Moses said, pulling a stool beside Zipporah. He took a cloth and wiped the perspiration from her face. She took his hand and placed it on her swollen belly.

"Our son is greeting you, Moses," she whispered.

Moses eyes watered when he felt the kicking movements. "I hate to see you in pain."

"I rejoice in this pain, for it brings forth the fruit of all our loving," she said turning on her side and gripping the ends of a pillow. Between the contractions she smiled and squeezed his hand. "It's starting now. Call my sisters to me."

He kissed her cheek then hastened from the tent as Naomi and Leah rushed back. Outside, Ruth was waiting for him.

"All will go well with Zipporah, so do not worry yourself," Ruth whispered. "I will take you to Jethro. He is in his temple praying."

They entered Jethro's writing room only to find him finishing his third cup of wine. "We will drink to the birth of a son," Jethro said, his voice slurred.

Ruth laughed and poured a cup of wine for Moses. "My husband's tongue is loose from the fruit of the vine, Moses. You may as well join him. The night may be long."

"None for me, Ruth," Moses said, placing the cup aside. He was determined to be completely sober when he held his child for the first time. It pained him when he thought of Naomi who no longer smiled. Would she ever know the joys of marriage and the miracle of childbirth?

Jethro took Moses' hand and forced him to kneel. He closed his eyes and muttered a prayer for Zipporah's safe delivery. "Grant me a grandson this time," he pleaded.

As they waited, Moses admired the hundreds of scrolls stored on the shelves. "Zipporah told me that you have scrolls from many lands. Why do you collect so many?"

"As Priest of Midian I study the commandments of all the gods, both good and evil. I admire some of your Egyptian gods, such as Nehau who punishes those who defraud their neighbors, and Fentiu who hates those who steal and plunder the land. And there is the two-headed serpent god who comes from the torture-chamber to punish those who defile the wives of man."

"I was taught the commandments of Ra and his son, Osiris. Speak more of Elohim who protects my beloved this night."

"He is the chief God whom the lesser gods worship. He is the God who spoke to Abraham. From my studies of the commandments and laws, it came to me in a dream that Ra, Yahweh, and Elohim are different names for the same God. That is because they seem to speak with same voice, calling for mercy and justice."

"What does God require of us?"

"It is so simple I almost overlooked it. He calls us to give bread unto the hungry and water unto those who thirst, clothing to the naked, and a boat to the shipwrecked mariner. He demands that we love one another. His name is Love and the jewels in his crown are justice and mercy."

Moses' eyes brightened. "I read those very words on the tomb of Pharaoh Amenhotep III. The High Priest of Egypt told me that Ra spoke them when dawn was young."

"Now you know why I meditate day and night. The true God of heaven, no matter what name men call him, is slow to anger. He commands us to wear the twin crowns of mercy and justice," Jethro said, handing Moses one of the scrolls. For the next hour they sat together and read by lamplight.

Timna threw open the door, shouting, "Moses, a man child has been born." Overcome with emotion, Jethro grabbed Moses and kissed his cheeks. Both men ran to the narrow door and, out of respect, Moses stepped back, allowing Jethro to exit first. Once outside Moses raced past him. In the birth tent Zipporah sat propped up on three woolen pillows holding the child to her breast.

"Here is your son, Moses," Zipporah said proudly.

He fell to his knees beside her and kissed her cheek. Wiping tears from his eyes he took the child and lifted it over his head. "God of Abraham, this is our son whom I now name Gershom. I offer him as a sacrifice to your service as you require." After he kissed the child's forehead, he turned to Jethro and held the child out to him. Jethro's eyes seemed apprehensive and fearful as his hands began to shake.

"The child will not break, dear husband," Ruth said, taking the baby and placing it in his arms. "You have waited long for this moment." Jethro cradled his grandson and kissed his forehead three times.

Zipporah held out her arms and welcomed Moses. "There is a Presence here with us this night," she whispered. "Can you sense it?"

Moses wiped the tears from his eyes and nodded. "Yes, my love."

"You named our son Gershom. What does it mean?"

"It means I am a stranger in a strange land." Moses saw the disappointment in her eyes.

"You are not a stranger in my arms, Moses. Our people are now your people."

"You are right." Moses said, turning to Jethro. "Father, will you circumcise my son on the eighth day?"

Jethro shook his head. "It is Elohim's law that male children are circumcised when they are twelve; at the time they become men."

"How can this be? The scrolls that the Hebrew elders gave me say that God demands sons be circumcised on the eighth day, and I am Hebrew."

"You are now a citizen of Midian and a son in the House of Jethro. Sons will be circumcised in the twelfth year," Jethro said adamantly.

Moses felt a gentle tug on his arm and turned back to Zipporah. Despite himself, he could not conceal his sense of frustration.

Zipporah held out her arms to comfort him. "All will be well. Let your heart be joyful, for God has blessed us with a beautiful son."

CHAPTER 8

And Pharaoh said to his people, "The people of Israel have become too mighty and influential. Unless we deal wisely with them, they will keep multiplying. If we go to war there is the danger that they will join our enemies, so I am ordering all of them out of Egypt."

Exodus 1:9-10

Jethro's caravan approached a hill overlooking the coastal city of Ezion-geber. He signaled for the fifteen drivers to rest their camels. Moses followed him to a bluff overlooking the Midian capital. "You are standing at the northern tip of the Gulf of Aqaba. This port city has a population of more than thirty thousand souls," Jethro shouted above the howling wind.

A network of single-storied dwellings hugged the shoreline like white lace decorating the sea's blue skirt. The sight invigorated Moses. It reminded him of towns that lined the river Nile.

Jethro stretched out his hand. "This is the capital that we seized from the Edomites."

"Did you not say the Edomites were your trading partners and cousins? What led to the war?"

"For centuries Midian, Moab and Ammon maintained an alliance with Edom. We used this port to trade with Egypt, Nubia and Ethiopia. When Zeeb was crowned king of Edom ten years ago, he placed a port tax on members of the alliance. Our Midian confederation united and defeated him and made it our capital. When the council meets tonight, King Zeeb will be present for the first time since that war."

"Why has the council been called?" Moses asked.

"We are here to consider a decree issued by the new Pharaoh of Egypt. I have been told it could have grave consequences for all of our nations."

"A new Pharaoh now sits on the throne of Egypt?" Moses asked, stunned by the revelation.

"Yes. The Pharaoh is Mer-ne-Ptah from the upper kingdom of Egypt, the land of the burnt faces. His mother is Nubian. He distrusts all foreigners, especially Hebrews."

"Our people are not foreigners. We have lived in Egypt for more than four hundred years," Moses said, feeling lightheaded. He had dreamed of returning to Egypt one day. Could it now be possible?

"Four hundred years is but the blink of an eye to the Egyptians. They count their history in millions of seasons," Jethro said as he waved to Zipporah who rode beside them.

Zipporah's shoulders ached from traveling all day on a donkey with the one-year old Gershom strapped to her back. She dismounted and handed Gershom to Moses. "Father, shall we camp here and rest before entering the city?"

"Yes, but only long enough to eat our meal. Moses and I must be at the Hall of Chiefs before evening," Jethro said.

Zipporah made a fire, using dried cow dung for fuel, then spread a table cloth on the ground. After reheating a pot of lamb stew thick with rice, she called to Jethro, "Start eating while I go for Rehob."

When she returned with the young man, he sat beside Moses. "Moses, this is my cousin, Rehob, my uncle's youngest son," Zipporah said, patting his back. "He serves as our trader. While you and father are at the council meeting, I will be with him selling our wool."

When Rehob turned and smiled, Moses almost choked on a piece of mutton. The young man's long eyelashes, smooth beardless chin, and full lips were those of a woman. He was more beautiful than many women Moses had seen in Egypt. When he kept smiling, Moses' eyes dropped and his face flushed.

Rehob whispered to Zipporah, "Is your husband always this shy?" She smiled as she broke chunks of bread from the loaf with her hands and handed it to each of them. Rehob opened his packet and placed a cake on the cloth. "I brought a date cake my mother taught me to bake."

"Rehob is a wonderful cook," Zipporah said enthusiastically. "When we celebrate our holidays, he comes over and cooks for us."

"I soak my dates overnight in honey and spices. It's a recipe that has been in our family for generations." Rehob offered a slice of cake to Moses. "Would you like some?"

"I don't think so," Moses replied curtly, as he scooped up rice and meat with his fingers.

"Well, what kind of dessert do you like?" Rehob asked, taken aback by Moses' attitude.

"Right now I would like to finish eating what's before me."

"Moses, you know you like date cakes," Zipporah said. "You liked mine."

"Zipporah, I have a lot on my mind. Please let me eat in peace."

After the meal Moses took Zipporah aside. "Speak of this cousin of yours. He has the face and manners of a woman, yet he is dressed in the garment of a man."

"Surely you have seen such men in Egypt. It is true he is a man, but God gave him the body and soul of a woman. Do you find him more attractive than me?" she said teasingly.

"Do not jest. Such men are an abomination in the sight of God."

"Not in Midian. God does not despise what he has created," Zipporah said, shocked by his lack of tolerance. She was relieved when he did not pursue the matter and turned away. From their position on the hillside, he pointed to the shoreline north of the city.

"There is the place where we spent our first nights together."

"It was on that shore this son of ours was made from all our loving. I have waited for such a moment to share more news with you." Zipporah searched his eyes for a response that did not come. "You will be blessed with another son before the winter rainy season."

Moses continued staring at the sea, giving only the slightest hint of a smile. Finally, he placed his arms around her and kissed her cheek. "Forgive me. I am pleased the Lord will bless us with another child," he said quietly. "If I seemed distracted, it was because Jethro told me there is a new ruler over Egypt. You know how I have longed to return to my home and be reunited with my family."

"But Midian is your home and we are your family," she said with concern. "Why do you wish to return to a place where men seek to take your life?"

"It is the land of my birth. My mother may still be living. I want to meet the brother and sister I have never known. Try to understand."

"You have seldom spoken of your mother and I did not know you had a brother and sister."

"I have told you of my birth. My birth mother urged me to flee from Egypt and come to the land of Midian. Before I left, she told me I have an older brother named Aaron and a younger sister named Miriam. I long to meet them."

Zipporah sighed then looked at the gulf waters. "Moses, I will follow wherever you go," she said, struggling to hold in her feelings. "My life would be meaningless without you. Aren't you happy living here in Midian?"

Moses took her hands and kissed both palms. "I love you as much as life itself. Nothing in heaven or on earth must ever come between us," Moses said as they walked back to the caravan. "But Egypt is my birthplace. My soul is rooted there."

The noise, smells and congestion of the open marketplace of the walled city of Ezion-geber reminded Moses of the Egyptian capital city of Noph. A pig broke out of its crate and knocked over three stalls. Zipporah laughed when two boys dived under a fruit stand and caught it. An angry merchant demanded the pig as payment for the damage to his property. The larger boy held the squealing pig under his arm and ran into the crowd with the merchant chasing him.

An enterprising man approached Moses. "I offer you doves, fat white doves. All have been blessed for your sacrificial offering to the gods."

"There is only one true God in Midian and your birds are unworthy of any sacrifice," Jethro shouted, pointing to the sick condition of the doves. "Come Moses. We must hurry to the palace. The hour draws near for the opening session of the Council."

Jethro gave final instructions to Rehob and Zipporah regarding bargaining for the best prices among the traders. As they had done on previous visits, Zipporah remained with Rehob and discreetly advised him if she felt a price was not right. Midian law excluded women from participating in the haggling over market prices for wool.

Zipporah loved the excitement of the market. She sought a place where she could keep eye contact with Rehob, and chose to sit on the steps of the platform used by merchants who demanded to speak to the crowd. Those who offered rare merchandise from distant lands were allowed on the stand to show off their products.

Because of Zipporah's beauty, no one asked her to leave. The merchant who had built the platform decided she was good for business. When several merchants tried to flirt with her, she showed them her wedding ring and reminded them that her husband was standing nearby. Zipporah communicated with Rehob through hand signals or slight head nods. With her help, his reputation as a skillful trader became well known among the merchants.

After the day's transactions were successfully concluded, Rehob and another trader walked over to Zipporah.

"Zipporah, I want you to meet my friend, Joash," Rehob said smiling. "He has invited me and several friends to his home to see his fruit trees. You know how I love fruit."

Joash looked to be twice Rehob's age. From his expensive robe and jewelry, she recognized him as one of the wealthy merchants she had seen earlier.

"I am pleased to meet you," Zipporah said, smiling. "Did you have a successful day?"

"Very successful," Joash said, taking Zipporah's hand. "Rehob, you never told me you had such a lovely cousin."

"Joash, are you trying to make me jealous?" Rehob teased, playfully slapping his hand. As they stood laughing, Zipporah was glad Moses was not there.

"Have you other sisters?" Joash asked.

"Yes, ours is a large family," Zipporah said.

"She has six sisters and they are all beautiful. Zipporah's my favorite. The only problem is she married a hateful Egyptian," Rehob said with contempt.

"Rehob, how can you say that," Zipporah said, distressed. "You just met Moses a few hours ago. When he gets to know you, I'm sure both of you will become friends."

"I know when men dislike me," Rehob said, clutching Joash's arm. "I hope you are right."

"I was counting on you to help me select gifts for my sisters," Zipporah said, pouting.

"There will be time before we leave for home. However, when we get back, Joash and I will be going to the arena to see the circus," Rehob said.

"Being from the country I doubt if you've heard of our famous circus," Joash said. "Would you like to join us?"

"Are women permitted?" Zipporah asked.

"Only in the company of men," Joash replied.

"I have heard whispers about the circuses. My father does not approve of them, but he never told us why. I'm married now and I don't think I should go without my husband."

Rehob stuck his finger in Zipporah's side and laughed. "Come on, dear cousin. You've always been an independent woman. This will be your last chance to be your free-spirited self. Besides, I doubt if your husband would approve."

"What will I do with my son?"

"Aunt Sarah has him. I'm sure she will keep him a little longer. By now she has sold all of her honey and eggs. You know how much she adores him."

"I'll think about it," Zipporah said with misgivings.

"We will return this afternoon when it is cooler," Rehob said. "Go find a place to rest."

"Take care."

"I always do." Rehob waved as he took Joash's hand and left the marketplace.

Zipporah returned to the caravan and found her aunt selling the last of her eggs. She knelt and kissed Gershom who was sleeping peacefully by her side.

"How did the sale go?" Aunt Sarah whispered.

"Far better than expected. My father and Uncle Eber will be proud when they learn how much we got for the wool."

"Where is Rehob?"

"He's with a friend. They should be returning later this afternoon."

"I'm glad you came. A little man walked by here with a basket full of snakes. It almost frightened me to death. See those fools crowded around him. If just one of those snakes gets loose and bites them, they will surely die."

"This I must see. I'll be right back."

"Zipporah, don't go over there. Think of your child," Aunt Sarah cried with alarm.

"I'll be extra careful, I promise," Zipporah shouted, elbowing her way through the crowd. In the center of the multitude she saw a small brown-skinned man sitting on a carpet playing a flute. His red trousers reminded her of the boy who had left his carpet with the elephant-headed god. The lid of the flute player's straw basket slid off and a hooded cobra rose. It swayed back and forth to the music of the flute. The man rose up, grabbed the snake with both hands and held it over his head. Those closest to him stepped back, giving Zipporah an opportunity to squeeze closer.

"Behold this sacred snake that once belonged to a god. If you place an offering in my basket, he will show you his wonderful powers," the flute player said.

Several merchants stepped forward and threw coins in the basket. The little man looked in the basket and shook his head. When Zipporah stepped forward and tossed a coin, he bowed to her.

When the man turned the snake loose, Zipporah moved closer while several others backed away. To her amazement, the snake turned into a rope and rose off the carpet to the height of a single story building. The little man picked up his basket, tied it on his back and began climbing the rope. When he reached the top, the man and the rope vanished. Reflecting on what she had just seen, Zipporah remembered her carpet with its elephant-headed god. Maybe it was the image of a god after all?

When Jethro and Moses entered the palace grounds, guards escorted them to the Hall of Chiefs. They took their seats at a long table where twenty representatives from the nations of Midian, Edom, Moab and Ammon were already seated. Jethro nudged Moses and pointed to the eight woolen tapestries suspended from the ceiling to the floor on iron rods. Each carpet depicted gory scenes of famous battles fought and won by the Midianites.

A white-haired man dressed in a purple robe stood up and pounded his staff on the floor three times. "I, Kaleb, Chief of the Midian Confederation, have called this meeting to consider a decree that has come out of Egypt. Present with their representatives are King Zeeb of Edom, Prince Malcolm of Ammon, King Balak of Moab, and five chiefs of the Midian confederation. Malcolm's father is sick and cannot travel."

Jethro nudged Moses and whispered, "Listen carefully. The Edomites are from the seed of Esau, son of Isaac, the grandson of Abraham. They have no love for Hebrews. You will learn why soon enough."

"Which one is King Zeeb?"

"He sits directly across from you. Watch him closely. He is the one with the hooked nose and dark beady eyes. Such men are deceitful." Moses restrained himself from laughing. Jethro's own nose and eyes fit the description. In fact, Zeeb and Jethro could pass for brothers.

49

Kaleb signaled for the five men seated near him to stand, "These are my fellow chiefs of the Midian Confederation." Following lengthy introductions that included each man's victories in battle, Kaleb clapped his hands. "After you have had your fill, I will present our guest from Egypt. They are Hebrews that bring a message from their elders. Now let us enjoy ourselves."

Servants entered carrying bottles of palm wine, followed by steaming dishes of lamb, baked quail, dates, cheese and various assorted vegetables and breads. During the three-hour meal Moses studied the two guests. They ate in silence and did not inject themselves into any of the side conversations. At the end of the meal, Chief Kaleb smiled as loud belches of appreciation echoed throughout the hall. Moses turned his head to avoid the obnoxious odor.

"It pleases me that you have enjoyed your meal. The hour grows late and we will now hear from our guests. They speak on behalf of the twelve Hebrew tribes that reside in Egypt," Kaleb said as he motioned for his guests to stand. "Estrum is of the tribe of Benjamin and Asa is of the tribe of Levi. Let us respect and hear them." Moses' heart began racing at the mention of the House of Levi, his own tribe.

"We pay homage to the God of Abraham and Lot who, centuries ago, brought our forefathers safely from Ur of the Chaldees, that great city on the mighty Euphrates River," Asa said, bowing four times in the direction of each leader.

"Speak of the proclamation issued by Pharaoh Mer-ne-Ptah," Kaleb said.

"Brethren, I bring grave news. Pharaoh's decree, issued several months ago, calls for the expulsion of all Hebrews from Egypt. He says that if there is another war with the Hyksos those who have been branded foreigners will betray Egypt by joining them."

"Have not your people been in Egypt more than four hundred years? Could it be that some of your leaders betrayed the Egyptians during the rule of Egypt by the Hyksos?" King Zeeb asked bluntly. "Trickery and deceit are in the blood of the Hebrews to this day."

"Silence! Let there be no hostility at this table. Hear these men as they speak," Kaleb shouted.

"Our people have never betrayed our beloved country. There are Egyptian nobles who are jealous of our success. What they really want are our lands and property," Asa said calmly. "The expulsion order includes not only Hebrews, but peoples from the lands of Libya, the islands of the Mediterranean, and nations east of the Sinai. We must leave Egypt or be reduced to a status little better than that of slaves. Our lands and property are being confiscated as we speak."

King Zeeb stood and pointed at Asa. "Speak the truth. This happened because your people collaborated with the Hyksos during their hundred-year rule of Egypt. Where is your pride now, Hebrew?"

"Take your seat and be silent. This is not the time to speak," Kaleb shouted. Zeeb slumped into his seat as Kaleb turned to Asa. "What do your people want from us?"

"Help us return to the land of Canaan that was given to us by our God," Asa said.

Zeeb slammed his fist on the table overturning several cups of wine. "By all the gods, what you speak is madness. You Hebrews abandoned the land of Canaan for the fleshpots of Egypt. That land belongs to the Canaanites that dwell by the sea, and the Philistines that dwell in the mountains and by the river Jordan. They dwelled in the land thousands of years before the arrival of Abraham and his kin. They live in walled cities and are our peaceful trading partners," Zeeb shouted angrily. "Do not look to the Edomites for help." He held out his cup which was quickly filled by a slave.

"He hates all Hebrews," Jethro whispered. "It's in his blood."

Zeeb wiped his mouth on his sleeve. "We Edomites have long memories. We have not forgotten how your ancestor, Jacob, tricked his twin brother, Esau, of his birthright. Esau is the father of my nation," Zeeb shouted, waving his finger at the guests. "No shadow of a Hebrew will ever darken my country. Members of the Council, if you allow these stiff-necked people to enter your lands you will all live to regret it."

Zeeb's words set off a roar of threats and counter threats that angered Moses. Only Kaleb and his fellow Midian chiefs seemed sympathetic to the plight of the Hebrews, thanks to Jethro.

Moses started to leave but Jethro gripped his sleeve and cautioned him to restrain himself. "Stay seated. Chief Kaleb is about to speak. Hear him."

Kaleb pounded his silver goblet on the table, "I will state my position to this council only once." He spoke directly to King Zeeb. "My brothers, although we are separate nations we are of one blood. The Hebrews are being driven from the land of Egypt. We cannot allow our cousins to perish in the wilderness of the Sinai. My priest, Jethro, has spoken to our God on this matter. If we turn our backs to their plight, it will be an abomination in his sight."

"To which god did your priest speak?" Zeeb bellowed.

"If this thing happens, our God, Elohim, requires that we give his people sanctuary," Chief Kaleb said, undeterred. "If each of our nations open our doors, it will not become a burden on any one of us."

Zeeb rose to his feet and pointed at the guests. "Our lands cannot support the rabble hoards that will be driven from Egypt. Any Hebrew who trespasses on my lands will be put to the sword."

Moses could no longer restrain himself. Amid the shouts he slipped from his chair and left the hall. The last time he had felt such rage he had slain a man, and he felt that urge surfacing again. In the palace garden, Moses sat under a palm tree and wept for his people.

It was dark when Moses entered his room at the inn. He found Zipporah waiting for him. He lit a clay lamp and sat beside her on the mat. When he kissed her, he saw redness in her eyes.

"You've been crying. Did you miss me that much?" he asked.

"Yes, but that's not why I was weeping. I hope you will not be too angry when I speak of it."

"Have I ever spoken to you in anger? What has happened?" Moses asked with concern.

"My cousin's friend invited me to go to the arena with them. What I witnessed made me sick. I know I should have received your permission before going there."

"Rehob took you to the arena where circuses are held?" Moses asked with alarm.

"Do not be angry with Rehob. Fault me if you must," Zipporah said, touching his cheek. "I confess I was overcome with curiosity."

Moses lay back on the mat and placed both hands beneath under his head. "Jethro warned me you were a free spirit. I hope you have learned your lesson."

She moved closer to him. "I must tell you what my eyes have seen."

"Only if you insist."

Zipporah sat up and took deep breaths to calm herself. "When we entered the arena, there was an open pit, large enough to hold a hundred sheep. Wooden walls covered the sides of it. All around it were stone seats where the people sat."

"I know of such places."

"After we were seated, six young women were forced into the pit where they stood before the crowd. All were clothed in sheer skirts that only covered their waist. They huddled together to hide their bodies from the eyes of the screaming crowd. A cage door opened and a giant lizard crawled into the pit. Its body was twice the size of a man. Its forked tongue sniffed the air and the crowd cheered. The women screamed and ran to escape from it. All but one managed to get behind a wooden barricade that was close to the wall. When she tripped, the beast grabbed her leg and devoured her as the crowd cheered," Zipporah said, shuddering. "There was nothing left of her, not even blood. It stuck its nose over the barricade and dragged another girl out by her head. After it swallowed her whole, it seemed satisfied. Rehob's friend told us that such lizards are called dragons. They were captured in the jungles of some far island."

"Such beasts should not be used to fire the passions in men," Moses said as he tried to calm her.

As though in a trance, Zipporah stared into the dark corners of the room. "Men came and threw nets over the beast and dragged it away. The doors opened again and four little men ran to the center of the ring. Two were fair of skin and had long yellow hair. And two were black," Zipporah said, closing her eyes momentarily. "All were naked and stood no taller than our sheep. Their legs were bent like bows, and their fat bellies looked like the boars my father and I hunt. I thought they were wearing thick ropes that hung beneath their bellies to their knees, but I was wrong. When they found the four women's hiding place, their organs stretched from their fat bodies like snakes. The women screamed when the little men chased them around the pit."

"Please spare me this," he pleaded, placing his finger to her lips.

"I shared those women's pain, so open your ears and hear it," she cried, squeezing his hand. He nodded, and held her tightly in his arms. "The crowd rose and cheered when they caught the youngest girl with a net. While the one with yellow hair danced around them, three raped her in a manner too horrible to describe. Men came with whips and forced the other women to join them. I left my seat and tried to jump into the pit to save them, but Rehob and his friend held me back. If they had not restrained me, I would have killed them all." She shivered while resting on Moses' chest.

"Why do you insist on speaking of this?" Moses asked.

"Don't you know?' she asked. "I never dreamed that *men* were capable of using women in such a despicable way?"

"I only know that lust hides in the underbrush of men's souls," Moses said, placing his finger to her lips to silence her.

Zipporah pushed his hand away. "I never thought my countrymen were capable of such brutality."

"I have heard your pain, now speak no more of it," Moses insisted. "From this day you will obey me and never speak of such things. Is that understood?" Moses said, highly agitated.

"I will obey you," Zipporah replied. "I spoke because I saw my sister being violated, not just those poor women."

"I believe you," he said hoarsely. "Try to cleanse your mind of such horrors."

Zipporah stared at him wild-eyed. "How do I cleanse my mind when I saw the faces of Amalek and his sons torturing my sister? Naomi, who had never known a man, finally found the courage to tell me what happened that terrible day at the oasis. That beast tore her body with the edge of his staff, then raped her. Then he gave her to his sons who made her satisfy them with her mouth." Her fingernails dug into Moses' arm.

The rage that surfaced in Moses caused his body to quake. He had never fully understood why Naomi refused to look into his eyes until that moment. In the hour that followed neither spoke as she lay in his arms. The stillness in the room was broken when Gershom started crying. Moses stroked Zipporah's hair as she breast-fed their son.

"Some day justice will come upon this earth," Moses said quietly. "There are gods in Egypt that demand an eye for an eye, a tooth for a tooth, and a limb for a limb when such unspeakable crimes are committed."

"When a woman has been violated, should a man's organ be severed from his body?" Zipporah asked quietly.

"If the power was mine, his organ would be removed and he would be denied entrance into the temple of the Lord forever." He held her in his arms until she finally drifted into a troubled sleep.

After waking late, Zipporah took Moses to a stall in the marketplace where she showed him the robe she wanted to buy for Jethro. When Moses agreed, she haggled with the merchant and finally settled for half the asking price. Moses was impressed with her bargaining skills but thought he could do better. Jethro had given him permission to purchase a saddle. When they stopped at a harness shop where saddles were prominently displayed, a bearded merchant rushed out and seized Moses' arm.

"If it is a saddle you need, you have come to the finest shop in all of Midian," the merchant said, escorting Moses inside his shop with Zipporah following close behind.

"These are beautiful saddles. What are you asking for them?" Moses asked. He did not notice Zipporah trying to get his attention.

"What price are you interested in?"

Moses paused when Zipporah squeezed his arm. She slowly shook her head, cautioning him not to mention a price. Moses pointed to a cowhide saddle that had intricate silver plates embedded in the leather.

"That one is beautiful," Moses said, turning to Zipporah. "Do you think your father would be pleased?" She shrugged her shoulders, indicating she was not all that impressed.

"Ah, so you like that one? You have excellent taste. I will sell it to you for one thousand quenta. At that price you are getting a bargain."

Moses examined it carefully. "I offer you five hundred quenta," he said nonchalantly. The merchant laughed.

"Please don't insult me. I have offered you the most beautiful handcrafted saddle in this city and at a bargain price."

Moses paused and considered the price. "Seven-fifty," he said.

The merchant paused and made a sour face. "Eight hundred. I can't do any better."

Zipporah stepped between them and took Moses' arm. "Moses, there is a saddle shop on the other side of this plaza. They have saddles just as beautiful and for half this price," she said, pulling him toward the door.

"Do not go in haste," the merchant cried, blocking the doorway. "Look at the beautiful silver plates that I crafted with my own hands. For you my friend, I will accept your offer of seven-fifty quenta."

Zipporah tugged at Moses' arm. "Let's go. We can always come back."

The merchant tugged at his other arm. "Because you have the face of an honest man of God, I'll sell it to you for the five hundred quenta you suggested." Moses shook his head in amazement as he completed the purchase.

When they returned to the caravan, Moses was pleased to see the Hebrew man, Asa, talking with Jethro.

"Ah, I see you have bought a fine saddle," Jethro said.

"I must confess that Zipporah was the one who bargained for the price I wanted," Moses said, placing the saddle beside Jethro. "I learn more about this beautiful wife of mine every day."

"I have been speaking with this young man who is from your tribe of Levi," Jethro said.

"I hoped I would have an opportunity to speak with you," Asa said.

"I regret that I left before the meeting ended, but King Zeeb angered me," Moses said. "Come, sit beside me." The two men walked to a bench near one of the few trees in the marketplace.

"Jethro has told me how you came to be in Midian. I will tell the congregation of our meeting. I hope you and your father-in-law will do all you can to assist us."

"Jethro has the ear of the Midian chiefs. I'm sure he will persuade them to help our people," Moses said. "I long to return to Egypt, but they would arrest and stone me."

"The Pharaoh that now sits on the throne of Egypt is from the upper kingdom. He will not know or care about your past. All he wants are all Hebrews out of Egypt."

"I am now a humble citizen of Midian. I will pray for our people."

"We will need more than prayers. I am certain God will call you to his service. Prepare for that day, Moses," Asa said. He kissed Moses' cheek then turned and faded into the teeming crowd.

CHAPTER 9

> Now Moses kept the flock of Jethro his father-in-law, the priest of
> Midian; and he led the flock to the backside of the desert, and came to
> the Mountain of God, even to Horeb.
>
> Exodus 3:1

Ruth watched with pride as Zipporah nursed her four-week-old son. As she
shelled a bowl of peas, Gershom sat beside her sucking his thumb. When he
started pouting, she placed her finger under his chin and looked into his eyes.

"What a sad face. Be happy, Gershom. Your little brother will soon be big
enough for you to play with," Ruth said, ruffling his dark curls. "Soon you both
will be running across the meadow chasing butterflies."

"I hate him," Gershom mumbled with his thumb still in his mouth.

Ruth turned to Zipporah and whispered, "Place red pepper on that thumb. It
will break him from sucking. If he doesn't stop soon, his teeth will grow ugly
and fall out."

"I'm not worried about Gershom, mother. It's Moses who causes me
sleepless nights." Zipporah said, shifting the baby to her left breast.

"What's this you say?"

"Moses has not been the same since he returned from the council meeting
eight months ago," Zipporah said, her voice quivering. "When I told him we
would have another child, all he wanted to talk about was returning to Egypt
someday. This is the fourth week of our new son's life. He takes no pleasure in
him."

"You speak nonsense, daughter. I saw nothing but joy on his eyes when he
named the baby 'Eliezer.' It is a fine name. It means, 'God is my help.' Trust
your mother when I say all men have their moods. I should know for I have had
to put up with your father's all these years. This thing will pass."

"If only I could believe you. When he comes from tending the flock, he talks
only of Egypt and his other family. We no longer take walks along the path or sit
together by the stream like we used to. There is no joy in him."

Ruth ordered Gershom to open his mouth. She placed a raw pea on his
tongue then lifted him to the seat beside her. Zipporah's concerns had caught her
by surprise. She had to admit that Moses did seem to be moody in recent
months. Now that she recalled, he seldom joined in the happy chatter at the
communal meal.

"Your husband took the flock to graze in the pasture of Horeb, near the base
of the mountain of the unknown god. He will be there two more nights," Ruth

said. She reached over and placed her hand on Zipporah's shoulder. "I'm sure you miss him as much as he misses you. Go to your husband and remain with him for tonight. Take the newborn child with you. I will care for Gershom and see to it that your sisters do your chores."

"But I am unclean and will remain so for another week or more."

"It is not your body your husband needs just now, Zipporah. Comfort him with kindness, food and song. Moses has only the sheep and his thoughts of Egypt. Open your heart to his grief as only you can do."

Zipporah's face brightened. She reached over and hugged Ruth. "You are so wise, mother. Thank you, thank you."

With her new son strapped to her back, Zipporah rode a donkey to the base camp. She dismounted and called for Moses, but there was no response. She glanced at the forbidden mountain and quickly turned away. The sight of evening clouds resting on its summit convinced her that the god, Yahweh Sabaoth, was awake. Her heart raced as she entered Moses' crude lodge, hoping he might be resting. The structure, made from dead limbs and covered with deer hides, showed signs that he had been there. Two empty wine bottles and partially eaten goat cheese had been discarded on the earthen floor. She went outside to the fire pit. After examining the ashes she knew Moses had been gone for several hours. When the sheep came toward her, she became frightened; Moses would never leave them unattended for any extended period of time. She removed her backpack and placed the sleeping child on a bed of leaves. A tree had blown over during a windstorm. She climbed on its stump and shouted Moses' name in all directions. The returning echo from the mountain was all she heard. Frightened that harm may have come to him, her heart raced as she gathered wood and stacked it near the fire pit.

The whole valley glowed with a purple hue from the setting sun. Was this a good or bad omen? It was not far from this place where the Amalekite shepherd had escaped into the forbidden mountain. As darkness cloaked the valley, she called to the flock with the braying sounds she had learned as a child. The sheep responded by gathering near the lodge and settling down for the night. She made a fire in the pit, hoping it would keep predators away. A quick head count of the sheep revealed that, once again, Ga was missing. That explained why Moses was not there.

Of course she had camped out on nights like this before she married, although never so close to this mountain. She had come to rely on Moses' strength. Now she had to muster her own reserve of courage.

Jackals yelping in the distance alerted her to be on guard. She placed her quiver of arrows and the long bow beside the fire pit and held the sleeping child on her lap. Why would Moses endanger the whole flock with dark approaching, knowing there were wild dogs in the area? A chilly night wind began to blow. She wrapped herself up in a wool blanket. Perhaps Moses may have gone up the mountain to search for Ga. She forced the thought from her mind. Had not Jethro warned Moses that Yahweh Sabaoth was a jealous, brutal god? Maybe he had no fear of this god.

Zipporah marveled as clusters of stars appeared like faded sheets spread across the dark canvas of heaven. She placed her son in his pouch and strapped it to her back, then walked among the sheep reassuring them that their protector was near. Suddenly a lamb's cry alerted her to danger. Sheep scattered when two jackals nipped at the tail of a lamb. The ewe brayed as she tried to protect her lamb. Zipporah yelled, causing the jackals to retreat a short distance. Not wanting to waste an arrow, she placed a stone in her sling and let it fly, hitting the larger jackal's head. She listened to its painful yelps fading in the distant night. Alert to every sound, she circled the flock, taking no time to rest.

When the baby started crying, Zipporah removed him from the pouch and breast-fed him. She rose when she felt a tremor shaking the ground, followed by thunder that seemed to come from the direction of the forbidden mountain. She detected what appeared to be a flicker of light on the mountainside. Again there was the rumble of thunder, yet the night sky was clear. The thought that Moses might be trapped on the mountain terrified her. What if the mountain god was holding him prisoner?

The sheep huddled together, their nervous braying echoed off the nearby foothills. She walked among the flock speaking softly, "Be still my children, I will protect you." As though they understood, the sheep grew quiet and settled down to rest.

Zipporah dropped to her knees and removed the garment from her child. Turning toward the mountain she lifted the baby over her head.

"God of this mountain, I beseech you not to take the life of my husband. If it is a sacrifice you require, I offer you my son, only spare my husband."

"No sacrifice will be needed, Zipporah. The Lord requires only me."

Momentarily frightened, Zipporah clutched the child to her breast, but her fear quickly gave way to joy as she recognized Moses' silhouette in the half-light.

"Moses!" She ran toward him but stepped back when she saw his face. For an instant she was not sure it was he. His face was ashen, the hairs on his temple had turned white. There was a perplexed stare in his eyes that frightened her.

"You've come from the forbidden mountain, haven't you?" she whispered, her voice trembling.

"Yes," he replied, barely audible.

Zipporah backed away. "Why did you go there? Our father warned you about the god who dwells there. He might have killed you."

Moses took her arm and led her into their lodge. Totally exhausted, he collapsed on the goatskin rug and rolled on his back with his hands propped under his head. Zipporah lit the oil lamp and held it up to better inspect his face. Whatever had happened, she knew he would never be the same. She waited for him to speak but heard only his labored breathing. She placed her hand on his chest. His skin felt cold, despite the warmth in the lodge.

"Do not shut me out. Speak of what happened," she whispered as she kissed his cheek.

Moses took deep breaths then sat up on one elbow. "I followed Ga's tracks to the base of the mountain. That's when I saw it...half way up the mountain side," Moses said as his eyes grew wider. He seemed to be staring through her.

"What did you see?"

"There was a flame that drew me to it. When I came closer I saw a burning bush, yet the fire did not consume its branches. I went closer to see this thing," he said, pausing to catch his breath. "A voice spoke to me from out of the fire and told me to remove my sandals for I was standing on holy ground. Then the voice said, 'I am the God of your father, Abraham.' I fell to the ground and covered my face, for I was afraid."

"How can this be? Elohim is the God of Abraham."

Moses clamped his hand over her mouth. "Do not speak, just listen. I heard the voice of God. I saw his form in the fire, and the earth shook as he spoke."

Zipporah pushed his hand away. "How can you be so sure it was our God? It could be a trick."

"The God on this mountain told me wondrous things. He has heard the cries of my people in Egypt."

Zipporah placed her hands to her ears, not wanting to hear any more. She looked at the empty wine jugs, wondering if he had too much to drink and had imagined it all.

"Rest for now. By morning you may find it was all a bad dream. When we return, speak to father about this," Zipporah said as she picked up the restless baby and rocked it.

A deep sadness clouded his eyes. Her doubting had upset him. She moved beside him and kissed his lips. She felt his tension ease when he leaned over the sleeping child and returned her kiss.

"Sing once again the love songs of Osiris," Zipporah whispered. "Songs that brought added joy to our nights."

"I will sing only to the God of the mountain. All others have blown from my thoughts like drifting sand," he said, staring into her eyes. "In time you will share my joy and the wonder I have known this night,"

"Rest while our son sleeps," Zipporah said, trying desperately to hold back her tears. "I will keep watch over the flock."

59

CHAPTER 10

And Moses returned to Jethro and said, "Let me go I beg of you, so
that I can return unto my brethren which are in Egypt, to see whether
they are yet alive." And Jethro said to Moses, "Go in peace."

Exodus 4:18

Zipporah followed Moses into Jethro's writing room where they were
greeted by the pungent aroma of incense. Its sweet scent came from a three-
legged brass censer that sat on one corner of his table. Jethro was on a ladder,
making room on his storage shelves for the papyrus scrolls he had recently
purchased from an Ethiopian merchant.

"What brings you to my study at this late hour?" Jethro asked as he climbed
down the ladder and motioned for them to sit beside him. When he held up his
clay lamp, he saw the concern on their faces. "Has anything happened to the
sheep?"

"We have just returned with the flock. They are safe. God has blessed you
with two new lambs," Moses said.

"That is good. So why have you come looking so worried?"

"My husband went up the forbidden mountain in search of my sheep,"
Zipporah blurted out. She flinched when Moses pinched her arm and glared at
her.

Jethro stared at Moses with disbelief. His hands trembled as he rolled up a
papyrus scroll and put it aside.

"Does she speak the truth? Let me hear it from your lips, my son."

Moses saw the terrible strain on Jethro's face as he pulled his stool beside
him. "She speaks the truth," Moses said, trying to compose himself.

Jethro raised his arms and cried, "In the name of Elohim, what possessed you
to go up that mountain knowing the danger that could befall this house?"

"You asked me to take the sheep to graze in the valley of Horeb. Zipporah's
sheep wandered off. There were jackals in the nearby hills, so I went searching
for her. When I came near the base of the mountain, I saw a burning bush on the
side of it. The flames continued to burn but the bush was not consumed, so I
climbed up the slopes to see this sight."

"Did you forget who dwells in that mountain?" Jethro asked, his voice
strained.

"No, but the beauty of the flame drew me to it. Then I heard a voice calling
to me from the flames," Moses replied.

Jethro's face began twitching. He placed his hands over his ears and shook
his head sadly.

Zipporah threw two empty wine bottles on the table. "Do you remember telling me about the Egyptian god who came from Pan-Amsu, who judges those who pollute themselves? Could it be you drank too much before you went up there?" she asked accusingly.

"How dare you question me?" Moses shouted, his voice quivering as he rose to his feet. "I was not drunk." It was the first time he had spoken to her in anger. As their eyes met, he felt remorseful.

Jethro raised his hand for silence. "My children, do you not see what is happening? Already the seeds of distrust have been sown in this family."

"Hear me, father." Moses dropped to his knees and took Jethro's hands. "I have heard the voice of God. He spoke to me and showed me his marvelous powers. He told me his name is I AM."

"You heard the voice of Yahweh Sabaoth, the warrior god, the god of volcanoes who rained fire on the cities of Sodom and Gomorrah, killing the wicked and innocent alike," Jethro said. "His other name is Jealous. In his possessive rage he might have killed you for little or no reason. Why would you place your life and that of this family in jeopardy?"

"Please hear my words," Moses pleaded. "The voice from the flames said, 'Go, gather the elders of Israel together, and tell them the God of Abraham appeared unto you, saying I have surely visited them, and have seen that which is done to you in Egypt, and I will bring you up out of Egypt unto the land of the Canaanites, into a land flowing with milk and honey.'"

"This mountain god cannot be trusted," Jethro said, throwing up his hands. "You heard the discussion at the Council of Four Nations. We are at peace with the Canaanites. If your people go there, it will inflame the whole region. I have asked the council to give your people sanctuary within our borders, just as I gave you sanctuary."

"I heard what the members said. Only the Chief Kaleb spoke for my people. God told me that many Hebrews have already fled and are dying of hunger and thirst in the Nubian and Libyan deserts. They will perish without someone to lead them. The God of our father, Abraham, has chosen me to be their leader."

"What assurance has he given you?" Zipporah asked, wondering if there were two spirits living in the mountain, the God of compassion and a god of war.

Moses turned to her, angered that she continued to interrupt at such a critical moment. "The Lord said to me that the Hebrews will be provided with what is needed by their neighbors. The Egyptians will allow my people to take their jewels of gold, their flocks, weapons and their slaves."

Zipporah could no longer restrain herself. "Why would the Egyptians make such allowances if they want to get rid of the Hebrews? They treat your people as outcasts, do they not? If you go there, you will only be killed."

Moses' face flushed as he stepped toward Zipporah and pointed to the door. "Leave us."

Stunned by the force of his words, Zipporah backed away. Never had she seen such anger in him. She hesitated, but Jethro waved his hand and motioned for her to obey. She went outside where the night air cleared her head. After drawing water from the well and splashing it on her face, she sat and reflected on the teachings of her father. For years, travelers had often discussed their gods and systems of beliefs around their campfires. From her study of Jethro's scrolls, she convinced herself that Elohim, the universal God, was merciful and kind. He commanded all peoples to live in peace and to love one another. She remembered her pledge to remain at Moses' side at all costs. It frightened her to think Moses might put his trust in a vengeful god, known for his jealous rages. She wept as she went to her bed and tried to rest.

Moses sat beside Zipporah in the morning light with his hands resting under his chin. She sat up and rubbed her eyes.

"Have you slept?" Zipporah whispered.

"How can I sleep when you doubt me?" Moses said. The weariness in his voice saddened her.

"Can you not understand my fear for us and our sons?" Zipporah replied, placing her hand to his cheek.

Moses removed her hand. "Do not touch me. Your doubting has caused great pain."

"Forgive my unbelief," she said as she tried to lean her head on his shoulder, only to have him rebuff her again.

"Listen to me carefully. When God told me to go into Egypt and lead the Hebrews out of that land, I told him many would not believe that he had sent me. It was then he showed me marvelous signs that took away my doubts."

"What kind of signs?"

"When I first saw the bush I grew fearful and ran away. The voice called me back and told me to cast my staff upon the ground. When I obeyed, it became a serpent, not unlike the one you killed on the mountain trail. The voice commanded me to take the serpent by its tail. When I did, it turned into a staff again."

Zipporah could not restrain herself from laughing. "Moses, I have seen men do such tricks in the marketplace at Ezion-geber. A man from the east removed a hooded snake from a basket and after it danced to the sounds of his flute, it turned into a rope that extended into the air. He climbed to the top of the rope and vanished."

"How can I convince you?" Moses cried, grabbing her shoulders and shaking her. "God told me to place my hand in my bosom and it became leprous as snow."

Terrified, she struggled to move away from him. "He told me to put my hand in my bosom a second time and when I did, my flesh was whole and clean." He turned his hands over to convince her.

Reluctantly, Zipporah took his hands and examined both sides as perspiration covered her face and neck. "Your words frighten me."

"I too was frightened."

Zipporah laughed nervously and stroked Moses' hand. "I cannot imagine you being frightened of anything."

"Do not doubt my words," he said, pulling her closer. "My God said there would be doubters who will refuse to hearken unto my voice. Now I find my wife is the first of the doubters. God told me to take water from the river and pour it on dry ground. I found water that had collected in a hollow rock. When I poured it on the ground, it turned to blood."

Zipporah felt nauseated and struggled to break his grip. How could she overcome the fears of a lifetime? She shuddered, convinced more than ever that it was Yahweh Sabaoth, the god of volcanoes, who showed Moses his powers. "I beg you not to perform such magic."

"If you no longer doubt, it will not be necessary," he said sternly. "Your father has given me permission to go to Egypt with his blessing. He said for me to go in peace."

Palpitations fluttered in Zipporah's chest as she sank to her knees. "I will open my heart to all you have told me," she replied, hoping he believed her. When she laid her head on his lap he began stroking her hair. Eli started crying, ending the tension they both felt. She went to the child, opened her gown and nursed him.

"When will you leave for Egypt?" she said.

"When my brother comes," Moses said, taking a cloth and wiping perspiration from her face. "God told me in a dream that Aaron will arrive after the next full moon."

"What of our children and me?"

"You did not think I would leave you behind, did you?" Moses leaned over and kissed her cheek. "Despite your doubting, you will always be the most precious rose in my heart. I told Jethro I will take you and our sons with me to Egypt and he agreed."

"Tomorrow I will begin preparing for the journey," Zipporah said.

"Have no fear, Zipporah. Our God will walk beside us. He will be our shield and protector," Moses said. "I go now to tend the sheep."

Zipporah wept silently, knowing their idyllic days were now numbered. She softly hummed a tune and rocked the child until it slept.

CHAPTER 11

And the Lord said to Aaron, "Go into the wilderness to meet Moses." And he went, and met him in the mount of God, and kissed him.

Exodus 4:27

The hot breath of early morning air and blowing dust obscured Moses' vision. It would be another hot day, the fourth in a row. He placed a scarf over his mouth and cleared his nose to relieve his dry nostrils. During the night the heat had disturbed his sleep. He had slipped quietly from Zipporah's side, and sat under a palm tree pondering the experience on the mountain. It seemed unbelievable that God would choose him to lead the Hebrews to the promised land. He doubted if he was capable of giving such leadership. At dawn he felt totally exhausted as he signaled the dog to help him move the sheep to the west pasture. By afternoon the oppressive heat had spread across the meadow like a red tide washing over some remote shore. Moses watched a trail of dust that could be seen in the shimmering landscape. Four men on camels moved slowly in his direction. Jethro had told him to be on the lookout for a caravan from Egypt. When the riders approached, Moses walked out to greet them.

"I welcome you in the name of Jethro, Priest of Midian," Moses shouted. His smile faded when he saw blood on the lead rider's left sleeve. "What has befallen you?"

"Our caravan was ambushed by Amalekites from the Wilderness of Zin. Those who traveled with us took shelter in the hills but we fear they may have perished," the wounded man said. He signaled his camel to kneel. "I am Brunu and these are my countrymen." After the drivers dismounted, Moses examined his wound.

"I am Moses, son-in-law of Jethro. This cut must be treated. With your permission I will clean it for you."

"You kindness will be rewarded," Brunu said. Moses took the men to a shade tree where he cleaned the wound with olive oil, then poured wine into the cut. Satisfied the wound was clean, he bound it tightly with strips of cloth. As they rested, Moses offered Brunu dates and wine.

"Where do you journey?"

"We are returning to the kingdom of Ammon. For more than a month we have been in Egypt trading our spices for grain," Brunu said as he adjusted the sling. "As we approached the border of Midian, the thieves came upon us without warning. They were forty or more in number. Their leader, a one-eyed man, demanded tribute. When we refused, they waited until dark then attacked us."

"Were there any travelers coming to Midian in your caravan?"

"Yes. A Hebrew," Brunu said, sipping his wine. "He agreed to pay us upon our arrival at your capital, Ezion-geber. I fear he may have been slain or taken captive."

Moses sprang to his feet. "What is his name?"

"He called himself Aaron. Do you know him?"

Moses felt lightheaded. Beads of perspiration covered his face and neck. He dropped to his knees and pounded his fist on the dry ground. "He is my brother," he cried in anguish. "My God told me of his coming. Come, we must make haste and report this to my father-in-law. He will send a messenger to the Chiefs of Midian."

Midianite cavalry arrived at Jethro's compound the morning of the following day. After conferring with a captain named Aken, Brunu agreed to escort them to the canyon where the ambush had taken place. Moses volunteered to join them when Jethro gave him permission to take his horse.

The company of seventy horsemen arrived at the mountain pass by late afternoon. The clear desert air made the wind-scarred slopes stand out in vivid relief. As they searched the area, Moses saw vultures circling above the sand stone cliffs.

"It was up there among those rocks our men sought safety." Brunu pointed to a plateau above them. "The sky is filled with birds of death. I count seven of them. It is a bad omen."

Aken selected twelve men to scale the steep slopes. Brunu and Moses volunteered to accompany them. As they clawed their way, Moses was impressed that Brunu's wounded arm did not slow him. At the first plateau they discovered a broken lance wedged between two rocks. Below it lay a necklace of bright stones and red feathers sprinkled with blood. Moses knew it belonged to an Amalekite who had been killed or wounded. At the next plateau they discovered the remains of five men whose bodies had been stripped of their clothing and weapons. Just above them, vultures feasted on human flesh wedged between two rocks. Moses shouted as he climbed higher and chased the scavengers off. The skulls of the dead had been bashed open. Moses turned away when he saw pools of dried blood on the ground and rocks. Brunu examined the skulls then turned to Moses. "Your brother is not among these dead."

"How can you be certain?" Moses said hopefully. "All that remains are their teeth and bones."

"I knew these men by their teeth. These were my kinsmen. Your brother may have escaped or been taken prisoner."

Moses leaned against a rock and stared at the sky as he muttered a silent prayer. He turned to Brunu. "I have a premonition that I will find my brother in the fields of Horeb, near the Mountain of God."

"If you are convinced he has escaped, you will have to look for him without us," Brunu said. "I will go with Aken to hunt down the Amalekites. They must be punished for their crimes. I hope you find your brother alive."

After descending the mountain, Moses watched Aken and his men mount their horses. In the final moments he was tempted to ride with them but an overwhelming compulsion forced him homeward. What if his premonition was wrong? He quickly dismissed the thought.

"Take care, Moses. If we find your brother we will return him to you," Brunu shouted as the cavalrymen raised their lances and rode off. Their bloodcurdling war cries echoed off the canyon walls. Moses stood in the trail and watched them disappear into a cloud of red dust.

Upon his return, Moses told Zipporah he wanted her to accompany him to the forbidden mountain. He insisted that she leave both children in Ruth's care. Zipporah was pleased that Moses had asked her, but she feared he might force her to follow him up the slopes of the mountain.

"I go to meet my brother. When he arrives, you will know it was our God who guided him to me."

They arrived at base camp just as winds began blowing at gale force. With their visibility impaired, Moses led Zipporah to the lodge and was relieved to find it intact. He pulled down a deerskin over the opening to protect them from blowing dust. Zipporah opened a jar, poured oil in the clay lamp and lit it. Once settled, she removed her garment and stretched out beside him. When Moses remained unresponsive, she kissed his lips and tickled him.

"Do not touch me," he said, pushing her hand away. "We are resting near sacred ground."

The steely expression in his eyes frightened her. His lips moved silently as he gazed at the thatched roof of the lodge. Zipporah blew out the lamp and found herself terrified of this god who demanded her husband's loyalty. She flinched when Moses touched her shoulder.

"Forgive me if I offended you," he said. "This night you will know the power of my God, for I am certain he will deliver my brother from the den of the Amalekites."

When he turned his back and slept she recalled the nights he taught her the mysteries of loving. Her body ached to be held and cuddled.

With the first rays of morning light, Moses gathered firewood and went hunting while Zipporah slept. She awoke to his gentle touch an hour later. He handed her a quail that he had killed with his sling. The winds were calm enough for her to make a fire in the stone pit. After cleaning and roasting the bird, they ate without speaking.

As the day heated, Zipporah could sense doubt gnawing at Moses. He paced back and forth, fearing the Amalekites may have killed or enslaved his brother. Even if his brother arrived it might not be enough to convince her that the god of this mountain was the God of Abraham.

"Should I have gone with the cavalry in their pursuit of the thieves?" Moses asked. Anguish spread across his tortured face. She embraced him and kissed his cheek. The ground suddenly shook, throwing them off balance.

"What is happening?" she cried.

"God is awake," Moses said, staring at the mountain peak. He cupped his hands to his mouth and shouted, "Aaron." His echo returned from the arid hills at the base of the mountain.

His outburst startled Zipporah. She tightened her arms around him. Suddenly, from the direction of the hills they heard a faint sound.

"Don't speak," Moses whispered, clamping his hands over her mouth. They stood still and listened. "Is anyone there?"

"Yes. I come in peace," a voice answered.

Moses grabbed Zipporah's shoulders and shook her. "Did you hear it?" he cried, his eyes blazing with excitement. "Someone's there. I'm certain it is my brother."

He removed a smoldering log from the fire and waved it frantically, sending smoke signals above the camp. Zipporah grew concerned. What if it was a trick? He could be endangering their lives.

"We are here," Moses shouted. "Who comes?"

Suspicious of strangers, Zipporah placed an arrow in her bow and tightened her fingers on the string. It was not far from this place that she had killed an Amalekite to protect Moses. When he ran toward the mountain trail, Zipporah followed several paces behind, cautiously watching their flank. She stopped abruptly when she saw a stranger standing on the trail. Moses ran toward the man, never doubting who he was. The stranger removed the gray hood from his head and waved. As she drew nearer, she noticed that his mixed gray hair and beard were covered with dust, his gray robe tattered and threadbare. Both men hesitated momentarily as they searched each other's eyes, then they embraced and kissed.

Moses stepped back and held the man at arms length. His sun burned head, with its receding hairline, revealed he was in his middle forties. No words were necessary at that moment. Both alternated between tears and laughter as they continued hugging and kissing each other's cheeks.

"The God of Abraham has brought you here, my brother. He told me of your coming in a dream," Moses cried. "I knew I would find you near the base of His mountain."

"I was sent by the Hebrew elders to find you. With God's help I escaped the jaws of death."

"Speak of our mother and sister. Are they in good health?" Moses asked, wiping tears from his eyes.

"Our mother is frail and in poor health," Aaron said. "Our sister, Miriam, sends her blessings."

Moses beckoned Zipporah to come closer. "This is my brother whom God has brought to me."

Zipporah covered her hair with her shawl as she approached them. "I rejoice that God has delivered you from the Amalekites," she said quietly.

"Aaron, this is Zipporah, my wife," Moses said. The brother showed no emotion as he approached her. His gaze left her feeling uncomfortable.

"You are married to a woman of Midian?" Aaron asked, obviously displeased.

"Yes. She is the daughter of Jethro, the Priest of Midian," Moses said with pride. "We have two sons."

"You will be welcomed in my father's house," Zipporah said, then turned to Moses. "Can we leave soon? Our children need us."

Aaron took Moses' arm and led him a short distance away. "This marriage could complicate my mission. We must speak of it when we are alone."

Moses called out to Zipporah, "My brother and I must go to the place where I met our God. There we will build an altar of stones."

"Should I return home or wait for you?"

Moses gestured toward the lodge. "Remain and prepare us food, for we will be hungry by the time we return."

Zipporah stood on the path and watched as Moses and Aaron walked toward the mountain. She felt troubled. Why did she have this uneasy feeling that his brother did not approve of her? When she stretched out on the rug, she knew she still did not trust Moses' mountain god. Would that distrust soon apply to Moses' brother? Unable to put the thought out of her mind, she closed her eyes. "Forgive me for my unbelief," she whispered. Confused and shaken, she wondered to whom she was praying, Elohim, Yahweh Sabaoth, or Osiris?

CHAPTER 12

And Moses said, "O my Lord, I am not eloquent...I am slow of speech, and of a slow tongue."

Exodus 4:10

Aaron found it difficult to breathe as he followed Moses up the steep mountain trail. He paused and took several deep breaths, then turned and stared at the valley. As he sat on a rock and wiped the sweat from his face, he admired the beauty of the lush grassland with its meandering stream winding through gently rolling hills. Moses pointed out Jethro's compound where a trail of smoke could be seen drifting slowly across the near windless landscape. A cluster of Acacia trees marked the spot. "You see before you the Valley of Arad. It belongs to Jethro and his kin." He noticed tears flowing down Aaron's cheeks. "Why are you weeping, brother?"

"Our family owned such land in the region of Goshen. It has been in our family for six generations and we were forced to leave it without compensation. When Pharaoh's expulsion order was given, Egyptian officials came and ordered us off our land," Aaron said, his voice quivering.

"Where did our family go?"

"We were ordered to the city of Pithom. Our people are gathering there for the exodus. We need a strong leader to guide us. When Asa and Estrum returned from their meeting with the kings and chiefs of the four nations, they spoke of you. That is why the elders sent me here. Our God wants you to lead us to our promised land."

"I know. God told me of your coming. Come, let us go to the place where I met our Lord."

When they reached the first plateau, Moses turned to Aaron and pointed to a bush whose twisted trunk extended from a crack between two massive stones. "This is the place," Moses whispered. With his finger on his lips, he cautioned Aaron not to speak. With hand gestures, he signaled for him to remove his sandals. They walked toward the bush, unmindful of the flat stones that burned the soles of their feet. Just short of the bush Moses dropped to his knees and prayed silently as Aaron looked anxiously in all directions. Both men flinched when a falcon flew from the bush, screeching in protest. Moses pushed the branches aside and found a nest with two chicks. The loud protest of the mother falcon pierced the air as it circled above them.

"It was here I saw the form of God," Moses whispered reverently.

"No man has seen the face of God and lived," Aaron replied.

69

"I did not see his face, only his form. This bush was on fire. There are no words to describe the wonder and beauty of it," Moses said, taking Aaron's hand and pulling him closer. He plucked several leaves and rubbed them across his forehead. "A voice called out to me, demanding that I return to Egypt and lead our people to the land were our forefathers dwelled. When I inquired who it was speaking to me the voice said, 'I am that I am. Therefore say to the children of Israel, I AM sent me unto you.' I feared if I returned I would be put to death for killing an Egyptian taskmaster."

"This is wonderful news," Aaron said. "You should know that those who would judge you are no longer in power. A new Pharaoh rules Egypt and Nubia."

"Travelers have told me all that has happened, but I did not want to take this burden upon myself. I am content to remain in this peaceful land. When God ordered me to return, I told him that I was not eloquent and slow of speech."

"You thought you could lie to God?" Aaron said with amusement.

"You speak the truth, for he became angry with me. The light from that bush glowed so brightly that I could no longer look at it. The earth shook beneath my feet and his voice sounded like thunder as he said unto me. 'Who hath made man's mouth? Or who makes the dumb, or deaf, or the seeing, or the blind? Have not I, the Lord?'" As Moses repeated the words, his voice quivered. "He told me of your coming, saying you could speak on my behalf until such time that he would guide my tongue and teach me what to say."

"You don't seem to be slow in speech now," Aaron said grinning. "But there is another matter I must speak to you about."

"What is it?"

"This wife of yours. She is a Midianite," Aaron said, unable to disguise his contempt. "You have been chosen by God to lead us. No foreign woman is worthy to be the wife of one chosen to lead our people to nationhood."

"But I am now a son of Midian," Moses said, refusing to get upset. "Zipporah is the light that gives meaning to my existence, such as it is. Do not speak against her for she is pure of heart. Come, let us gather stones and build an altar to our God."

"But you have transgressed the law by marrying a woman of Midian. You must separate yourself from her."

"If I had transgressed God's law, would he have chosen me to lead our people? Listen carefully. You must speak no more of this."

On the fourth night of the quarter moon, Jethro invited relatives and friends from the neighboring villages to a feast to celebrate Aaron's safe arrival. An elaborate wool rug was placed on the ground at the center of the compound where the guests laughed and joked as they drank Jethro's finest wines. Ruth and her daughters served a feast of spiced vegetables, breads, dates, roasted lamb, and baked quail. When all were filled, Zipporah and her sisters changed from their cooking garments into flowered blouses and red skirts. The seven daughters ran to the center of the dining area and danced to the accompaniment of flutes, drums and bells played by Rehob and his brothers. Zipporah moved toward Aaron and threw a flower in his lap. He flinched and brushed it away as though it were a scorpion.

The guests shouted and clapped as the sisters twirled and tumbled to the beating of drums and tambourines. At the end of the dance Rehob stood up and blew kisses to the guests as everyone cheered. Aaron turned to Moses and whispered, "I take no delight in this shameful exhibition."

Moses stared at his brother momentarily, then laughed as his refilled Aaron's cup.

"Come brother, enjoy the night. It is the custom of the young women and men of Midian to dance on such festive occasions."

"Such dancing is an abomination in the sight of the Lord," Aaron whispered reproachfully. "You have been chosen to lead thousands, yea, hundreds of thousands of our people out of the land of bondage. Our God will require strict obedience to his laws if this exodus is to succeed. The ways of the heathen will not be tolerated."

Moses extended his hand to Aaron and pulled him to his feet. He turned to the guests and said, "My brother has come through the desert of the Sinai. The sun has tired him and he is in need of rest. You will excuse us. Let the music and the dancing continue."

Moses lead Aaron into the tent reserved for travelers. Aaron collapsed on the bed that Ruth had prepared for him. "I did not mean to offend your guests, but this burden we will soon undertake is heavy," Aaron said, lifting himself up on one elbow.

"Hear me well, my brother. My adopted people are not heathens, and you must not treat them as such," Moses said sternly.

"I meant no disrespect to you or your wife. But the sight of that young man with his face painted like a woman offends me."

"Let us not speak of this again," Moses said, mindful of his own attitude toward Rehob.

"Have you spoken to your father-in-law of our journey?"

"Yes, this morning. He has given me his blessing. When our people leave Egypt we will need weapons to protect ourselves. Jethro will ask the chiefs of Midian to sell us arms and supplies."

"Do you intend to bring your wife and children?"

"Yes. Did you think I would leave them behind?"

"You would be wise if you did. They will only hinder you. I must be truthful, the elders will not accept a woman that is not of our faith and race."

"My wife and I are of one flesh," Moses said, trying to control his temper. "Are the elder's hearts made of stones? Have they forgotten these people are also the descendants of Abraham?"

"Your Midian wife does not know the God of our fathers."

"You are mistaken. Zipporah and her people know our God. They call his name Elohim."

"Have your sons been circumcised as the Lord demands?"

Moses hesitated, as it was still a sensitive issue for him. "My father-in-law is the Priest of Midian. Midian sons are circumcised at age twelve, signifying they are entering manhood."

"But you are Hebrew. The sons of Israel must be circumcised on the eighth day. You must circumcise them before you reach Egypt. If it is not done the wrath of God will fall upon your head."

"As long as I am in my father-in-law's house, I will honor his wishes. Of this I am sure, Jethro walks with God."

"But does he walk with the true God of Abraham?"

"By what measure does our God judge men? I came to Jethro ragged and he gave me garments. I was starving and he gave me food, drink and offered me work as the shepherd of his flock. I was lonely and he offered me his daughter, Zipporah. I have been blessed beyond measure."

"God demands that you circumcise your sons on the eighth day," Aaron insisted indignantly.

"Does God judge a man by his foreskin or by what is in his heart?" Moses said quietly, as he leaned over and kissed his brother's cheeks. "Rest well, my brother. Soon we begin the Lord's work."

Zipporah and Timna walked across the meadow carrying their slings at their side. The sheep dog slowed, alerting them that some creature was in the tall grass. When Zipporah whistled the dog sprang forward, flushing out a hare that darted across the field. Timna's sling whined as she twirled it and released a stone. The missile hit its mark as the hare tumbled over and quivered. The dog quickly retrieved it and returned it to Timna.

"Good girl," Timna said, holding up the hare by its ears. "Trogee is learning fast."

"Your skill with the sling has greatly improved," Zipporah said.

"Moses helped me. While the flock is grazing, we practice together. I used to get excited and would miss most of the time. He taught me how to remain calm and cast my stone to the right place."

"Timna, there is something I must tell you. Moses has been called by God to lead his people out of Egypt. He has accepted the call."

"Does that mean he will be leaving us?" Timna said with alarm.

"I'm afraid so."

"Why does he have to leave? Don't the Hebrews have their own leaders?" Timna protested.

"I knew from the moment we met he was destined for something special. This will be especially hard on you, but I am taking the children and going with him."

"No! You can't leave us," Timna cried, hugging Zipporah's waist. "It's not fair. It's not fair."

Zipporah cupped her hands to Timna's cheeks and looked into her eyes. "You will learn that life has its storms. My husband goes into a storm and I must be at his side," she said. Timna hugged Zipporah tighter. For a brief period, neither spoke as they clung to each other. Timna's dog, Trogee, nuzzled and pawed at them when she became impatient. They wiped their tears and petted the dog's head, then walked arm in arm back to the compound.

CHAPTER 13

So Moses took his wife and sons and put them on a donkey, and
returned to the land of Egypt, holding tightly to the rod of God.

Exodus 4:20

A refreshing afternoon shower greeted the caravan that arrived at Jethro's compound. As drivers from the kingdom of Moab rested their animals for the night, Zipporah knew her life would never be the same. From the hour she learned she would accompany Moses to Egypt with their sons, she had not been able to shake off her depression. Adding to her discomfort was Aaron's attitude toward her. She sensed his unbridled hostility and suspected he found her unacceptable to be the wife of Moses. How would the Hebrews treat her when they arrived in Egypt? When she finally spoke to Moses about her fears, he smiled and kissed her.

"My people will learn to love you as I love you. They are a gentle, caring people."

That evening Jethro invited the caravan chieftain to dine at the family table. After eating and discussing trade matters, Moses successfully bargained for passage to Pithom, a city in the Egyptian province of Goshen. Hebrews from throughout Egypt were gathering there to begin the exodus.

The next morning, Zipporah rose early and took her sons to the staging area which seemed to be a mass of confusion. Drivers were busy preparing for their continuing journey. When all her sisters joined them, Timna helped Gershom count thirty-three camels and twenty horses. All were laden with trade goods. The sisters laughed when a camel resisted its driver by spitting in his face. The driver cursed and retaliated by ramming a pole under its tail.

Moses and Jethro led a camel and two donkeys into the corral. The camel was weighted down with supplies for the trip. It was decided that Zipporah would ride the saddled donkey with the baby strapped to her back. Jethro insisted Moses take his horse so he could assist the caravan guards in case there was trouble.

Zipporah was glad that Aaron would not be making the trip with them. He had departed for Egypt a week earlier to prepare the way for Moses. A blast of the Ram's horn signaled their departure within the hour. Ruth and her daughters kissed and hugged Zipporah and the children. Timna screamed and became so hysterical that Leah and Katurah had to pry her arms from around Zipporah's waist.

"Take me with you," Timna pleaded.

Jethro placed his hands over his ears. "Stop before you cause a stampede," he shouted. "We must have a reverent attitude at such a time as this."

"Reverent attitude you say," Ruth muttered under her breath. "You allow Moses to take our daughter and grandchildren through that desert, knowing the Amalekites may be waiting for them. This is madness."

Jethro's face softened. He turned to Ruth and cupped her face with his hands. "It is God's will, dear wife. We must place our trust in him. Elohim walks with them," Jethro said, leaning over and kissing her forehead. "The chieftain of this caravan is my friend. He will protect them with his life." Ruth pushed his hands away and went to Zipporah, unaware that Moses had overheard her remarks.

"It saddens me that Ruth still doubts me," Moses whispered.

"In time she will know the truth," Jethro said, wiping tears that flowed into his mustache and beard. "May Elohim's love protect you from your enemies. This will be my prayer night and day."

Moses did not reply. He was certain his God would have to use more than the power of love for this exodus to succeed. A God that was strong in battle was what he needed.

Leah took Zipporah aside and whispered, "Rehob wants to see you. You will find him in our tent."

"Why doesn't he come here?"

"You should ask him."

Zipporah left the baby with Leah and ran to the tent. "Rehob, why are you here and not outside with the family?"

"I thought it best that I see you alone. I didn't want to upset your husband. You do know that both he and his brother despise me."

"That's not true. Why could you say such a thing?"

"I'm not blind, Zipporah. They look at me as though I'm worse than swine. I'm surprised you haven't seen it. But of course, love often blinds us. I just wanted to say goodbye to you in privacy. Take care of yourself and those sweet, sweet boys." Rehob bit his lip then kissed her cheek. She struggled to hold back her tears after he opened the flap to the tent and left.

The final blast of a Ram's horn was followed by the guttural calls of the camel drivers, signaling everyone to their assigned positions. Moses lifted Zipporah and the baby onto the donkey, then took Gershom's hand.

"You will walk with me for now," Moses said, pushing strands of hair from the boy's eyes.

"Why are we walking, father?"

"Our horse must be well rested during our journey. If enemies come upon us, I will ride this horse and help drive them away. If you get tired, I will carry you on my shoulders."

"I won't get tired, father," Gershom replied proudly. "May I hold the reins?" Moses glanced back at Zipporah who smiled and nodded her approval.

Amidst the confusion of shouting men, braying animals and swirling dust, Zipporah covered her younger child's face. Smiling bravely and fighting tears, she waved to her family. The caravan moved slowly onto the dusty highway. Her concern for Gershom soon faded when he kept pace with Moses and did not seem to tire.

By late afternoon the caravan arrived at the Azur oasis with its three wells and a shaded grove of date trees. Moses pitched his tent under a tree near the edge of the grove. Zipporah gave thanks for the temperate breeze that blew in from the direction of the gulf.

"I must speak with the caravan's chieftain," Moses said as he kissed her cheek. "I won't be long. He trotted to the front of the caravan where he found the chieftain seated under a tree beside several of his drivers.

"You are approaching the mountain pass where the Amalekites ambushed a caravan returning from Egypt," Moses said, pointing to the mountain range in the distance. "It would be wise to send some of your men ahead to search the pass before you enter it."

After wiping his mouth on his sleeve, the chieftain motioned for Moses to sit beside him. "My caravan will not be troubled by the Amalekites," he said, cutting a slice of cheese and offering it to Moses on the tip of his knife. "That's because I pay them tribute. A few skins of wine and a block of salt are highly prized by them. You have no need to worry."

"They violated the borders of Midian when they attacked the caravan returning to Ammon."

"Do not concern yourself, Moses. You and your family will soon be enjoying the sights of the Nile and the beautiful gardens of Pithom, if only for a short time," the chieftain mumbled with his mouth full. "It is regrettable that your people are being forced out of Egypt. Egypt will lose some of its most gifted and talented sons. Pharaoh's expulsion order requires them to be out in three months or their lands will be seized without compensation. Those remaining will be little better than common laborers."

"I know of this. In some provinces it has already happened."

"Jethro told us that you have been chosen to lead the Hebrews to the land of Canaan. Why did the Hebrews choose you, the son-in-law of the Priest of Midian?"

"They did not choose me. God commanded me to take my people to our promised land."

"You take your people to a land where the Philistines and the Canaanites have dwelled since the dawn of time. They are a powerful people who live in walled cities."

76

"God told me he gave the land of Canaan to Abraham and his descendants. He has commanded that I take them there. I put my trust only in him."

"Your god is greedy or mad. Abraham purchased several hundred acres of land for himself and his family when he arrived in Canaan. His grandsons relinquished their birthright when they abandoned their land four centuries ago," the chieftain said. "Go rest and pray, Moses. You will need your god's protection when you bring your people out of Egypt." Moses suspected the chieftain thought his mission was suicidal.

While returning, he thought it wise not to tell Zipporah about his conversation, knowing it could only upset her. Resting beside their campfire, he listened as she told the children stories. She looked so beautiful in the soft moonlight that highlighted her hair. How fortunate to have such a wife to comfort him in times of stress. When the children grew tired, he took them inside the tent and remained with them until they fell asleep.

To give them privacy, Zipporah had tied a canopy to trees near their tent. Moses felt exhausted when he stretched out beside her. He hated the tension that had plagued him recently. Why was he always preoccupied with thoughts of the coming exodus, even when he held her in his arms? He watched as she undressed and took the combs from her hair, letting it hang loose.

"What if the stars are gods and they are watching us," Zipporah said, pressing closer to him.

Moses searched the night sky and pointed out a star cluster. "There is Isis and next to her is Osiris. They are smiling down on us." He moaned when she began massaging him. There was an assertiveness about her that he had never experienced before.

"Would Isis approve if I kissed you here?" She did not wait for a reply and soon thereafter, felt the tension draining from his body.

"Isis never makes a glutton of herself?" he whispered, restraining her. She pouted, then crawled over him. With their coupling, the soft cooing of a dove could be heard in the tree above them. "You are like a cluster of lilies from the valley of the Nile," Moses whispered. "Your cheeks are comely and your lips more beautiful than all the roses of Sharon."

"Take your pleasure, then rest between my breasts," Zipporah whispered hoarsely. In the crystalline sky, the star cluster exploded and showered the heaven with trails of light. She whispered a prayer to both Isis and Osiris, giving thanks that they had not allowed Moses' mountain God to interfere.

When Eli started crying, Zipporah whispered, "Why do babies always cry at such precious moments as this?"

The blast of a ram's horn startled Zipporah from a restful sleep. She reached for Moses but he was already up and loading the donkey. She went to him, placed her arms around his neck and kissed his lips.

"Did you sleep well?" he asked, squeezing her tightly.

"In your arms I always sleep well," she said, smiling. "I had a marvelous dream. We were walking on the beach. Later that night the stars circled us as we made love. Then that ugly rams' horn sounded and woke me."

"I will take you to other beaches," Moses said. "The chieftain has ordered us to our stations. Prepare the children while I finish packing."

Within the hour the caravan continued its slow pace through the narrow pass that led into the Sinai desert. Moses pointed out the spot where the ambush had taken place the month before.

"In those hills is where Aaron escaped from Amalek. I have been assured by the caravan chieftain that we will not be troubled by him or his men," Moses said, hoping she believed him.

As the sun began to set, the caravan came to a sudden halt. A scout rode by on horseback shouting for everyone to hold their positions in line. Situated near the end of the caravan, Moses strained to see what was causing the delay. He became impatient and started toward the head of the column on foot. A camel driver cautioned him not to go further.

"Our leader holds council with a band of Amalekite tribesmen. Keep your wife and children out of sight and do not show yourself. It would not go well for any of us if they learned that a Hebrew family is traveling with us."

Moses shielded his eyes from the sun's red glare. He heard shouts, followed by the thunder of horses' hooves. Out of a cloud of dust rode 40 horsemen at a full gallop. Moses ducked behind a camel as they passed. The lead rider turned the horsemen toward the mountain trail and rode out of sight. He was certain the man at the head of the column was Prince Amalek. He waited until the caravan reached the next rest stop before inquiring of the chieftain if it was Amalek.

"Yes, Moses. How do you know him?" the chieftain asked.

"When I first arrived in Midian, he and seven men seized the wells at the Ezon oasis. They ravaged one of Jethro's daughters. I fought Amalek and made him pay for their crime."

"You fought Prince Amalek and his men and made them pay tribute?" the chieftain said skeptically. "If what you say is true then it is far better he did not know you travel with us. He would return with a larger force. I hate to think what would happen to you and that lovely wife of yours."

"Our God will be our strength and protector," Moses said, as the tightness in his chest increased.

"You had best bribe Amalek if you can, and pray he does not remember you. If he learns you are the leader of the Hebrews, you will have to fight your way through the Sinai. Prince Amalek worships Molesh, the fire god. He and his followers sacrifice children and virgins on his altar," the chieftain said. "As for your god protecting you, there is no better contest than when gods join men in battle. If such comes to pass, I am sure the gods of Egypt will be watching the contest from Mount Sinai and placing wagers on the outcome. Men will bleed and die while your god and Amalek's god, Molesh, scuffle in the desert sands."

Moses was not amused.

CHAPTER 14

And it came to pass by the way of the inn, that the Lord met Moses and sought to kill him.

Exodus 4:24

Two Egyptian sentries standing guard outside of the walled city of Pithom signaled the arrival of the caravan with the beating of brass gongs. Zipporah persuaded Gershom to ride the donkey while she walked beside Moses. With the month long journey nearing its end, she wanted to be at his side when they entered the city. As they passed through the arched gate, her excitement grew. She no longer felt tired, despite carrying Eli strapped on her back all day. When she reached Moses' side, she squeezed his arm. Soon they were caught up in the thick crowd thronging the narrow street.

"The Egyptians call the gate we just passed under the Passage of Peace," Moses shouted, trying to make himself heard over the noise of the massive crowd with their carts and animals.

"I have never seen such tall buildings," Zipporah called out breathlessly as they passed a sandstone temple. She got a brief glimpse of the massive statue of the god, Osiris. Thanks to Moses' teachings, she could now read the hieroglyphic inscription etched on the forty-foot obelisk that stood in front of it. When the caravan halted in the congested street, Gershom darted into the crowd.

"Gershom, come back," Zipporah screamed. Moses and Zipporah found themselves being jostled as they pushed frantically through the throng after him. When they reached the temple, they found him standing on the base of the obelisk.

Moses grabbed Gershom's arms and shook him. "You must never run off. Is that understood?" he shouted. "You could get lost or stolen and we might never find you."

"Yes father," Gershom said, rubbing one arm while pointing to the hieroglyphic figures. "What do those drawings mean?"

Zipporah hugged Gershom tightly and said, *"Ausar, maaxeru, sebebi heh unt-f er er t'etta neb nebu suten suteniu aqi neter neferu ma sen.* Osiris, triumphant, traversing eternity, his existence being forever, Lord of lords, King of kings, Prince, God of the gods, who lived with you."

"You read the inscription perfectly. I'm proud of you," Moses said. He lifted Gershom on his shoulders and headed back to their place in the caravan. "This is a great city but it is not as impressive as the capital, Noph. Before we

80

leave for Canaan, I hope to show you the Pyramids and the Sphinx at Giza. My adoptive family often took me there as a boy. I still dream of its splendors."

After a delay, the caravan continued through the narrow streets until it reached the plaza in the heart of the city. Thousands of people haggled with merchants over articles and foods of every description. The more profitable merchants equipped their stalls with colorful awnings that protected their customers from the blistering heat.

Never in her life had Zipporah seen such an abundance and variety of food. A market woman motioned to her, "Come buy my fine melons, my leeks, my cucumbers, garlic and onions. This hen will make a delicious meal for your family. These sun-dried caterpillars are delicious when cooked with tomatoes and a pinch of garlic."

Zipporah purchased a melon and slices of goat cheese. While they rested in the shade someone shouted, "Are you Moses?" Two men dressed in black robes pushed their way through the crowd. When Moses nodded, they rushed to him and kissed his cheeks.

"I am Reuben, the elder of the House of Simeon and this is Abidan of the House of Benjamin," the older man said. He motioned for Moses to move under the shade of a merchant's awning. "When Aaron told us of your coming, we prayed that you would have a safe journey. Our people rejoiced when they heard that God had chosen you to lead us from this land."

"Why is my brother not here?" Moses asked.

"He has journeyed up the Nile to the city of Hermopolis to inform the congregation of your coming. We expect him to return within 20 days or more. Our people are to assemble here to begin the exodus to the land promised us by our God," Reuben said. "The elders are anxious to hear your plans."

"Our first task will be to raise an army and train it. Aaron spoke of many Hebrews who have been expelled from the armies and navy of Egypt. It is from their ranks I will appoint my commanders. The chiefs of my adopted land have agreed to sell us arms," Moses said.

"Well spoken, Moses. One such leader is Joshua. You will meet him this evening."

"My family and I are weary and in need of rest. Our journey has been long," Moses said, taking Zipporah's hand. "This is Zipporah, my wife, and these are my sons."

Reuben stared at her then turned to Moses. "I have reserved a room for you at the inn. It is only a short distance from here."

Reuben's cold reserve confirmed Zipporah's fear. She took the reins of the donkey and walked behind Moses as they made their way out of the plaza. They arrived at a two-story building located on a narrow street. The innkeeper, a stout man with a wooden leg, took them up a flight of stairs to a single room on the second floor. He led Zipporah to the window and pointed to the enclosed courtyard separated by a wall.

"On the other side of that wall are two pools. The one with the red tile is for women and girls," he said, handing her four bath cloths.

Zipporah nodded her thanks as she shrugged off her backpack. Leaving the children with Moses, she rushed to the marble-edged pool and enjoyed her first bath in months. Beyond the wall she could hear Moses and the children's laughter. As she relaxed in the sun-heated water, she realized they had come through dangers seen and unseen. She felt remorseful for having doubted Moses' God. At the proper hour she would tell him so.

When she returned to the room, she portioned out slices of the melon. Moses gave thanks for their safe journey and for being free of desert dust and grime.

"Can we return to the plaza when it is cool?" Zipporah said enthusiastically. "There is so much to see."

"There will be time later," Moses said, placing his arms around her waist. "The elders have invited me to meet with them and the time grows near. I regret I must leave you on our first night in Egypt."

"Do not worry about us," Zipporah said, rising on tiptoes to kiss his lips. A knock at the door caused her to step back. When Moses opened it, a slender, dark-skinned woman entered carrying a bowl of fruit.

"My master, Reuben, asked me to bring you this gift," the woman said, avoiding Zipporah's eyes as she handed her the bowl.

"Thank your master," Moses said, intrigued by her ebony face and flawless skin. "Are you Hebrew?"

"Yes, my lord. My master has taught me the commandments of your God. Your God is now my God."

Gershom pulled the woman's skirt. "I'm Gershom, and that's my brother resting on the bed."

"What is your name?" Zipporah asked, as she restrained Gershom and made him sit beside Eli.

"I am Shina," she said, adjusting the strap on her white linen dress that had fallen below her shoulder.

"Are you Egyptian?"

"No. I am from Ethiopia. My nation met defeat at the hands of the Egyptians. My family was brought here as prisoners of war," Shina said, her head bowed.

"Where is your family now?" Moses asked.

"My father and brothers have returned to Ethiopia. My father is a prince whom the Egyptians held for ransom. Our king paid the ransom but it did not include me."

"Do you wish to return to your home?" Zipporah asked.

"No. I am content to remain as a member of the congregation," Shina said.

Zipporah thought it strange that a woman whose father was a prince would choose to remain a slave. Or was she a slave?

"The meeting of the elders will begin shortly," Shina said, glancing quickly at Moses. "My master asked me to escort you to the House of Worship. It is only a short distance from here."

"Wait outside for me," Moses said.

When she stepped outside and closed the door, Moses took Zipporah in his arms. "If you are awake when I return we will celebrate our arrival," he whispered.

"I may rest, but not for long. I'm too excited to sleep." After he left, Zipporah went to the window and watched the flow of people in the crowded street below. A thick cloud blocked her view of the stars. There was no breeze and the room was extremely hot. She removed the children's clothing, placed them on a mat and waved a reed fan over them until they slept. Just as her eyes grew heavy, a knock at the door startled her. She opened it, thinking Moses had returned. Two women dressed in black blouses and ankle-length skirts brushed by her without speaking. They gawked at the sleeping children then turned to face her.

"We are from the Hebrew congregation," the older of the two women said. Zipporah guessed she was in her eighties. The younger woman appeared to be in her thirties.

Zipporah smiled as she nervously pulled two chairs to the center of the room. "I am pleased you have come. Will you sit?"

"Cover the nakedness of your sons," said the woman sternly. "There is an urgent matter we must discuss with you." Zipporah felt uneasy when they adjusted their skirts and took their seats. She spread a cotton cloth over the children.

"The elders are meeting with your husband at this hour. It concerns them that you have not honored his wishes."

"I do not understand. How have I not honored my husband?" Zipporah said with alarm.

"Your sons have not been circumcised according to Hebrew laws," the woman said. "Our God is offended by the sight of these boys. Their foreskins will be removed and you must not interfere. Aaron told us you are a strong-willed woman. Do not oppose your husband in this matter."

Zipporah rose and stood behind her chair. "My husband is a citizen of Midian. Our sons will be circumcised according to the laws of our God. Surely you know my father is Jethro, the Priest of Midian," Zipporah said indignantly. The women sat momentarily, then placed their shawls over their heads and hurried from the room. Zipporah slammed the door behind them and locked it.

83

Gershom sat up rubbing his eyes. "Why were you shouting, mother?" he asked. "Who were those women?"

"Go back to sleep, Gershom," Zipporah said. When he started pouting, she sat beside him and ran her fingers through his hair. She reclined on the mat but was unable to rest. A loud clap of thunder shook the inn, waking both children. The room grew darker as strong winds began blowing through the open window. She tried to close the shutters but was driven back by the force of the wind. The night sky filled with multiple streaks of lightening, followed by the continuous roar of thunder. Just as she gathered her sons in her arms, a blinding flash of light filled the room, followed by a single clap of thunder. When the room shook, she was certain an angry god had pounded his fist on the roof. Gershom and Eli screamed as they huddled closer to her. As suddenly as it began, the storm passed. Zipporah finally relaxed after her sons fell asleep. The room was cool now. She rested her eyes and prayed for Moses' return.

Just as she nodded, a heavy pounding on the door startled her. Had those dreadful women returned? The room was pitch dark as she fumbled in the dark. She paused at the door. "Moses, is that you?"

"Open the door."

Zipporah recognized Reuben's gravel voice. When she unlatched the door and opened it, he refused to enter. Behind him stood the innkeeper holding a lamp.

"Where is my husband?" she asked.

"Your husband has felt the wrath of God. I have come to take you to him." The darkness turned gray as Zipporah placed her hands to her mouth to stifle her scream.

"What has happened to him?" she cried, grabbing the sleeve of his garment. He slapped her hand.

"It is not for you to ask. Be thankful he still lives," Reuben said. He grabbed Zipporah's wrist and pulled her into the hall. "My wife will remain with your sons."

A woman stepped from the shadows and entered the room. She was the younger of the women who had visited earlier. Zipporah could only think of Moses as Reuben pulled her down the steps and into the crowded street. Pushing their way through the mass of humanity, they arrived at the Hebrews' place of worship, a handsome stone building. As they entered the courtyard, Reuben pointed to an olive tree. Its trunk was split down its middle and was smoldering from a recent fire.

"There is the place where the finger of God came from the heavens and almost killed your husband."

"The finger of God?" Zipporah muttered, as Reuben pushed her through the temple door. She saw six men standing over Moses who lay prostrate on an olive wood table. She rushed to him but the elders restrained her. Moses turned and looked at her. Burns covered parts of his swollen face, arms and upper chest.

"He has been burned," Zipporah screamed as Reuben held her arms. "How did this happen?"

"Hold your tongue, woman," Reuben shouted. "God has punished your husband for bringing his sons to us uncircumcised." Zipporah stared at Reuben's ashen face, unable to comprehend what she had heard. She shoved her elbow into his ribs with such force he doubled over and had difficulty breathing. The elders gasped and backed away, having never seen such strength displayed by a woman.

Zipporah ran to Moses, knelt and placed her hand on the scorched hairs of his head, carefully avoiding the blisters on his swollen face. She turned to the elders and shouted, "God is merciful. He would never harm the servant he has called to lead your people." Angry groans filled the hall as the elders backed away, whispering among themselves.

Moses whispered through swollen lips, "Zipporah, return to the inn. This thing will pass." She shook her head, pleading to remain.

"Only a woman of Midian would not honor the wishes of her husband," Reuben whispered. "She defames God by her disobedience."

"Go to our sons. Do not make matters worse," Moses pleaded.

Zipporah wept as she left the room. As she prepared to close the door she heard Reuben's remarks. "Who is this insolent woman of Midian? She will surely bring a curse upon all our heads."

Moses remained in the room at the rear of the temple for three weeks. Every day Zipporah came to bathe him and apply the special ointment Egyptian doctors had given her. His recovery was much slower than expected. It concerned Zipporah that Moses refused to speak about what had happened. Every time she mentioned it he grew moody and remained passive for hours. With each passing day his depression seemed to worsen.

During the second week of his convalescence Aaron returned to the city, bringing their sister, Miriam, his son, Eleazar, and his seventeen-year-old grandson, Phinehas. Upon hearing of Moses' condition, they rushed to his bedside. Much to their relief, they found him sitting up.

Miriam kissed his hand. "So this is my brother. I only wish our mother had lived to see this day. The Lord our God has answered her prayers."

"Our mother is dead?" Moses asked. Before him sat a woman with weather-hardened features who appeared to be in her late thirties. Her infectious smile was just what he needed at that moment.

"Yes, Moses. Do not grieve for her. She rejoiced, knowing God has chosen you to be our leader." Miriam wiped the tears from his cheek then went to

Zipporah. "Moses, what a beautiful wife and child you have. Aaron told me you have two sons," Miriam said. She kissed Zipporah's cheek and offered to take the child.

Zipporah felt relieved as she returned Miriam's kiss. Aaron and his son, Eleazar, had not acknowledged her with so much as a glance when they entered the room. And something about the gaze of the brooding youth, Phinehas disturbed her. He had remained in the doorway staring at her.

"I trust my brother did not upset you," Miriam said. "It was rude of him not to acknowledge you. The expulsion of our people has made him bitter. He hates all who are not of our race and faith. Once Moses has taken us to the promised land, I hope he will rid himself of hating."

"But our people are cousins. Why would he, or any of your people, hate us?"

Miriam sighed. "You are not Hebrew. I know it should not matter but the behavior of men and gods is often hard to comprehend. All we can do is to love our men with open hearts."

"I rejoice that you have offered me your friendship," Zipporah said. "Now I feel I can endure any hardship."

"Sisters we will be until death separates us," Miriam said, placing her arms around Zipporah's shoulders.

After four weeks, Moses felt well enough to return to the inn, though he was still troubled by bouts of depression. Zipporah noticed subtle changes in his behavior toward her and the children. He rarely spoke and spent long hours by the window meditating and reading scrolls that the elders had given him. Most nights he refused to come to bed, but sat at his table writing into the wee hours. Frustrated by his moodiness, she sat beside him and mustered the courage to speak of his injuries.

"Now that your wounds have healed, will you speak of what happened?" Zipporah asked.

"I have no memory of it," Moses said wearily. "The elders told you the finger of God struck me down and I believe them. I should never have brought our sons here uncircumcised."

"But the sons of Midian are circumcised at age twelve. It is the law given to us by Elohim."

"This is the dawn of a new age. The God I now follow calls himself a 'Man of War.' He is preparing me to do battle with our enemies. Every night he whispers in my ear, telling me wonderful and terrible things."

Zipporah couldn't believe what she was hearing. "You are frightening me. What terrible things?"

Moses placed his finger to her lips. "You are a woman, Zipporah. There are some things you will never understand. These scrolls I am writing contain the laws that will govern our people."

Zipporah sat quietly, baffled by his words. When she picked up a scroll, he snatched it from her hand.

"Never touch these scrolls again," Moses snapped. "The words of God are only for the eyes of the elders." The terror in his eyes frightened Zipporah. This was not the courageous Moses she had married.

"We have always read my father's scrolls together. Our joy was in reading and discussing them."

"Those days are over," Moses said. "These are the days of purification. You will learn the ways of a Hebrew wife and mother and obey me from this day forward. Worthy is the wife who honors her husband's wishes."

Zipporah bit her lip in order to restrain herself from speaking. With each passing day she became more dispirited. Nothing she did seemed to please Moses. In desperation, she decided to seek Miriam's guidance. The following morning she took the children and met Miriam at the plaza.

"Miriam, I need to speak to you in confidence?" Zipporah said.

"Of course. Are we not sisters?"

"I'm worried about Moses. Although his wounds have healed, there is no joy left in him. He sits brooding and working at his writing table for long hours. He takes no time for his family."

Miriam reached over and patted Zipporah's hand. "Do you not see what is happening? In his meditations, our God is speaking to him. He is not brooding, Zipporah. God is instructing him on the laws that will soon govern our people."

"The elders say your God sought to kill him. Why would God try to kill my husband?" Zipporah asked, her eyes blurred with tears. The shock on Miriam's face surprised her.

"Never question God, Zipporah," Miriam whispered. "God has a purpose for everything he does. As the wife of Moses, you must learn to fear our God. He rewards those who love him and obey his laws."

"How can I stop my heart from questioning?" Zipporah asked.

Miriam did not reply as she shook her head. She took Zipporah's hand and smiled. "There is a garment shop near here. Nothing cheers the heart of a woman more than haggling for something new to wear. Just put your trust in God and follow me."

When Moses' energy finally returned, Zipporah felt the need to be held and loved. While the children slept, she went to the secluded pool, bathed and anointed her body with sweet oils. Upon returning, she found Moses resting in bed with his hands crossed under his head. She sat at the dressing table and dabbed perfume behind her ears. After applying sienna-colored powder that highlighted her cheeks, she darkened her eyes with an ash-based eyeliner, using a small mirror Miriam had given her. Standing before him, she twirled to show off the sheer gown she had purchased at the garment shop. Then she noticed a ceramic wine bottle beside him. Had Moses been drinking alone? Why did he not wait for her? She removed the gown, lay next to him and kissed his lips. He remained passive and stared at the ceiling as though in a trance. Her trail of kisses moved below his navel. To her astonishment he rudely pushed her face aside.

"What has come over you?" she whispered, shocked by his rejection.

Moses made no reply. He left the bed and returned with a wet cloth. Too frightened to protest, she did not resist as he washed the powder and eyeliner from her face.

"Why are you doing this?" she cried. "Speak to me."

"God has punished me for the last time," he whispered. By dim moonlight she saw fear in his eyes. His breathing increased as he stared at her body.

"What have you done to anger him?" she asked as she reached out to touch his face. He held her wrist and pulled her to him.

"The games we have shared in the past must cease," he said adamantly. "It is an offense in the sight of God for a Hebrew wife to paint herself the way pagan women do. I no longer take any delight in your perfume or the suggestive ways you dance. Nothing must distract me from my work."

"Pagan! I think you've had too much to drink," Zipporah said, laughing nervously.

"It is not wine that pains me," Moses whispered, pressing both thumbs to the corners of her lips, stretching them. "These lips are impediments to me now."

She pushed his hands away. "Have not our lips delighted each other?"

"Yes, and by allowing it, I have polluted myself and now I must atone for my sins."

"You have nothing to atone for. God would not harm you because we loved fully," Zipporah cried. She cringed as his hands tightened on her shoulders and pressed her to the bed.

"A Hebrew wife must be submissive," he whispered in her ear.

"You are hurting me. This is not the way we love," Zipporah cried as she struggled to break his grip. The expression in his eyes frightened her. Was Yahweh Sabaoth using him to punish her?

The silent struggle ended with the full weight of him pressing down on her. She gritted her teeth and remained passive, not moving or speaking during the planting of his seed. She heard familiar sounds that signaled a pleasure she no longer shared. With a final gasp, he released her. After kissing her forehead, he turned his back and slept.

Zipporah curled up on her side, holding her hands to the pit of her stomach. She struggled to understand the change that had come over him. Gone was the foreplay that had been the prelude to their joyful nights. Gone was the tidal wave both rode until they breached in the comfort of each other's arms. Would she forever be denied the cuddling, the kisses, the tasting, with its warm afterglow that lingered until slumber came? She had been on the verge of accepting Moses' God and had planned to tell him so. She had doubted when the elders told her God almost killed him. Now, the very thought of his God frightened her. Miriam would be pleased to know she feared him. She rose quietly and sat by the window staring into the ink-black night.

CHAPTER 15

> Then Zipporah took a sharp stone and cut off the foreskin of her son, and cast it at Moses feet, and said, "Surely a bloody husband thou art to me."
>
> Exodus 4:25

Zipporah struggled to understand the nightmare she had endured. No matter how hard she tried, she could not understand the sudden changes that had come over Moses. Was Yahweh jealous of their love? Or was some unknown god trying to destroy their marriage? Fearfully, she remembered the tale of a god who loved a married woman. That god had become so jealous he had killed the husband and raped the wife before dragging her to the underworld where she lives with him forever. Was the seed of Moses or some foreign god implanted in her womb? The thought of becoming pregnant terrified her. She lit a candle and placed it on the nightstand beside their bed. Reaching over, she shook Moses.

"Wake up. We must talk."

"Wait until morning," Moses grumbled.

"I can't wait until morning," she said, punching his shoulder. "What is happening to us?"

Moses rubbed his eyes and raised up on one elbow. When he saw the redness in her eyes, the full realization of what had transpired came flooding back.

"Speak to me," she said, wiping her tears. "What came over you last night?"

"If you had opened your ears you would know what has happened," Moses said, sadly placing his hand to her cheek. "In time you will understand that what we shared in the past was nothing more than lust that pollutes the souls of men. The carnal act is sacred when husband and wife lie together. It is for the creation of new life and should not be profaned."

"Profaned? What was profane about the way we loved?" she cried.

"Must you force me to speak of it?"

"Yes, you must speak of it. When we first loved on the beach at Aqaba, you told me Osiris was smiling down on us. Look upon the beauty of our children. They are the fruit of all our loving."

"That was before I met the one true God. He demands that we purge ourselves of unclean acts. It is an abomination for women to taste the seed of men," Moses said, embarrassed by his own words.

Zipporah's eyes narrowed as she moved closer to him. "Whose lips first woke my body to the glories of love's pleasure? Must I now remain passive

90

while you take me? Must I bury the fire that burns within me whenever you plant your seed?"

"I have confessed my sins," he said with growing frustration. "Try to understand that the glory of the Lord came upon me when I stood on his holy mountain."

"His glory almost killed you," she cried. "What more does your God require of you?"

Moses hesitated then gripped her shoulders. "He spoke to me in a dream saying, 'I have made you a god unto Pharaoh and Aaron your brother will be your prophet.'"

Zipporah gasped. "You, a god? Why would he make you a god?" she whispered.

"Pharaoh is a living god who is revered by the Egyptians. He made me a god to confront his powers. Now do you understand?"

"No, I will never understand it," she said, shaking her head. "Was it a man or a god took me against my will last night?"

"Why do you vex me?" he shouted as Zipporah collapsed on the bed and wept. He reached over and gently stroked her hair. "It does not mean I love you less."

"Your God frightens me. What more does he require of you? I need to know," she asked bitterly, pushing his hand away.

"Do not speak in anger," he said, squeezing her wrist. "God demands that our sons be circumcised. Only then will his anger be cooled toward us."

"Are you saying your God almost killed you over the foreskin of our sons?" Zipporah cried. "If this is so, then he is the mountain god, Yahweh Sabaoth, and not the God of Abraham." She grimaced when Moses' hand tightened on her arm.

"You have offended my God," Moses shouted.

Zipporah broke his grip and slid away from him. "I did not hesitate to kill the Amalekite who attacked you. You are my husband whom I love more than life itself. I will no longer offend you or your God. I do not have the strength to defy both of you."

Moses' heart pounded as Zipporah went to the table and picked up the sharp stone she used for chopping vegetables. She went to the mat where Gershom was sleeping and knelt beside him.

"You wish our sons circumcised?" Zipporah said, glaring at Moses. Before he could act, she rolled Gershom on his back, stretched the foreskin of his organ and cut it off cleanly. Moses sprang from the bed and slapped the stone from her hand as Gershom's screams filled the room.

Zipporah flung the foreskin at his feet. "A bloody husband you are to me," she spat at him scornfully. "I hope your god is satisfied and will free you from his anger."

The screams of both children drew their attention from each other. Moses tried to comfort Gershom as he poured wine over the cut then held him on his lap. Zipporah took Eli and retreated to a corner where she rocked him in her arms.

When the children finally slept Moses whispered, "I fear you will never understand what is required of me. Unless you accept my God without question, there is no hope for us."

"You are right. I will never understand it. I only want the loving husband who taught me to love and be loved. You and your god are strangers to me."

"The Moses you knew is no more. God has made me a new being."

"And I am Zipporah, daughter of the Priest of Midian," she said, lifting her head proudly. "I married a kind, loving man, not a god. I think it best that you return me to my people."

"I will pray to God then consult with the elders regarding this," he said composed.

"To which of the gods will you pray, Moses?" Zipporah asked bitterly. "Your god of war, or Elohim, the God of Abraham?" Moses made no reply as he kissed his sleeping son's forehead.

Zipporah wept periodically, not having slept the remainder of the night. No matter how hard she tried, she could not understand the events that followed Moses' injuries. She wondered if she had done anything to provoke him. Did she have a right to question the demands of God that their sons be circumcised according to Hebrew laws? Should she have declared herself a Hebrew wife and not questioned their customs? Could she be the wife of one who was now a god unto Pharaoh?

At the first sign of morning light, Zipporah quietly dressed and covered her head with a shawl. She quietly left the room and entered the streets where merchants were heading to the plaza to open their stalls. She moved with liquid grace, flowing with the crowd until she came to the Temple of Osiris.

At the entrance she whispered a prayer before climbing the Temple's marble steps. Upon entering the massive hall, she slowed her pace to observe the brilliantly colored relief paintings that decorated the columns. She imagined that all of the figures were looking at her. In the center of the hall sat the god, Osiris. The statue was so tall she had to stand back to see its face. She dropped to her knees and lifted her arms.

"Hail to you, great Lord of Right and Truth. I come not as a stranger, for I have heard from my husband's lips his songs of praise to you and your wife. In his arms I knew a love that sprang from his devotion to you. He taught me your commandments that called all men to turn from wickedness and from that which causes pain and grief," Zipporah cried as her voice echoed throughout the chamber. "Now my beloved has embraced Yahweh Sabaoth, the jealous god of war. He has turned from me, causing pain and sorrow. If I have acted with insolence, forgive me. If I have judged him hastily, forgive me. Speak to me in my hour of sorrow."

Zipporah flinched when she felt a hand on her shoulder. She looked at the face of an old man dressed in a rustic colored loincloth, whose soft eyes smiled at her.

"Osiris has heard your prayers, my daughter," the priest said.

"What should I do?" Zipporah asked, her voice breaking.

"Return to your father's house, my child," he said.

The priest offered his hand and helped her to her feet, then turned abruptly and left her standing in the shadow of Osiris. When she looked up, the morning sunlight was shining through an open window, illuminating the stone face. Zipporah was certain Osiris was smiling down at her.

CHAPTER 16

And the Lord said unto Moses, "See, I have made you a god unto
Pharaoh, and Aaron your brother will be your prophet."

Exodus 7:1

Two blasts of the ram's horn signaled that the time of the caravan's departure
was nearing. Zipporah took her sons to the plaza where Moses was making final
arrangements for their passage to Midian. While waiting, she haggled with
merchants for earrings, scarves and a prayer shawl for members of the family.
Gershom tugged at her skirt when he spotted Miriam and the woman, Shina,
making their way through the crowd.

"Aunt Miriam, here we are," Gershom shouted, waving his hand vigorously.

"I'm glad we found you in this mob," Miriam said, kissing his cheeks.

"I am pleased you came," Zipporah said. Miriam helped her remove Eli
from her back pouch. "You have been a true sister to me. I will miss you."

"You speak as though we will never see each other again," Miriam said as
they walked over to a bench next to a fountain. "Moses told me what happened
between the two of you. He will be lost without his family. You must never give
up hope. I am confident one day you will be reunited."

"Moses will not miss me. He has his God," Zipporah said bitterly.

"Do not speak disrespectfully of your husband or God, Zipporah," Miriam
said, visibly upset.

"Why shouldn't I? Ever since the elders told Moses it was God who almost
killed him, he has been a stranger to me," she said, fighting back tears.

Miriam shook her head sadly. "Now I understand why Moses thinks it best
that you return to Midian. With that attitude, you will only hinder his mission."

"Your elders hate me because I am a Midianite," she said scornfully.

"You must put such foolish thoughts out of your head," Miriam said,
impatiently. "Let us speak of other things. Shina has been chosen to serve as
Moses' maidservant after you depart."

Zipporah glanced at Shina. Gershom was showing her the glass bowl he had
just purchased for Ruth.

"Was it my husband's wish?" she asked, trying to sort out her feelings.

"No. Reuben thought it best that Moses have someone to serve his daily
needs. So do not worry about him. I'm sure you both will be reunited when we
reach Midian. We will rest there before proceeding to the promised land. Take
this time of separation to learn about our God and fear him."

"I do fear him, but how can I not question when your God almost killed my husband?" Zipporah said, squeezing her hands that began trembling. "As a child I was taught to love God. Does your god demand fear rather than love?" Miriam gasped as she shook her head in disbelief.

Zipporah glanced up and saw Moses making his way through the crowd, carrying a bundle wrapped in strips of brown linen. Gershom leaped from his seat and ran to him.

"Father, are you coming with us?" Gershom asked hopefully. "Mother said we have to go home without you. I don't want to go through the desert if you are not with us. Who will protect us?"

"You must not be afraid, Gershom. God will protect you," Moses said as he lifted Gershom in his arms. "I must remain here and do God's work."

"It's not fair," Gershom protested. "I'm big enough to stay and help you."

"When you are older, you will understand. Now stay with Aunt Miriam while I speak with your mother." Moses took Zipporah's arm and led her to the other side of the fountain. "I needed to speak to you in private."

"Does it concern your maidservant?" Zipporah asked sarcastically.

"It does not," he said, irritated that Miriam had spoken to her about the arrangement. "Your trip to Midian will be long and tiring. I am sending one of my trusted officers to serve as your protector. His name is Jacob, the son of Reuben."

At the mention of Reuben's name Zipporah's eyes narrowed. "I trust the son will not be as hateful and despicable as his father?"

"Do not speak ill of Reuben. He is a man of God," Moses said, highly agitated. "Listen carefully. I am entrusting these scrolls to your care. They are for Jethro's eyes only. I am instructing you not to break the seals and read them."

"I will honor your request," Zipporah said, placing the bundle on her lap. "You have refused to speak of the night you were injured. I wish to speak of it."

Moses hesitated then replied, "Yes, what is it?"

"Shortly before we married, we stood before the forbidden mountain and took shelter from a storm."

"How could I forget. You fought at my side when the Amalekite shepherds attacked us."

"When the sky grew dark and lit up with fire, it frightened me. We saw the terrible finger of a god reach down from heaven and strike a tree, splitting it. The poor sheep that took shelter beneath it was killed. I told you it was your mountain god, Yahweh, but you insisted it was the Egyptian god of flame, who came from the womb of Het-Ptah-ka and I believed you."

"Why do you speak of this?"

"Could it have been that god of flame who touched the tree where you were standing the night you were injured? It was still smoldering when Reuben brought me to you."

Moses stared at her. "I have no memory of standing under a tree," he said reflectively. "Must I remind you that the elders witnessed the hand of God striking me. They are men of God and would not lie. I deserved that punishment, so speak no more of this, and listen carefully."

"As you wish," Zipporah said, biting her lower lip to restrain herself.

"In the ninth month of Thoth my people will be forced from Egypt. I have recruited an army that will become God's instrument for his divine plan. The route we will take is outlined in the scrolls I have placed in your care. Also recorded are the laws that our God has given me," Moses said as he held her hand. "Tell your father we are counting on the weapons and supplies promised us by the Midian chiefs. I pray you will have a safe journey."

Zipporah impulsively threw her arms around his neck and kissed his lips. He restrained her as he glanced at the milling crowd, relieved that none of the elders was present to witness so public a display of affection.

Zipporah and her sons encountered few hardships as the caravan followed the trade route along a coastal route of the Sinai Peninsula. Easterly breezes from the Red Sea cooled the sun-scorched earth, making the trip tolerable. The Hebrew elders had paid the caravan chieftain a handsome price to take the southern route around the Wilderness of Paran after receiving word that Prince Amalek had been crowned king of the Amalekites. The route led them toward the Kibroth oasis, located at the base of Mount Sinai.

When the caravan stopped for the night, Zipporah reminded Gershom not to wander off. While she prepared their evening meal, he amused himself by chasing horned lizards that quickly buried themselves in the loose desert soil. He paused when he saw what looked like a mouse, only its ears were pointed and it stood on hind legs that were as long as its body. The little creature's front legs were short and it used its long tail to balance itself as it hopped beneath a bush searching for seeds and insects. Out of curiosity, Gershom came closer, moved a branch and peeped under the bush. The creature stared at him with its buttonlike eyes then, with bounding leaps, sped away. As Gershom chased after it, a vulture with a wingspan longer than Gershom's outstretched arms, swooped down and seized it. Despite Gershom's cries of protest, he could only watch as the bird flew off with its prey. He returned to Zipporah crying.

"If father were here, he would have killed that ugly bird for eating that little hopping mouse," Gershom sobbed.

"What you saw was a jerboa, Gershom. You will see others before we reach home," Zipporah said, ruffling his hair. "When I was your age, I caught one and kept it as a pet."

"You did!" Gershom said, wiping his eyes. "What happened to it?"

"I had to feed it worms, bugs and seeds every day. After seven days I got tired of feeding it so I set it free."

"If I catch one can I keep it?" Gershom said, his eyes sparkling.

"Only after we get home. But you must promise to love it and feed it every day. All of God's creatures need love and care, Gershom. I loved my jerboa, but I had lots of chores to do and sometimes I forgot to feed it. So that's why I let it go."

"If I catch one I promise to love and feed it every day, mother," Gershom said, snuggling closer to Zipporah. After eating, he slept next to Eli and dreamed his little jerboa had escaped from the ugly bird.

At daybreak the caravan made good progress before encountering a harsh afternoon windstorm. The chieftain sent word that the caravan would rest at the village of Dophkah, thirty miles from the Mount Sinai oasis. The delay was particularly hard on the women and children as the wells at Dophkah were low on water. When the winds finally subsided, swarms of black flies descended on the village leaving painful stings on all exposed areas of the body.

Zipporah sat under a lone acacia tree trying to protect Eli by fanning flies from his face and arms. Unable to tolerate the heat, he kicked off the cotton sheet she had placed over him. His exposed arms and legs soon became a mass of welts. Gershom had gone to play with several village boys. She had no idea how he was coping with the heat or the flies.

A village woman standing in the doorway of a thatched mud hut watched Zipporah trying to quiet Eli's unrelenting screams. She beckoned her to bring the child into the dwelling. When Zipporah followed her into the crude hut, the woman smiled and held out her arms for Eli. Zipporah hesitated as her eyes adjusted to the dim light that came from a single narrow window. The stench of urine burned her eyes and nostrils. In the middle of the room was a table covered with the remains of pigs' feet that had been the woman's meal earlier that afternoon.

In one corner sat a small wooden statue. Zipporah knew from reading Jethro's scrolls it was an image of the fire god, Molech. The crude carving revealed a grotesque face with its mouth stretched open. Two shark's teeth protruded from its upper jaw, and the lower jaw was filled with human and jackals teeth. At its base sat a bowl covered with dried blood. What kind she could only guess.

When Zipporah refused to hand over Eli, the woman picked up a fetish doll and offered it to him. Eli turned away and buried his face against Zipporah's breast.

"What a beautiful child you have," the old woman said, her voice high pitched and cracked. Zipporah observed the woman's sad vacant stare.

"Do you have children?" Zipporah asked, clutching Eli tighter.

"I have two sons. All my daughters were sacrificed to my god. Now my womb is barren and I have no others to offer my Lord," the woman said, unable to take her eyes off Eli.

Zipporah felt a sudden chill, despite the sweltering heat in the room. She turned when she heard a male voice shouting her name. When the woman opened the door, Zipporah stepped outside where she saw Jacob on his horse. The animal pranced about using its tail to swat the swarm of flies attracted by its sweat. Until that moment she had not seen much of him. When Moses first introduced Jacob, she was so unhappy she had kept her head bowed. Now when he dismounted and walked to her she was surprised. His rugged features and broad shoulders reminded her of a more youthful Moses.

"I've been looking for you. A village child saw you come here," Jacob said, staring at the old woman. "You should be careful where you take your child."

"This kind woman invited me into her dwelling to escape the flies," Zipporah said, turning and placing a coin in the woman's hand. The woman rushed to the corner of the room and returned with a duck struggling to free itself.

"Take this duck. It has been blessed by my god."

Jacob tried to suppress his laughter. "A duck blessed by Molech. I hope it won't make you sick."

"We have seen little of you while we journeyed, and only at a distance," Zipporah said as she restrained the duck from flapping its wings.

"I came to serve as your protector, not your manservant. I've been scouting ahead of the caravan." Jacob noticed the dust on her face and the condition of her clothing. "We are not far from the oasis at Mount Sinai. If you wish, I will take you there now. You will be able to bathe and rid yourself of this pestilence."

Zipporah hesitated, weighing the risk of leaving the protection of the caravan. Her "protector" was the son of Reuben, the elder who despised her.

"When will the caravan leave here?"

"Before the sun sets. However, the chief of the caravan may decide to wait until morning. Come, you will have the pool at Kibroth to yourself if we leave now."

The prospects of bathing for the first time in weeks overcame her reluctance. "I will go with you after I find my son."

When she returned with Gershom, she gave him permission to ride with Jacob. It was still light when they arrived at the oasis.

Jacob pointed to the mountain's four barren peaks. "There is Mount Sinai, the place where it is said the gods rest." Zipporah felt frightened when she saw smoke rising from one of its peaks.

"There is nothing to fear, Zipporah. The gods always belch after a good meal. While you take your children to bathe, I will pitch your tent," he said, grinning.

Something about him disturbed her and she didn't know why. The itching in her scalp prompted her to take the children to the pond without hesitation. Three women carrying jugs of water on their heads greeted her as they passed. They were part of the permanent community of sixty-seven people living at the oasis.

Gershom ran to the marble-edged pond filled with lilies. "Look at the fish, Mother. I've never seen a yellow one before. I'm gonna catch me one." Gershom promptly removed his loincloth, then splashed through the lily pads trying to catch a fish with his bare hands.

Zipporah removed her dusty traveling garment and laid it beside her light cotton dress. Confident they were alone, she sat with her feet dangling in the water and bathed Eli. When Gershom finished swimming, she placed Eli in his care. She lowered herself into the water and swam on her back. When she surfaced, she saw Jacob standing on the edge of the pond holding Eli. Unable to cover herself, she remained low in the water and waded towards him.

"Is it lawful for a Hebrew man to look upon the nakedness of a woman?" Zipporah asked.

"It is written that man will not look upon the nakedness of his mother or his sister. You are not my mother or my sister," Jacob said smiling.

When Zipporah reached the edge of the pond, she rested her arms on its marble edge. Her waist-length hair spread on the water, covering her body like a wide net.

"Since you are my protector and not my manservant, I do not need your help to dress, so leave us," Zipporah said, her chin now resting on her arms.

"I am protecting your sons," Jacob said as he lifted the giggling Eli over his head. He almost dropped the child when Zipporah lifted herself out of the water and sat on the edge of the pool with her head lifted defiantly. Her sculptured body reminded him of the bust of the goddess, Isis.

Amused by his astonished expression, Zipporah reached under her garment and removed a knife from its sheath. She placed it at her side and patted the handle once. His eyes remained fixed on her as she stood up and slipped the linen dress over her head. After strapping on the belt, she said nothing as she took Eli from him and gestured for Gershom to follow her. Jacob remained at the pond trying to regain his composure. Never had he met a woman with such exquisite beauty and self-confidence.

"Maybe it was one of the lesser gods of Egypt who had tried to kill Moses after all. Jealousy does strange things to both men and gods," Jacob muttered to himself as he prepared to bathe.

Gershom watched while Zipporah readied a cooking fire in an open pit. He cried when she placed her foot on the duck's neck and slit it with her knife. As she roasted the bird over the open fire, she comforted him by telling his favorite stories. Jacob came from the pool and sat beside them.

"Did you enjoy your bath?" Zipporah asked as though nothing had happened.

"Yes, but I would have enjoyed it more if you had remained," he said, tossing a dry twig into the fire pit. "I must return to the caravan, but I will be back shortly. You will be safe here. Merchants from Ezion-geber have just arrived. They've come to get first choice of some merchandise being traded. I suggest you remain close to your tent. Do not let Gershom wander from your sight."

"I have met many merchants. My cousin and I travel to our capital to sell our wool. I have no fear of my own people."

"The goods I speak of are not sold in any marketplace. It would be wise if you followed my advice," Jacob said, eyeing the roasted duck. "Am I to partake of that bird?"

"Of course. You will be our taster, unless you fear it will make you sick." She pulled off a leg and thigh and handed it to him. After they had eaten in silence, he mounted his horse and headed back to the caravan. In the comfort of her tent, Zipporah rested beside her sons. Above her she heard the sharp whistling sounds of some strange bird. Why was it calling out so late at night? Did it feel the same loneliness she felt at that moment? When she finally slept, she dreamed she was in Moses' arms, only to have him leave when he heard his God calling him.

Zipporah awoke in the darkness to the sounds of barking dogs. She tightened her gown around her waist and stepped outside. A refreshing breeze was blowing from Mount Sinai. The only lights were from a dozen flickering campfires. A hand on her bare shoulder startled her.

"I did not mean to frighten you. Why are you not resting with your sons?" Jacob asked.

"The dogs were barking and woke me," Zipporah said. "When did you return?"

"We just arrived. Come sit beside my fire pit and warm yourself. Desert nights at the base of Mount Sinai can get very cold."

Zipporah followed him a short distance, certain the children would not wake. She watched as he tossed slabs of dried cow dung on the fire.

"I wonder where my husband is tonight," she said, staring up at the starry night sky.

"Moses should be in Noph, the Egyptian capital, about now. He and Aaron were granted an audience with Pharaoh. After Pharaoh issued his expulsion order, our people's lands, personal property and slaves were seized without compensation in several provinces. Moses hopes to convince him to right this injustice and allow our people to leave in peace under the protection of the army we recruited."

"A living god speaking to a living god," she muttered reflectively. "Why is there so much hatred between Egyptians and Hebrews? And why does your father hate me?"

"The priest and several royal families close to Pharaoh envy us. They want our property after we are forced out of Egypt. The thought of Egyptians living in my mother's home fills me with rage," Jacob said, trying to control his anger. "As for father, he fears your influence on Moses. Your husband was chosen by God to be our leader. You are a woman of Midian and that is unacceptable to him. The elders are convinced your people do not worship the true God of Abraham."

"But your father and the elders know we worship the same God. Both our peoples are from the seed of Abraham. Abraham's son, Midian, is the father of our nation."

"The elders say your people turned their backs on the true God of heaven," Jacob said quietly. "Moses is expected to set an example for us. He should never have brought his sons to Egypt uncircumcised."

"My husband is a citizen of Midian. He obeys the laws of our God, Elohim."

Jacob did not respond as he sat watching her. Lights from the pit highlighted the soft features of her face. He felt aroused by the nearness of her. "It is said that Midian women make their men forget their God."

"How so?" Zipporah asked.

"Is it true Midian women prefer giving men pleasure with their lips?" Jacob moved closer to her.

Zipporah's eyes narrowed and she slid away from him. "How dare you ask me such a question?"

"I meant no offence," Jacob said, adjusting his garment to conceal his growing erection. "I tell you this because such pleasures are an abomination in the sight of God."

"Are such pleasures an abomination in your sight, Jacob?" Zipporah asked, pointing to the bulge in his garment. "You men disgust me."

"I will speak of this no more," Jacob said, embarrassed by her disclosure.

"See that you don't," Zipporah said, clutching her gown against the blowing wind. "Did your father instruct you to entice me to your bed?" By the expression in his eyes, Zipporah knew she had stumbled on the ugly truth.

"How can you think so ill of me?" Jacob blurted out, completely unnerved by her frankness.

"Aren't you afraid I might make you forget your God?" she said. Her smoldering eyes narrowed as she leaned closer to him. "If I let you seduce me, it would give the elders proof that I am unsuitable to be the wife of Moses. They would insist that Moses divorce me." She watched as Jacob tried to regain his composure, having been totally stripped of his defenses.

"I would never betray Moses, not even if my father asked me," he replied.

Zipporah was not convinced. She sat up when she heard the dogs barking again. The sounds came from a nearby tent. "Why are those dogs here?"

"Do not ask," he said as he slid closer to her. She pushed him away and rose to her feet.

"I go to rest. Do not follow me." Zipporah returned to her tent and threw herself on the rug. After a restless period she finally slept. It was near dawn when the barking started again. Angered by the noise, she dressed and stepped outside. In the gray dawn all of the campfires had been extinguished. Out of curiosity, she followed the sounds to a nearby tent where voices could be heard haggling over the price of the dogs.

"Why do you insult me? My dogs will draw large crowds to your circus," a gravelly voice protested. "They have proven their worth in the Pithom arena." Zipporah felt sick at the mention of the circus.

"Show us proof before we pay your price," a high-pitched voice countered.

"I will give you all the proof you need," the gravel voice said. "Bring me the slave girl, Iza and put her in the cage."

Zipporah stood petrified, recalling the scenes from the Ezion-geber circus. When she heard the woman weeping, her anger turned to rage.

In the morning Jacob found Zipporah preparing breakfast beside a fire pit. "Are you still angry at me?" he asked, reaching out gently and touching her shoulder. She drew away.

"Aren't you afraid I might use my powers to cast a spell over you?" Zipporah asked as she poured eggs onto a hot stone griddle. When the eggs were cooked to her satisfaction, she offered him some on a clay plate.

"Did you rest well?" Jacob mumbled with his mouth full.

"How could I sleep with dogs barking half the night?" Zipporah said as she cracked more eggs. "I know those dogs are used to arouse the passions of the crowds at those horrible circuses," Zipporah said, avoiding his eyes.

"How did you learn of this?"

"What does it matter? If you plan to stay, speak of more pleasant things."

"Your husband gave you scrolls to be delivered to your father. They speak about such evils."

"He has forbidden me to read his scrolls," she said, staring at him quizzically.

"I am free to speak of what is written."

"Are you one of his elders?" Zipporah asked.

"No. I served as your husband's scribe before he made me one of his captains."

"If it will not offend your God, speak of it."

Jacob moved closer to her "God spoke to Moses saying, 'Those who give their children to be burned at the altar of Molech will be stoned to death. If any man lies with a beast of the field, as he would a woman, he and the animal will be put to death. And if a man lies with a man, as he would a woman, both will be put to death, for these are things that delight the god, Molech.'"

Zipporah flinched as she thought of Rehob. She wondered if Moses had spoken to Jacob about her cousin's preference for men. Was this yet another attempt to test her attitude concerning the Hebrew God and his laws?

"Will there be justice for men who place defenseless women in cages with dogs for their entertainment?" Zipporah asked, struggling to remain calm.

"I'm sorry if I upset you," Jacob said.

"I have seen men become worse than wild beasts. I am convinced the gods of evil destroy what good there is in the hearts of men."

"Zipporah, you amaze me," Jacob said. "As for those barking dogs, when the merchants came to feed them this morning they found them dead. Someone came in the night and shot arrows into their cages, killing them. Two slave girls were unchained and escaped into the desert on horses stolen from their masters."

"I'm glad for them."

"Now, I wonder who could have done that?"

Zipporah stared into Jacob's eyes. For the second time her implacable stare unnerved him.

CHAPTER 17

And it came to pass the self-same day, the Lord did bring the children of Israel out of the land of Egypt by their armies.

Exodus 12:51

A vicious sandstorm delayed the caravan from reaching the border of Midian by one week. Jacob rode to Zipporah's tent to inform her they were only a day's journey from her home. He found Gershom sitting outside trying to calm his screaming brother. When Gershom saw him, he burst into tears. Jacob quickly dismounted, took the baby from Gershom and rocked him.

"Where is your mother?" Jacob asked, anxiously glancing in all directions.

"She's sleeping and I can't wake her up," Gershom cried between sobs.

"Everything will be fine. I'm here now. Hold your brother while I go to your mother." Jacob placed the child back in Gershom's arms. When he entered the tent, he found Zipporah semiconscious. Her face was bathed in perspiration and her garment was soaking wet.

"Zipporah, speak to me," Jacob cried, lifting her into his arms. He panicked when he felt the heat from her body.

"He's trying to kill me too," Zipporah mumbled through parched lips, her eyes half closed.

The prospect of her dying frightened him. After placing the children with a camel driver's wife, he removed the containers of drinking water from a camel's back. Despite her weak protest, he removed her garment and sponged her body from head to foot. Where before he had been obsessed with her beauty, now he remained focused on his single purpose. After her body cooled, he dressed her. While she slept, he nailed a cowhide between two poles and hired four shepherds to carry her.

The next evening the caravan arrived at Jethro's compound. Zipporah's sisters screamed and cried when they saw her condition. In the confusion, Jacob stood aside and watched helplessly.

Jethro insisted on questioning Zipporah, but she turned away and refused to speak of the circumstances leading to her separation. The fever returned and by nightfall she became delirious. Ruth placed her in the tent reserved for guests, fearing her ailment might be contagious. Jacob insisted on remaining close by while her sisters applied wet cloths to cool her body. Family members went to the temple where they sat in a circle and prayed. The prayer vigil lasted two days, with family members taking only short breaks.

On the evening of the third day, Naomi placed her hand to Zipporah's head. "Sister, the fever is gone. God has answered our prayers," she cried, clasping her hands. "Soon you will be well."

With Naomi's help, Zipporah sat on the side of her bed and sipped a cup of water. "There still is a sickness in me. I am with child, but there is no life in it," she whispered hoarsely.

"What are you saying? Only God knows such things," Naomi cried.

Zipporah placed her hands over her abdomen. "The seed in my womb was planted against my will."

Naomi's eyes widened. "Did some man force himself upon you?" she whispered.

Zipporah bit her lip. "At times I'm not sure," she said, vacantly. "My husband took me while under the spell of Yahweh Sabaoth. He became a stranger to me, someone I did not know."

Naomi gasped and stared at Zipporah. "What you speak is nonsense. No one, even a god could make Moses stop loving you. He is the sweetest, gentlest man I know," she cried, placing her hand to Zipporah's forehead. "It is the fever that is making you speak ill of your husband. When you have recovered, I'm sure the child will bring you added joy."

"Yahweh Sabaoth, the god we feared, has made my husband one of his gods," she whispered, somberly. "From that hour Moses began to change. He is no longer the man I loved and married. This child is withering in my womb. It cannot live being only part human and part god."

"Stop it. I can't bear to hear you say such things," Naomi cried, placing her hands over her ears.

Zipporah reached out and held Naomi's hands. "I did not mean to frighten you. Tell father I will speak with him soon," she said.

Jacob's frustration over Zipporah illness gave way to admiration as he observed the sister's single-minded devotion to her. He was relieved when Naomi told him that her fever had broken. On the fourth evening, Ruth invited him to dine with the family. The sisters brought dishes of lamb stew, boiled cabbage, dates and bottles of red wine out to a wool carpet that had been placed under a spreading cedar tree. Family members seated themselves around the edges of the carpet and bowed their heads as Jethro blessed the food. Jacob finally relaxed and took the opportunity to get acquainted with the sisters. By the end of the meal, he decided that Zipporah was the most beautiful and intelligent of them all.

"Will Zipporah be joining us?" Jacob asked as Jethro filled his wine cup. "It would be good if she could be present when we discuss the plans for the exodus."

"I cannot say. She is still weak," Jethro mumbled with his mouth full. "I am anxious to discuss the contents of the scrolls Moses sent me. We will go to my temple after the meal. Where is Moses now?"

"Moses and Aaron should be in the Egyptian capital by now. They were granted an audience with Pharaoh. Moses will speak to him concerning those of our people whose lands and properties have been taken without compensation. However, under the expulsion order, most of our people have been granted permission to take their personal possessions, their flocks and slaves with them. We have some weapons for the army we are training, but we are relying on your chiefs to supply us with much more. It is urgent because the movement of our people will begin within the month."

"How large a group will Moses be leading?" Ruth asked, as she poured more wine.

"By last count, ninety thousand," Jacob replied.

Jethro coughed, sending a spray of wine over the uncovered dishes. "Ninety-ninety thousand souls marching through the Sinai?" he said, sputtering to clear his throat. "It is impossible. So great a multitude will die of thirst within weeks. I have spoken to our chiefs and they have agreed to send arms and supplies, but I had no idea your departure would be on such a grand scale."

"Israel will be grateful for any support we receive from our cousins. We will be especially grateful if we could rest in Midian before proceeding to the promised land. As for our numbers, we place our trust in God. He has promised to guide and protect us."

No one noticed Zipporah walking toward them holding her hands over her abdomen. "What if the Hebrews are defeated? Where will they go?" Zipporah asked. Naomi and Leah joyfully rushed to help her. Jethro kissed her cheeks when she sat beside him.

"God is good," Jethro said. "Come eat, my daughter. We will discuss the coming exodus in the privacy of my prayer room."

During the two-hour meal Jacob forced himself to eat, having totally lost his appetite. After the meal he helped Zipporah to her feet and held her arm as they followed Jethro to his prayer room. The number of scrolls stored on the shelves astonished him.

"I am pleased you are recovering," Jacob said. "You had us worried."

"I have not recovered yet," Zipporah said, easing herself down on Jethro's cot. "You did not answer my question. Where will your people go if they are driven out of Canaan?"

"If you had faith, you would not ask such a question. Yahweh has promised to help us vanquish our enemies," Jacob said, observing the dark circles under her eyes.

"The peoples of Canaan are not your enemies," Zipporah said defiantly. "They have been at peace with us for many seasons. Even if you conquer them, I fear there will never be peace."

"Zipporah, I must insist you remain silent," Jethro said, raising his hand. "Never speak when your tongue is bitter." After lighting three candles, he unrolled the papyrus scroll and motioned Jacob to move closer.

"I have read the scrolls Moses sent me. I see you are the scribe who wrote these laws for him." Jethro said, pointing to Jacob's signature in the margin.

"That is true. These are God's laws that will be enforced when we leave Egypt. He has promised Moses that ten commandments will be given him when he reaches Mount Sinai." Jacob was disturbed by Zipporah's cold stare. Would her bitterness over the separation influence Jethro's attitude and jeopardize his mission? With the Hebrews counting on the Midianites for weapons and supplies, it was hard to conceal his anxiety.

"Tell me of this covenant God has made with your people," Jethro said.

"God has declared Israel his chosen people. The land of Canaan will be His special treasure. He will establish a holy kingdom with a government headed by priests from the tribe of Levi. Our nation will be a light unto all nations of the earth."

"Can such a nation be built on a foundation of punitive laws such as I have read in these scrolls?" Jethro asked. "They read like the laws of some Egyptian gods, such as an eye for an eye, a tooth for a tooth, a limb for a limb and a life for a life. This is not the way of the God I know."

"These laws are to purify our people and rid them of sin. Enchantments, wizardry, prostitution, adultery, and all unclean carnal practices must be stamped out," Jacob said, with a quick glance at Zipporah. "The terrible punishment of the Lord will extend to the third and fourth generation of those who refuse to obey and turn their backs on Him."

"Father, may I speak?" Zipporah said, unable to restrain herself.

"Only if you speak with kindness, Zipporah." Jethro said tenderly, as he helped her to her feet. She saw Jacob's jaw tighten as she followed Jethro to his writing table.

"You should rest, Zipporah," Jacob said. "You do not want to say anything you may regret later."

Zipporah sat beside Jethro and held his hand. "Did you not teach me that our God spoke to Abraham, saying he would be the father of many nations? Did he not bless Midian, his son by Katurah, and from his seed our nation grew and prospered? As a child, you taught me to sing hymns of praise, not to those gods that dwell on mountains and dark caves, but to Elohim, who calls us to care for the hungry, give water to those who thirst and clothes to those who are naked or shipwrecked."

Jethro tenderly held Zipporah's hands. "You must rest my daughter. Do not trouble yourself with such matters. It will only make you ill again."

"I cannot rest," Zipporah said, wiping tears from her cheek. "The god who spoke to my husband on the forbidden mountain is Yahweh Sabaoth. His name is Jealous. Moses calls him a 'man of war.' His god almost killed him, and from that day my husband turned his back to me."

Jethro placed his finger to her lips to silence her. "Keep silent, my child."

Jacob backed toward the door. "You have offended our God," he cried.

"Yes, and I will do it again!" Zipporah snapped at the point of exhaustion. "My God is Elohim, the merciful. He sends forth light into the darkness and knitteth together the girdle of righteousness." She buried her face in her hand and wept uncontrollably.

"Zipporah has desecrated the name of God," Jacob shouted, glancing into the dark corners of the room. "How can Moses sing a new song with a wife of unclean lips? It was God's punishment that came down upon her head." Before Jethro could reply, Jacob left the room, slamming the door behind him. Jethro placed his hands to Zipporah's cheeks. "If Moses succeeds in bringing his people out of Egypt, you must accept the truth that our God walks with him. If such comes to pass, you and your sons must return to him. Is that understood?" He watched as Zipporah rested her head in her arms and made no reply.

Zipporah stood at the foot of the mountain staring at its sun-drenched peaks. In the three months since her return, her bouts of depression had worsened. The evening clouds cast shadows on its sunken crevices. She mustered her courage, remembering the times she had been too fearful to come near this mountain or even look at it. Soon there would be no need to fear ever again.

During the early morning hours she left her sons in Leah's care and made her way to the base of the mountain. She began recalling the events of previous months that had driven her to this place. Jacob had returned to Egypt without speaking to her. Two months later, Jethro had called her into his study and told her that the Hebrews had successfully crossed the Red Sea and were heading toward Mount Sinai. She had sat beside him shivering when he spoke of the message he had received from Moses.

"Moses speaks of the great wonders that the Lord has performed for Israel. There have been many hardships, as I predicted. When his people were on the verge of starving, a great wind blew flocks of quail into their camps, providing them meat. He writes of water coming from dry places where there was no water," Jethro said as his face clouded. "Then came Amalek with his army. Israel defeated the Amalekites, driving them back into the desert. Now I am certain that our God walks with Moses."

"Yahweh Sabaoth is a god of war," Zipporah mumbled under her breath. *"I saw with my own eyes what his jealous rage did to my husband."*

"You speak heresy, Zipporah," he shouted. *"Go to your place of rest and repent before it is too late."*

Later that night, Zipporah had woken with cramps in the pit of her stomach. For months she had prayed that her womb would be cleansed of the unwanted child. Were her prayers being answered?

Reflecting on all that had happened, she felt chilled as she ascended the mountain trail. She adjusted her pouch, making sure the desert flowers and the small bundle she carried would not be crushed. She chanted a hymn Moses had taught her before they married. "Lord of the wind, O Weigher of Righteousness, guide me to the chamber of right and truth. May your emerald light encircle me that I may see your shining face."

The sun was setting when she reached the place where Moses had built his altar. Close by was the bush where he said he had met his God. Its branches, now barren, had been shaped by seasonal windstorms. The excessive slant of its twisted limbs, like black bony arms, all pointed toward her. It was as though they were warning her not to come closer. The few remaining leaves were now a brilliant red. She felt no fear and stepped closer to look at the falcon's abandoned nest. All that remained were bits of cracked eggshells, broken bones and traces of rabbit fur.

Zipporah sat cross-legged in front of the bush. She closed her eyes and meditated, hoping the bush would catch fire so she could make her final peace with Moses' God. The wind grew colder, causing her to shiver. She opened her pouch and removed the male fetus she had miscarried the night before and placed it on the stone altar. After spreading flower petals over it, she took a knife and carefully removed the minuscule foreskin.

Two ravens circled overhead as Zipporah returned to the bush and placed the foreskin in the nest. When shadows from dark clouds covered the area, she grew impatient. Maybe Moses' God did not rest here during the night. Removing her flint stone she started a fire with twigs and dry grass. Taking a burning twig to the bush, she tossed it into the nest. Flames, whipped by a sudden gust, spread to the branches and quickly consumed the bush, forcing her back from its heat. When the last sparks died and the embers cooled she vented her rage by scattering the ashes with the soles of her shoes.

Zipporah walked to the edge of the cliff and stared into the darkness below. Beyond the valley she could see the faint glow on the waters of the gulf where Moses first loved her. The joyful memories were blotted from her mind by all that had happened in Egypt. The winds increased, causing tears to race across her cheeks. In the depths of her depression she hesitated momentarily, closed her eyes, then jumped. As she plunged downward, a strong current of wind slowed her fall. A powerful gust, like some invisible hand, lifted her back to the summit and tossed her onto the rocky ground with such force it stunned her. Zipporah found herself lying prostrate before the stump of the burned bush. She reached out, scooped the ashes into the palm of her hand and rubbed them on her face. Above the phalanx of dark clouds that hid the setting sun, spear-like rays of light spread across the canopy of heaven, painting the sky a delicate reddish hue. For a moment she thought she was in the world of the spirits as its blush illuminated the ground around her. She returned to the cliff, raised her arms and embraced its warmth. At that moment she felt her spirit lift as though she were one with both earth and heaven. Here she remained until the lights grew dim and the sky faded to deep indigo. She marveled, as a single star seemed to skip across the heavens, showering the darkness with its trail of light, then fading as it plunged into the valley below.

Zipporah felt renewed, certain that the powerful breath of Elohim had saved her and restored her will to live. As the shadows of night crept over the summit, the firmament filled with countless stars, all bright like tiny drops of pearl. She took shelter from the wind in a shallow cave. At dawn she made her way down the mountain singing a chant she had composed during the cold, sleepless night.

"The palm of God did lift me from the pit of death, and blew within my soul the will to live again. Without shape or form, He kissed my cheek and whispered in my ear that I am loved."

She arrived home at midmorning, confident she could face the world with renewed courage and strength.

CHAPTER 18

When Jethro, the priest of Midian, Moses' father-in-law, heard of all that God had done for Moses, and for Israel his people, and that the Lord had brought Israel out of Egypt; Jethro returned Zipporah and his sons to where Israel was encamped at the mountain of God.

Exodus 18:1-2

Zipporah sat at Jethro's workbench reading a scroll by candlelight. Deeply engrossed in her reading, she did not notice when Jethro entered his study for his evening meditation. He paused momentarily, then removed the scroll from her hand and rolled it up.

"My daughter, your husband forbade you to read his scrolls. He told you they are for the eyes of the elders and priests only," Jethro said. "Why do you not honor his wishes?"

"I feel no obligation to honor him," she replied bitterly.

"Although you are separated, you dishonor me if you do not obey him."

"I never meant to dishonor you. Why do I have to obey a man who turned his back to me? His people do not respect us or our God."

"Zipporah, you are the wife of Moses and the mother of his children. Happy is the wife who is obedient and virtuous in her heart. By doing so she places a crown upon her husband's head."

"Have you read all that is written in these scrolls?" Zipporah asked, indignantly.

"Yes, every word. God has brought his people out of Egypt and given Moses laws that will govern them. It is not for me to question what is written here." Jethro's face softened. "This is a time to rejoice. Are you not pleased that the Hebrews have defeated the Amalekites and driven Amalek back into the wilderness?"

"But Amalek lives," Zipporah cried. "You taught me Elohim is a just God who is slow to anger. Here it is written that if men walk contrary to this god, he will chastise them seven times. In his fury, they will be reduced to eating 'the flesh of their sons and the flesh of their daughters will they eat.' Their cities will be laid waste and their sanctuaries desolated."

Jethro's hands trembled as he feverishly unrolled the scroll and spread it before her. "Listen to these words. 'You will not afflict any widow, or fatherless child. If you afflict them in any way and they cry unto me, I will surely hear their cry and in my anger I will kill you with the sword.'" He rolled the scroll back up and placed it on the shelf. "The God who walks with Moses hates injustice. During the period of this exodus, God must be harsh with those who do not obey him."

Zipporah shuddered. "Father, these laws state that men will not lie with men, for if they do, both will be stoned to death. My beautiful cousin prefers the company of men. Rehob would be stoned if he were Hebrew. Their God hates what he has made with his own hands."

Jethro wiped his brow and slumped on his stool. "I forbid you to speak of such things," he said sternly, waving his finger in her face. "I am now certain that their God and our God are one."

Zipporah took Jethro's hand and caressed it. "Cannot evil be overcome with goodness and mercy? Must justice only be accomplished with a sword or by stoning?" she whispered softly.

"You must remain silent," Jethro shouted as his eyes watered. "Zipporah, you are my greatest joy. You can honor me by returning to your husband."

"Please hear me. Who was it who taught me to think wisely? Am I now required to close my mind and place my thoughts in the wine bottle of blind obedience?" Zipporah pleaded. "I have felt the terrible fury of Yahweh Sabaoth. He almost killed my husband. This vengeful god may one day destroy Midian. Do not force me to return to Moses." Jethro slapped her face but she made no outcry.

"Ungrateful daughter, look what you made me do," Jethro cried, and stared at his trembling hands. "Tomorrow I lead the relief caravan to Moses' encampment to bring weapons and supplies sent by our chieftains. You and your sons will go with me. Your place is at the side of your husband. Go now and prepare yourself for the journey."

Zipporah fought to hold back her tears. It grieved her to think she unnerved him to the point that he would strike her.

"Forgive me father" she cried.

"Just go," he shouted, his voice quivering as he waved her away. "I will remain here all night praying that our God will forgive you for blaspheming his name. Let us hope his vengeance will not fall upon this house." She saw the hardness leave his eyes when she wiped blood from her lip. "You have always been an obedient daughter. Why do you bring nothing but shame and grief upon my head?"

Zipporah walked to the door and hesitated. "Last night I climbed the forbidden mountain so I could speak to Moses' God. When I arrived at the bush I placed the spoiled fruit of my womb upon the altar Moses had built."

"What are you saying?" Jethro cried in anguish. "Have you lost the child?"

"Yes, and in my grief for the loss of my husband I threw myself off the cliff. It was the breath of Elohim that lifted me back to the summit," she said, in awe.

Jethro gripped the table and staggered. Before Zipporah could reach him, he fainted and slumped at her feet.

Moses woke from a troubled sleep when he heard rams' horns trumpeting from the hills at the base of Mount Sinai. He dressed and rushed toward his command tent, only to be met by panicky men, women and children running in all directions, adding to the dust whipped up by hot desert winds. Women screamed as men shouted for their wives to find missing children. Moses suddenly found himself surrounded by what threatened to become a mob.

"Tell us what is happening?" a mother asked. "Why are the horns sounding?" Voices overlapped as people pulled at his garment.

Moses made no reply as he elbowed his way through the frightened masses. When he entered the tent, he found Aaron and Joshua waiting for him.

"Have the Amalekites returned?" Moses asked, coughing to clear dust from his throat.

"No. Great news, Moses. The caravan from Ezion-geber has been spotted north of here. It stretches for miles. It is the relief caravan promised us by the Chief Kaleb and your father-in -law. Yahweh has answered our prayers," Aaron cried.

"Joshua, have the men saddle my horse. We will ride out to meet them," Moses said with jubilation. Moses and Joshua made their way to the corral. Hordes of people followed, shouting as they blocked their path. Moses tried to elbow his way through, but the sheer numbers made it impossible. Men fought each other to get closer to him.

"Are the Amalekites upon us again? We do not have the strength to fight them a second time. Meet their demands and pay any tribute they ask," an elder shouted.

"We are starving. We are out of food and there is not enough water." The mood of the crowd grew ugly.

"Our children are sick and dying," a father cried, holding his dying child above his head.

When Joshua drew his sword, the people backed away. Moses reached the corral and mounted his horse. He raised his hand in a futile effort to calm the hysterical mob.

"Listen to me," Moses shouted.

"We have listened long enough," a bearded man shouted, holding a club over his head. "This fanatic does not talk with God. We have been tricked into leaving Egypt with him. He gives us nothing but snakes, roots and locusts to eat. Each day we bury our dead in this desert. It would have been better if we died at the hand of the Lord in Egypt than let this fool kill this whole assembly with hunger."

Joshua rode beside the man, snatched his club and struck him over the head. The crowd lowered their voices as Joshua waited for other challengers.

"Listen to Moses," Joshua said, waving the club to make sure all remained quiet. "We have marvelous news."

Moses rose up in the saddle. "Where is your faith? Did I not tell you that our God walks beside us?" he said pointing eastward. "God has spoken to our cousins in Midian and they have responded to our cries. I go to meet my father-in-law, the Priest of Midian. Just beyond those hills he leads a caravan laden with food, weapons and healing herbs. Soon you will know the power of the God of Abraham. He has opened their hearts and made them generous." The angry muttering quickly gave way to laughter and cheering. Men hugged each other as women dropped to their knees and gave prayerful thanks.

Moses, Joshua and Aaron rode through the encampment as the crowd, now numbered in the thousands, moved aside and made a path for them. Moses looked into the dusty, emaciated faces of his people and saw signs of hope for the first time in weeks.

Jethro rode his camel to a hill overlooking the desert valley of Jezreel. As far as he could see were thousands of tents. Never in his life had he seen such a sight. How so many people could survive these past months in the desolate Sinai he could only attribute to the power of God.

Jethro turned to the caravan commander. "Ekron, what do you think of this vast multitude?" he asked.

The commander shielded his eyes and scanned the horizon. "The oasis at Mount Sinai is not adequate to quench the thirst of such a horde. There are more people down here than in our capital city. It will take a caravan twice this size to meet their needs. Our cousins in Edom, Moab and Ammon, should be cursed for not sending them aid," Ekron said with concern. "I fear what will happen if the Canaanites defeat them. Where will they go?"

"They will not fail. Our God walks with them."

"There is a rumor among our people that it is the mountain god, Yahweh Sabaoth, who walks with them, not our God, Elohim."

"Do not listen to lies. It is Elohim that stands there on Mount Sinai. He helped them defeat the Amalekites," Jethro said as he rose up in his saddle. "Look. Riders are coming to greet us."

Ekron raised his hand and signaled for the caravan to continue toward the encampment. When the riders drew closer, Jethro recognized Moses at the head of them. After they dismounted, Moses fell on his knees before Jethro and did obeisance three times. Jethro pulled him to his feet and kissed his cheeks.

"How are Zipporah and my sons?" Moses asked out of curiosity.

"You will see them soon, for I have brought them to you, my son," Jethro said. Moses' smile faded as he stared at Jethro with disbelief.

"You brought Zipporah and my sons here?" he stammered.

"Yes, Moses. It is where a wife should be at a time such as this. But let us speak of other things. God has performed miracles by bringing your people out of Egypt."

"It will take more miracles if we are to succeed, for these are a stiff-necked people."

"We will speak more of this after the caravan is unloaded," Jethro said. "Do you not wish to see your wife and children now?"

Moses hesitated as he looked toward the encampment. He could tell by the rising cloud of dust that thousands of his desperate people were stampeding toward the caravan on foot.

"It is best that I enter the camp with you. As much as I want to see them, the security of this caravan must come first," Moses said, fearing the approaching mob might confiscate the supplies. He also needed time to reflect on a sensitive problem presented by Zipporah's unexpected arrival.

CHAPTER 19

> And Moses' father-in-law said unto Moses, "The thing that you do
> is not good. You wilt surely wear away, and this people that is with
> you. This thing is too heavy for thee, thou art not able to perform it
> thyself alone."
>
> Exodus 18:17-18

As the dust settled, Zipporah stared at the thousands of refugees standing behind the roped off area where the caravan's supplies were being unloaded. The smells from excrement pits and smoke from hundreds of campfires hung heavy over the camp, burning her eyes. Armed warriors brandishing swords and spears guarded the vital supplies. She rested against a canvas bag, breast-feeding Eli and cautioned Gershom to remain at her side. When word spread she was the wife of Moses, women waved their scarves and shouted greetings. She wondered how long it would be before Moses arrived. The thought of seeing him caused her emotions to shift like drifting sands. Although it had been six months since she had last seen him, their separation still caused her nightmares. Should she allow herself to hope that they might be reconciled? Her tension eased when she remembered their tender moments on the beach of Aqaba. Now in the incessant wind and heat, her thoughts turned to her children who were exposed to the choking haze and dust.

"Where is father?" Gershom whined. "Why doesn't he come to see us? Why are there so many flies here? Why does everything smell so bad?"

"Your father is busy helping these people. I'm sure he will come to us soon," Zipporah said as she fanned the flies from Eli's face with a cloth.

A young man, followed by a dark-skinned woman, entered the secured area. When they approached, Zipporah recognized Shina. Unlike the unkempt women of the encampment, Shina wore a knee-length white linen gown with one shoulder bare. It was obvious that she had dressed for the occasion of Zipporah's arrival. The stocky young man wore only a short garment wrapped around his waist. His woolly hair reminded her of the black men she had seen in the circus pit at Ezion-geber. He stood before her and bowed. "I am Lamech, one of your husband's officers," he said proudly. "Moses has sent us to escort you to a temporary tent that has been set up for you and your sons. Shina will assist with your needs."

"Moses is pleased that you had a safe journey," Shina said, offering to take Eli. Being arm-weary, Zipporah handed her the child.

"Will father come to see us soon?" Gershom asked, pulling her skirt.

"Your father is judging the people that come each day to seek his counsel. He will come to us after this day is over, but it may be very late." Shina motioned for Zipporah to follow her.

"I won't sleep, even if I have to stay up all night," Gershom said impatiently.

"Do not worry about your garment bags, Zipporah. Lamech will bring them to our tent," Shina said.

Zipporah wanted to get out of the sun, go to the pond and take a bath. It was strange being back at Mount Sinai, although she hardly recognized the place. It dawned on her that with the demands of so many people it seemed unlikely she would have an opportunity to bathe at the pond. She wondered how long it would be before Jacob made his presence known. During the journey home she had learned to appreciate him, despite their differences. She held Gershom's hand as they walked outside the guarded enclosure. The curious multitude moved aside to let them pass. Several of the women reached out and touched Zipporah's skirt as though it held some magical healing power.

The different facial features and skin colors of these people reflected the racial mixture common among the Egyptians. The thin faces and sunken eyes of the children alarmed her.

"These women and children are starving. Has not your God provided better than this?" Zipporah whispered. Shina made no reply as she opened the tent's flap for them to enter. When Zipporah saw the size of it, she shook her head. "There is not enough space for all of us."

Shina poured water into a bowl and handed Zipporah three towels. "We will stay here for only one night," she said with the hint of a smile. "Moses was unaware of your coming."

"Where can I find my sister, Miriam?"

"I am forbidden to speak of her," Shina said, turning away.

"Is she sick?" Zipporah asked with alarm.

"Do not ask about her," Shina pleaded. "Moses will tell you what has happened when he arrives." Zipporah felt a knot in the pit of her stomach, fearing Miriam could be sick or dying. She quickly composed herself when Lamech entered with her garment bags.

"I trust this tent will be acceptable for tonight. Other arrangements are being made for you, Shina and your sons," Lamech said, placing the bags aside. "These have been difficult days since we defeated the Amalekites. Do not be concerned if you hear women speaking of our enemy returning."

"Might they return?" Zipporah asked, tightening her arms around Eli.

"Moses thinks they will not, especially since your chiefs have sent us arms."

"Some broke into our encampment, raped several women and rode off with four of our children," Shina blurted out.

"Did they harm Miriam?" Zipporah asked, suddenly feeling lightheaded.

"No," Shina replied.

"I'm sorry you had to hear this," Lamech said, glaring at Shina. "Our army met their host at the valley of Rephidim. God helped us put Amalek's warriors to the sword. It is true, one raiding party broke into our encampment but most were slain."

"I'm sure Amalek has sacrificed the children to his bloody god," Shina said as though she deliberately wanted to frighten Zipporah.

"I will never sleep in peace knowing Amalek lives," Zipporah said, struggling to maintain her composure.

Jethro sat beside Moses on an elevated platform looking out over a column of ninety men and women. Behind the platform were the colorful standards of the twelve Hebrew tribes. The line of people waited patiently for Moses to hear their complaints and pass judgment. Jethro found it hard to believe that Moses would spend precious hours every day judging so large a multitude. He watched as the first man in line pushed his young wife toward Moses and forced her to kneel.

"My Lord, Moses, my mother told me that this wife of mine has been unfaithful while I fought at your side against the Amalekites. What should be the judgment?"

"Have you witnesses, other than your mother?" Moses asked.

"No, but she cannot look into my eyes. I know she's guilty and I demand a trial to see if she is lying." Moses noticed the disgusted look on the young woman face.

Moses motioned for the wife to rise and to step forward. "Your husband has accused you of being unfaithful. What do you have to say? Speak truthfully, my daughter."

"Lord Moses, my husband has always been jealous and his mother hates me. I have never known any man but him," the women said, looking directly into Moses' eyes.

Moses gestured for Aaron. "Take this woman to the tent of the Tabernacle. Have her take an oath then administer the test of bitter water." Moses motioned the woman to step closer. "My daughter, if no man has lain with you, give an oath unto the Lord then drink the bitter water offered you. If you have slept with any man other than your husband, the water will cause your thigh to rot and your belly to swell. If you have not slept with any other man, nothing will happen and you will go free. Your husband will atone for his jealousy by making payments in coins of silver to your family. Is that understood?"

"Yes, my Lord," she said cheerfully. She turned to her husband and waved as she followed Aaron. The husband kept his hands on his purse as he followed close behind her.

"The wife is not guilty," Moses whispered to Jethro. "The test works every time. The guilty ones usually faint or cry out, then confess their sins."

"What is the penalty if she was found guilty?" Jethro asked.

"Death by stoning. However, there are exceptions. It all depends on the wishes of the husband. He may sell or keep her as his slave," Moses said, motioning for the next man to come forward. Before Jethro could inquire about the penalty for adulterous men, a bony man of eighty years made his way up the steps.

"My Lord, the man I purchased in Egypt is hiding somewhere in the encampment and refuses to return and serve me. I want him found and punished."

"Is he Hebrew?" Moses asked.

"Yes. I have owned him ten years and now he has stolen his freedom by hiding from me."

"It is now our law that if you buy a Hebrew slave, six years will he serve you. On the seventh year he will go free for nothing."

"I protest, for I have given him a wife who has borne three children. He has taken all of them with him, leaving me to travel alone in my old age."

"If what you say is true, the wife and children will be found and returned as your property. I will instruct my commanders to find and return them to you." The man bowed and backed from the platform.

By the seventh hour, Jethro had seen judgment passed in eighty-three cases. At the point of exhaustion, Moses returned to his headquarters. Jethro took Moses aside and said, "My son, why do you sit alone when you judge these people?"

"The Lord requires me to teach and judge them every day. I must strictly enforce his statutes."

"If you keep this up you will surely wear away, both you, and these people that follow you. This burden is too great for one man alone. You will not be able to perform this task by yourself," Jethro said.

"I confess this thing I do is a heavy burden. What advice do you offer me?"

"You have in this encampment many educated men," Jethro said. "Seek out men of truth, those that hate covetousness, and place them over your people to be rulers of thousands, and rulers of hundreds and rulers of fifties. Let them judge the people in all seasons. Have it understood that in great matters they will consult with you. On small matters, such as you have dealt with this day, let them judge."

Moses fell to his knees and kissed Jethro's hand. "How can I thank you?"

"Thank God and implement it with his blessing, then you will be able to endure. God willing, your people will go to their promised land in peace."

"I will hearken to your wisdom and choose leaders from the various tribes as you suggest. Come, let me show you the tent that serves as our Tabernacle. It was made according to the Lord's instructions," Moses said as he escorted Jethro into a massive tent next to his headquarters. "The ten curtains are of fine linen in colors of blue, purple and scarlet. The altar is made of shittim wood, five cubits long."

Jethro walked around the enclosed area, examining the curtains and admiring the fine gold that was entwined in the cloth.

"It is good that your people were able to bring so much of their wealth with them," Jethro said. "I could not help but admire Aaron's breastplate, with its twelve precious stones."

"The stones represent each of our tribes," Moses said. "It did not matter to Pharaoh that we took our wealth and our flocks with us. As I suspected, Pharaoh's advisors wanted us out of Egypt, fearing our growing power and influence. They convinced him that we would betray Egypt if there was a war. It was jealousy and greed that caused them to drive us out, nothing else. When a plague killed thousands of people in his capital, he became convinced that our God caused it."

"Come Moses, it is time to go to your family. Zipporah and your sons are eager to see you."

Zipporah had just put Eli down for the night when Moses and Jethro entered. Gershom greeted Moses with loud yells, startling the baby.

"Father, why did it take you so long to come see me?" Gershom cried as he rushed into Moses' arms. Moses picked him up then turned and kissed Zipporah's cheek.

"It pleases me that my family arrived safely," Moses said. "I hope your journey was not too tiring."

"And I am pleased that God has protected your people," Zipporah said quietly. From the corner of her eye she saw Shina open the tent's flap and leave.

"It is good to see my son and daughter together," Jethro said, as he nudged Zipporah closer to Moses. "I know how much you love each other. Now let the love of God strengthen and protect you."

"Thank you, father. Please take Gershom outside. I wish to have a few moments alone with my husband," Zipporah said. Jethro dragged an unwilling Gershom from Moses' arm.

"I was not prepared for your return." Moses said, awkwardly embracing her. "I hope you will accept the role of a Hebrew wife. It will make my burden lighter."

"I will honor your wishes. Tell me where I can find my sister, Miriam. Your maidservant refuses to say what has happened to her."

"Shina is no longer my maidservant," Moses replied. "It pains me to tell you that my sister has leprosy. She has been confined in the leper camp."

Horrified, Zipporah covered her mouth to stifle her cry. "How long has she been there?"

"For thirty days. You are forbidden to see her. It is God's punishment. I must warn you that if you step into the shadow of a leper it will defile you. Your limbs will rot and fall off."

Zipporah stared at him in disbelief then slumped to the carpet. She had counted on Miriam's friendship. Without her, how could she survive in Moses' alien world?

"As much as I would like to remain, I must return to my headquarters. There are urgent matters that require my attention," Moses said, placing his hand on her head.

"When will you return?" Zipporah asked as he opened the flap of the tent.

"I cannot say. Stay close to the tent and do not let the boys wander off," Moses said, hesitating momentarily. "In the morning we will speak in private."

If Shina was no longer his maidservant, what was her new position? And what of Miriam and the curse of a leper's shadow? If the Hebrew God was punishing Miriam, what great sin had she committed? Did the curse apply only to Hebrews? Jethro had never warned his family to stay out of a leper's shadows, only never to touch them. She had taken food to a leper colony but could not remember if she had stepped into any of their shadows. She did remember one leper's prayerful thanks.

Jethro returned Gershom to Zipporah and kissed her cheek. "Have faith, my daughter. Rejoice that you are now reunited with your husband." Zipporah made no reply as he hurried to catch up with Moses.

CHAPTER 20

And Miriam and Aaron spoke against Moses because of the Ethiopian woman he had married; for he had married an Ethiopian woman.

Numbers 12:1

The first night in the encampment was miserable for Zipporah. She could not overcome an uneasy sense of foreboding after Shina had told her not to expect Moses that night. With no breeze, the cramped tent became extremely hot. She sat telling stories to Gershom until both children grew tired and slept. Relief came when cool desert winds blew in from Mount Sinai. Despite the comfort, she twisted and turned most of the night. The cries of children in a nearby tent kept her awake until almost dawn. She awoke to find a stranger seated on a stool beside her cot. Upset, she reached for her sheath.

"Careful with that. Don't you recognize me?" Jacob said.

"How long have you been sitting there?" Zipporah asked, drawing her garment around her exposed breast. She did not recognize him with his new growth of beard and dark sunburned face.

"Not long. Shina has taken your sons to the pool. They should be returning shortly. If Moses had known you were coming he would have been better prepared to receive you. All of you are to move into a larger tent near his headquarters."

"My husband would punish you if he knew you entered my sleeping area without permission."

"Would you trouble him over so trivial a matter?" Jacob said confidently. "Have you forgotten that it was I who bathed and dressed you after you became ill?"

"How could I forget? All the same, you have no right to enter here unannounced," Zipporah said. She recalled how she had protested when he undressed her and gently sponged her feverish body. She would not tell him that after she attempted to end her life, she had dreamed of him several times.

"Let us not begin by quarreling. Moses and your father are waiting to receive you," Jacob said, as he picked up her garments from the chair and tossed them to her. "We are pleased that Jethro arrived when he did. The people were on the verge of rebellion over the lack of food and water. Some traitors even spoke of killing Moses and returning to Egypt. They would rather risk the wrath of Pharaoh than remain in this desert."

122

Zipporah went behind a partition and returned dressed in a red blouse, ankle-length black skirt, and camel hide boots. The short boots were ideal for walking in the desert. She sat beside him and combed her hair, then tied it back with a leather string she had cut from the hide of a goat.

"My husband told me that Miriam has been confined to a leper camp," Zipporah said, with a worried frown.

"That is correct. What else did he tell you?"

"I was warned not to go there. He said the shadows of lepers are contagious. Do you believe your God punishes people by inflicting leprosy on them?"

"It's not important what I believe. If it is God's law, I do not question it."

"What if it is an unjust law? Some gods are very cruel and take delight in inflicting pain and suffering for the sport of it."

"What you say is true, but I hope you have the good sense not to ask such questions. If you are to remain the wife of Moses you must learn to accept and fear our God. It is the only way you can honor your husband," Jacob said. "If you don't, you might end up in the leper camp with Miriam."

"All my life I have loved God with all my heart," Zipporah said proudly. "I have done his will by taking food to lepers and caring for those who were poor and sick. These are things I was taught as a child."

Jacob watched her with admiration. In addition to her beauty, her intellect and courage astonished him. "I will confess, I have trouble believing the tale about the shadows of lepers," Jacob said, smiling. "I also have worked among them. Many a shadow has crossed my path and to this day I have remained clean. Of course, I am careful not to touch them and I always bathe after working among them. It saddens me to see the suffering they have brought upon themselves."

"I'm glad to hear you say that," Zipporah said, reaching over and touching his hand. "Jacob, I must see Miriam. Will you take me to her?"

His smile evaporated. "You would defy your husband and endanger your own life?"

"For Miriam's sake, yes. She's my sister and I love her."

Jacob shook his head. "And you would ask me to defy the orders of Moses?"

"So now you are loyal to him," she said. "All I ask is that you point the way. I will go by myself."

Zipporah waited as he pondered her request. It was obvious he knew something about Miriam's internment that he was not telling her.

"I'll think about it. Get yourself ready. I've come to escort you and your sons to your permanent tent."

"I have seen the plight of your people. I wish to live as simply as they do."

"You are the wife of Moses. Accept what he offers you," Jacob said with growing impatience. "You should know you are not the only Midian woman among us. There is a young woman who is betrothed to Zimri, a prince of the tribe of Simeon."

"Betrothed?" Zipporah said. "It pleases me that some of your people are not as closed-minded as your father." She could see by his pained expression that Jacob was not amused.

"Your tongue still has the sting of a scorpion. Finish packing and prepare for the move. I will wait outside," he said, leaving abruptly.

Shina returned with a jug balanced on her head. "I bathed your sons." She removed Eli from the back pouch and placed him on the rug. Gershom sat sucking his thumb, a sign he wanted attention. Zipporah gently squeezed the tip of his nose and hugged him.

"I appreciate your kindness," Zipporah said, wondering if Moses would continue her services or return her to Reuben. As for her own status, she decided to learn the customs of a Hebrew wife. She began by preparing food for her family and was unaware that Shina had quietly left.

Moses chose to sleep at his command center, having spent most of the night discussing plans with Jethro and his commanders. Jethro had informed Moses that the Midian chieftains had offered the Hebrews sanctuary for six months. With only three hours rest, he found it hard to rise. During the night he dreamed that God had told him not to delay in Midian, but to proceed through the Wilderness of Paran to the village of Kadesh-barnea. The village was only a short distance from the border of Canaan. This would be the staging area for the invasion of the Holy Land.

Moses sat up as Shina entered, carrying a platter of bread, cheese, braised mutton and a cup of goat milk. She took a cloth and washed his hands and feet. After the sponge bath, he watched as she glided about the enclosed area gathering the articles of clothing he would wear.

"Jacob will bring Zipporah and your sons to you shortly, my Lord," Shina said softly. "The tent you have prepared for us will be partitioned according to your wishes."

"Do I hear sadness in your voice?" Moses said, drawing her closer.

"There is no jealousy in me. Your happiness is my only desire," she said, with her head bowed.

"Zipporah is headstrong, but a devoted wife and mother," Moses said, kissing her cheek. "In time she will learn to accept you as my second wife."

"When will you speak of our marriage?"

"She will learn of it soon," Moses said.

* * *

When Jacob escorted Zipporah and her sons to the permanent tent, Moses and Jethro were waiting outside. Jethro seemed nervous when Zipporah kissed his cheek.

Gershom jumped into Moses' arms. "I missed you so much," he cried. "Where were you last night?"

"I had much work to do. Now stay with grandfather while I speak with your mother," Moses said, turning to Zipporah and taking her hand. "We must speak in private."

"I will take the children inside to escape this heat," Jethro said, taking Eli from Zipporah.

Moses lead her to a palm tree where they sat in the shade. "I trust you will accept what I have to tell you. I have taken Shina as my second wife. Accept her and remain faithful to me in all things," Moses said as though issuing a command. "It is lawful for a man to take a second, even a third wife."

Zipporah felt her throat constrict as she looked beyond him and saw Shina standing in the tent's entrance watching them. "I wish to be alone," she said, her voice quivering.

"I've never stopped loving you, Zipporah," Moses said. "I did not think I would see you again."

"My father insisted that we return to you. I had no say in the matter. Just leave me alone for now."

"As you wish," Moses said after a brief hesitation. He abruptly left and headed toward his command tent. Zipporah saw Jacob walking toward her and struggled to maintain her composure.

"Is there anything I can do for you?" Jacob asked, noticing her tears.

"Yes, I need to find Miriam. Will you help me or not?" Zipporah said bitterly.

Jacob looked to make sure Shina was not within hearing distance. If he helped her, it would be for the wrong reasons. His own father had urged him to seduce her for Moses' sake, and she had guessed the truth. Countless times he had envisioned her sitting naked beside the pool at Mount Sinai. The memory had become an obsession. Could he contain his desires, knowing how vulnerable she was now? "I will warn you again. You take a great risk by going there."

"It's a risk I must take. My sons sleep soundly at night. I will go when the hour is late."

"Then I will point the way, but you will go alone. Shina must not know of this."

"How can I thank you?"

"We can discuss that later," Jacob whispered. "When the time is right, I will bring you a pass to show the guard. Go to your children."

Shina showed Zipporah the partitioned areas where they would sleep, then fed Gershom the dates and bread that Moses had left for them. Zipporah accepted Shina's offer to help her unpack. After she breast-fed Eli, they worked beside each other without speaking. Zipporah realized this was not the shy woman she had met in Egypt. As the day drew to a close she tried to sort out her feeling about Shina. It was not a part of her nature to hate anyone. Yet the thought of Moses taking Shina to his bed was unimaginable.

By late afternoon the encampment grew quiet as everyone took shelter from the blistering sun. Zipporah, Shina and the children stretched out a thick wool carpet. Gershom spent time counting the yellow flowers that decorated its borders while Eli played with a wooden lion Moses had brought him.

"Thank you for helping me with the children," Zipporah said.

"Your sons are beautiful," Shina said quietly. "But you must warn Gershom not to wander off. It is not safe."

"Do you fear another raid by Amalek and his warriors?"

"Yes, but there are also predators that are here among us."

Zipporah sat up and pushed her hair back from her face. "What do you mean?"

"Women have been raped and several children molested. A few guilty ones have been caught and punished by Moses, but there are others hiding out there."

"What is the punishment for those who rape women?" Zipporah asked, remembering Naomi.

"Their organs are severed from their bodies and they are never allowed to enter the Tabernacle as long as they live," Shina said nonchalantly.

"Is it Moses' or God's law?" she asked, remembering that Moses had told her castration should be the punishment when women are raped.

"It is God's law, of course," Shina replied. "Do you remember Phinehas, the grandson of Aaron?"

"Yes, why do you ask?"

"Keep Gershom away from him. I don't trust him around children."

"He's Moses' nephew," Zipporah said, alarmed by her words. "Have you spoken to Moses about this."

"No. Just trust me and keep him away."

Emotionally exhausted, Zipporah sat on her bed and braided her hair. She buried her face in her pillow and finally slept, only to be awakened hours later. The tent was now dark. After a brief period she realized Shina was no longer there. Zipporah dressed and went outside. In the distant hills she saw the glow of campfires and a thin crescent moon rising above Mount Sinai.

She flinched when she felt a light touch on her elbow. Jacob drew her into the shadows of the tent. "I'm sorry if I frightened you, but we must be careful," he whispered.

"I'm alone," she replied bitterly. "I don't expect Shina to return anytime soon. You knew my husband had taken another wife, didn't you?"

"Do you want to go to the leper camp or not?" he said, pushing a package into her arms. "Change into these garments. I will show you where a horse waits and give your directions to the camp."

"Remain here while I change," Zipporah whispered, going behind the partition.

"You once sat before me unclothed. There was no shame in you then," he said with a sheepish grin.

"I am now a devoted Hebrew wife," Zipporah replied sarcastically, slipping the drab cotton garment over her head. Her children were sleeping soundly and she felt confident they would not wake before she returned.

When she emerged, he smiled. "You would look beautiful even if I had brought you a sack cloth filled with ashes." As she tied a black scarf over her head, he impulsively pulled her into his arms and kissed her.

Zipporah hesitated, then slapped his face. "Never do that again," she said, wiping her mouth. It did not remove the warm tingle from her lips.

"I will make no such promise," he whispered.

"Then after this night stay away from me." She followed him to the corral and hesitated before taking his hand to mount the horse. He gave her a tablet to give the guard, and instructions on how to reach the camp. She nodded and looked back at him as she rode off. Beyond the maze of tents, she approached the distant campfires near the base of the mountain.

When she arrived at the gate of the leper camp, a guard lifted his lamp before opening it. "Who comes at this hour?"

"I bring herbs and bandages for the sick," Zipporah said, handing the guard the clay tablet.

"Dismount and let me take a look at you."

Zipporah hesitated, then slid off the horse. A heavyset black man held his tablet to his lamp. After reading it, he gestured for her to come closer.

"Why do you come at this late hour?" he said, holding the lamp close to her face.

"The needs of these people are great. They suffer day and night."

"Your pass is in order. I have learned to be extra careful, even in this place. Our enemies come in the night to trick us. Recently a spy came through here dressed in the rags of a leper."

"May I enter now?"

127

He smiled as he lowered his lamp. "Yes, but be careful. These people have sinned and the punishment of God is great upon their heads."

"Where can I find the sister of Moses?" Zipporah asked as her heart began pounding.

He stared at her suspiciously. "Why do you seek her?"

"She is my friend and sister."

He turned and pointed to a nearby campfire. "You will find her over there caring for the children of these poor devils. Be careful. God has placed a special curse upon her head."

Zipporah held the reins and guided the horse toward the glow of the campfire. What was this "special curse?" At the fireside she saw a woman seated on the ground with an infant in her arms. By the flickering light Zipporah could see the woman's chalk-white face.

"Miriam?" Zipporah asked as she walked next to her.

When she stepped into the light, the woman stood up and backed away. "Zipporah? Do my eyes deceive me?"

"I'm here, sister," Zipporah said. Miriam dropped to her knees and began weeping as Zipporah took the child from her arms and carefully placed it on a torn blanket.

"Why have you come to this place and at this hour?" Miriam asked between sobs. "Surely you know why they have placed me here?"

Zipporah sat beside her and kissed her pale cheek, unmindful of the risk. "When we first met you said to me that sisters will we be until death separates us. So do not weep. All that matters is we are together. I will never abandon you."

CHAPTER 21

And the anger of the Lord was kindled against (Aaron and Miriam) and he departed. And the clouds departed off the tabernacle, and, behold Miriam became leprous, white as snow...

Numbers 12:9-10

The putrid smell of rotten flesh caused Zipporah to cover her mouth. She watched Miriam clean pus from the open sore on a child's leg. The smells brought to mind the day she stumbled across the decaying body of a lamb filled with maggots and flies.

Miriam was grateful for the clean bandages and herbs Zipporah gave her. "You never get used to this," she whispered as the child kicked and screamed.

"What sin has this child committed to deserve such punishment?" Zipporah asked.

"None. It was the sin of the mother. She slept with an Egyptian. The night she died she told me she had been raped. If she had been truthful, God never would have brought this punishment upon her head," Miriam said as the child grew quiet. "When did you return?"

"We arrived two days ago. My father headed the caravan that brought supplies to your people. Moses told me you were here and I came against his wishes," Zipporah said, wondering what kind of God would inflict leprosy on an innocent child. And so what if the mother *had* been raped, she thought.

"Then you know of his marriage to that woman," Miriam said sneering.

"Yes, but that does not concern me now. What can I can do to relieve your suffering?"

"Suffering? I'm not suffering," Miriam said indignantly as she waved her hand in Zipporah's face. "This whiteness that robs me of my skin color is not leprosy."

"Then...why are you here?"

Miriam leaned forward and gritted her teeth. "Because the elders are angry with me for opposing Moses' marriage to that woman."

"Speak not ill of Shina. I'm sure she had no choice in the matter."

"Don't be naive, Zipporah. I saw the way she fanned herself in Moses' face. She began weaving her spider's web the day you left Egypt. My brother was lonely and yielded to her charms," Miriam said, shaking her head angrily. "Aaron and I warned him to stay away from her."

"If Aaron objected, then why are you the only one being punished?"

129

"Because I continued protesting, that's why," Miriam said bitterly. "Moses tried to silence me from the day I found out he was sleeping with Shina. It angered him when I spoke to the elders about it. Reuben just laughed in my face. As prophetess to my people, I told them no good would come of it. The elders declared that God had made me a leper and they sent me here."

"I thought Shina was Reuben's slave," Zipporah said reflectively. "He must have given her to Moses knowing she would come between us. Reuben despises me because I am a Midianite."

"She was never his slave. Listen to me. Reuben and the elders feared your influence over Moses," Miriam said, as she placed the child on a bed of straw. "As for this condition, Aaron knew this whiteness in my skin had been coming on for years. He refused to speak on my behalf because he is afraid to challenge Moses." Miriam rolled up her sleeve and showed Zipporah the brown patches of her skin that had not turned white.

"This is terrible. I've got to find a way to get you out of here."

"You've got enough troubles. Don't concern yourself or you might end up here with me." Miriam pointed to an open sore on the child's cheek. "That's leprosy. I spend my days caring for these poor children."

"You are an inspiration to me," Zipporah said, wiping tears. "Even in this terrible place you do the Lord's work."

"The elders seem to have forgotten that God made me a prophetess. He will deliver me from this place of death."

"I hope you are right," Zipporah said. "Why is there such a great sadness among your people?"

"When we arrived at Mount Sinai, Moses went up into the mountain and did not return for more than thirty days. When the mountain shook and erupted with fire and smoke, we feared he had been swallowed up in all the fires that spewed from its lips. The people wanted a god to lead them, so Aaron ordered those among us who had gold to give it to the elders. They melted it down and fashioned a golden calf to honor the Egyptian god of the two horns, whose name is Sais."

"Before Moses met his God, I remembered him telling me that Sais is one of the gods who caution men not to speak falsely."

"I'm impressed," Miriam said. "Well, Moses finally returned, bringing with him two tablets on which were written ten commandments. When he saw us celebrating around the golden calf, he became so enraged he broke the tablets and ordered the calf melted down."

"Did his God become angry also?"

"Yes. He spoke to Moses in a dream, telling him to gather the sons of Levi," Miriam said as she paused to catch her breath. "Then He ordered them to search out the leaders of the revolt and slay them. Before the day ended, more than three thousand of our people were slain."

Zipporah gasped. "Three thousand of your own people? What punishment was given Aaron?"

"Aaron went unpunished because he confessed his sins and God forgave him. Or should I say Moses forgave him. My brother returned to the mountain and received another set of tablets. He walked through all that ash and smoke you see spewing from that mountain."

"It is horrible that so many had to die," Zipporah said, shaking her head with disbelief.

Miriam gazed at the position of the stars. "The hour is late. Go in haste and do not risk coming here again."

"When I arrived at the gate, the guard was kind to me, but is he of your tribe? I thought only Hebrews were ordered out of Egypt."

"His name is El-Hor. He was born in Nubia, the land of the blacks. Nubia was once a province of Egypt; now a Nubian is Pharaoh of both Egypt and Nubia. Their blood has mixed with ours for centuries. Those who accepted our God chose to leave Egypt with us."

"I will never rest until you are free of this place," Zipporah said. "This injustice must not be allowed." She kissed Miriam's cheeks then mounted her horse and rode from the camp. When she arrived at her tent, the first light of dawn was touching the peaks of Mount Sinai. She removed the partition where the boys slept and found Eli missing. Her heart raced as she opened the partition to Shina's sleeping area. To her relief, Eli was resting peacefully beside her. Shina opened her eyes and stared at her but said nothing. Zipporah did not remove Eli from her arms.

The blowing of the Ram's horn signaled the congregation to rise for morning prayers. Moses sat under the shade of a broad canvas awning, surrounded by the tribal chiefs and elders. The colorful standards of the tribes fluttered in the breeze from spears buried in the ground behind their chairs. Jethro opened the meeting with prayer then asked the chiefs and elders to meditate in silence for the success of their journey.

Moses rose and cleared his throat. "Chiefs and elders, God has spoken to me concerning our journey to the village of Kadesh-barnea, located near the border of Canaan. I have sent Joshua and several of our men as spies to bring us information about the land of Canaan. It is only a half day march from Kadesh. Before we march, however, I have made a decision based on the advice of my father-in-law. From among your ranks I will choose seventy men to serve as judges." The chiefs smiled and nodded. "Until now I have judged our people and listened to their complaints. The seventy judges will administer justice and determine the punishment when the Lord's commandments are broken."

"This is a wise decision, Moses," Reuben said. "Now you will be able to devote your full attention to more serious matters."

"Our God has given me additional laws regarding the evils that continue to plague this assembly. Recently, two children were found dead, their bodies mutilated. If the man is caught, he will be burned alive. Now hear me. Any man who has carnal knowledge with a child, his daughter or his daughter-in-law will be put to death by stoning. If a man takes a woman and her mother to his bed, all three will also be burned at the stake," Moses shouted, trying to control his rage. Several chiefs glanced at each other but remained silent. "You will not marry two sisters, for they will become rivals. However, if the man's wife dies, he may marry her sister. I will remind you once again, if a man has carnal knowledge of another man or with an animal, they both will be stoned to death and their bodies burned. Now hear Jethro, my father-in-law, who brings a message from the Chiefs of Midian."

Jethro rose beside Moses. "The Chiefs of Midian are prepared to welcome you, our cousins, for ninety days. Accept our offer, for your people are in no condition to move to Kadesh-barnea, especially during the dry season. They are weary and in need of rest. Pray, stay with us and regain your strength before you take this burden upon yourselves."

Moses interrupted Jethro. "Father, I have heard the voice of God and he has warned me not to delay in Midian. Come with us, for the Lord will be pleased to count you as a member of our congregation."

"I am the Priest of Midian and must remain and tend to the spiritual needs of my people. However, my prayers go with you, for I know my God and your God are one," Jethro answered.

A chief stood to be recognized. "Oshea, the son of Num of the tribe of Ephraim, will speak," Moses said.

"It has been reported that the wells at the oasis at Kadesh-barnea are low on water. Should we not wait for ninety days? By then the rains will come to the Sinai."

"Would you defy the will of God? Many will perish if our faith is weak. Have you forgotten how water came from the rock at Elam when the Lord commanded me to strike it with my staff?" Moses said.

"Yet many of our wives and children perished before we pitched our tents at Mount Sinai." Oshea replied. Moses frowned and pointed to Chief Nahshom whom he was sure would support his decision.

"Nahshom of the tribe of Judah will speak," Moses said.

"We of the tribe of Judah are pleased with the advice that your father-in-law has given us. Twice our encampment has been at the point of revolt and twice it has been put down by the sword. Speak to God and ask him to let us rest in Midian for the ninety days. By then our people will be better prepared to seize the land of Canaan."

Moses raised his staff and pounded it on the ground. "The Lord our God has spoken," he shouted angrily. "The Ark of the Covenant, which houses the spirit of God, will go before us. Our God will be with us in battle. You will go to your sections and begin preparing the people for the march to Midian. We will rest there only seven days, then we march to Kadesh-barnea."

By nightfall an eerie silence had fallen over the camp. Zipporah lay awake, unable to sleep. She knew they would break camp at dawn. Just as she closed her eyes, she heard the voice of Shina calling her. The partition that separated their sleeping areas was drawn aside. Shina wore only a white skirt. Her brown breasts glistened from the olive oil that she had applied earlier.

"Why do you call me at this hour?" Zipporah asked.

"My lord Moses bids you come to him," Shina said.

The sight of her irked Zipporah, for it was obvious she had just come from Moses' bed. She slipped on the drab garment she had worn to the leper camp and walked the short distance to Moses' tent. Upon entering, she found him seated on his carpet with a bottle of wine by his side.

"Why did you send for me?" she asked.

Moses took her hand and pulled her beside him. "Does an obedient wife ask why her husband beckons her?" He untied the belt on his blue robe. "Why are you dressed like the women of the camp?"

"This is the garment I wore when I went to find my sister, Miriam," Zipporah said calmly.

The veins stood out on Moses' neck. "You defied my orders and went to that camp after I told you not too?"

"Yes, and I know why you sent her there," Zipporah said. "You are angry with her for opposing your marriage to Shina. I beg of you not to punish her in this manner. She is not afflicted with leprosy and you know it."

Moses squeezed her arm and shouted, "It is God who is punishing Miriam. Do not mention her name to me again."

The pressure on her arm brought back memories of their last night in Egypt. She squirmed as he held her chin and forced her to look into his eyes.

"You may use my body," she said calmly. "But I will not come to you freely until Miriam is released from that place." She stood, removed her garment and threw it at his feet. Standing naked before him, she saw the familiar hunger in his eyes.

"Do not defy me," he warned.

"Use me the way the foolish shepherd boys do their sheep. That way I will not have to look into your deceitful eyes," she cried as she walked to his writing table, leaned over it and gripped its edges. She could hear his heavy breathing as he stood behind her. Gritting her teeth, she prepared herself to receive him. In the silence that followed, she suddenly realized she was alone.

Zipporah dressed then sat at his table, drained and tearful. As she tried to compose herself, she saw a scroll and, beside it, two stone tablets with Hebrew words carved on them. She picked a scroll and read silently until she saw the words, 'For you shall worship no other God: for the Lord whose name is *Jealous, is a jealous God,* ... visiting the iniquity of the fathers upon the children unto the third and fourth generation of them that hate me.' Her hands trembled as she stared at the word *'Jealous.'* She placed the scroll aside and read the ten commandments carved on the stone tablets. It was then she recalled Moses reciting the confessions made by all spirits when they enter the Egyptian's Great Hall of Double Right and Truth. The commandments carved on the tablets were certainly not original. Was Yahweh one of the forty-three Egyptian gods that judge the dead? Or was he the Chief God whom all the gods worship?

Out of the corner of her eye, Zipporah noticed movement in the curtain. Out of curiosity, she walked over and examined it. The curtain had been cleanly cut with a sharp knife. Someone had been watching them! Frightened, she quickly left the tent. A cloud covered the moon, making the path difficult to see. She took only a few steps before bumping into someone. When her eyes adjusted to the dim light of a campfire, she saw Phinehas glaring down at her. He hesitated momentarily, then stepped aside and allowed her to pass. She stepped pass him and returned to the safety of her tent. It was only then she remembered Shina's warning.

The next morning Zipporah took Gershom and Eli to the pool and waited in line to fill her bladder bags. She wore the drab dress Jacob had given her. When guards offered to take her to the front of the line she refused. She spent time talking with the women, which caused a great deal of excitement. After filling her water bag, Gershom pulled the hem of her garment and pointed at Jacob.

"There's Jacob," Gershom said. "Can I go get him, please?" Zipporah nodded and he ran into Jacob's arms. Gershom took his hand and pulled him toward her.

"I see you are popular with the women of the camp," Jacob said, taking her water bag. "There has been less grumbling among them since you arrived."

"I told you I wanted to be among the people and share their hardships."

"I am pleased that you returned safely from the leper camp," he whispered. "How is Miriam?"

"She's well. She cares for the sick and dying and does not belong with lepers. I told my husband as much."

"You told him you went there?" he asked with concern.

"Yes, and I also spoke to Aaron this morning. He promised to intercede on her behalf." Zipporah touched his hand. "Do not worry, Jacob. You have nothing to fear."

"You are a remarkable woman, Zipporah," Jacob said, feeling relieved. "What do you think Moses will do now?"

Gershom pulled on her skirt. "Mother, who is that woman waving at us?" he said, pointing to the woman running toward them.

Zipporah raised her hand to shield her eyes from the bright sunlight. She uttered a cry when she saw it was Miriam.

"Zipporah, I'm free!" Miriam shouted.

Zipporah handed Eli to Jacob and ran into her sister-in-law's arms. As the two women hugged, kissed and cried, Gershom squeezed between them, determined not to be excluded from their joyful reunion.

CHAPTER 22

And all the congregation lifted up their voice, and cried; and the people wept that night. And all of the children of Israel murmured against Moses and Aaron. They said, "Let us choose a captain and return into Egypt."

Numbers 14:1-4

A vicious sandstorm slowed the movement of the congregation from the border of Midian through the Wilderness of Paran. Dust devils danced across the dry landscape like satanic spirits, adding to the misery of the travelers. Clouds provided some relief from the searing heat, but by the time the advance units of Moses' army arrived at the Kadesh-barnea oasis, the midday temperature had risen to oppressive levels.

Most of the Amalekite tribesmen who occupied the oasis had fled with their families, but not before their men put up stiff though brief resistance. The skirmish resulted in the deaths of seven Hebrew and four Amalekite warriors. Moses was disheartened to discover that the Amalekites had filled their wells with sand. It was clear they'd had advance knowledge of the Hebrews' arrival. Removing the sand and gravel would take several days with no assurance the wells could be fully restored. By the afternoon of the third day, men and horses were dying from heat stroke and lack of water.

As the twelve tribes arrived with their flocks, complaints were heard from their leaders as they staked out their positions around the oasis. Nights brought little relief from the incessant heat as the cries of the women and children sounded throughout the camp. By the fifth day, Moses and his officers realized they faced a major crisis. With complaints mounting, Moses issued a call for a special meeting of tribal leaders and elders. After all had assembled, Joshua announced that the wells had been cleared but water would have to be rationed for several weeks.

Elder Eban, from the tribe of Naphtali, rose and pointed his finger at Moses. "Hear me, Moses. Our people are dying from the heat and there will not be enough water even if the wells are fully restored. Our sheep and goats will soon strip the leaves from all the nearby desert shrubs. It would have been better that we had died in Egypt rather than perish in this hellish place. There are some who are whispering that the time has come to choose a new leader before we all perish. We are in no condition to fight a war."

Moses raised his hand for order, but the complaints grew louder. "Have you forgotten so soon how the Lord gave us manna to eat and how great flocks of quail were blown into our camp on the winds of a storm?" Moses shouted with growing irritation.

"Do not speak of what has happened in past months. Tell us how we are going to survive in this infernal heat without adequate water," Eban shouted. "Our woman and children are sick and dying. Our flocks are perishing. You dragged us to this place with the promise that God would protect us. Why did you not listen to the advice of your father-in-law? We could have remained in Midian until the rains came."

"God sent us here at the time of his choosing. He is testing your faith. Now listen to me. Joshua and Caleb have just returned from the land of Canaan. Hear their report." He motioned for Joshua and Caleb to join him on the platform. Both men held up their arms and appealed for calm.

"We beg you not to speak against Moses," Joshua shouted. "We have returned from a fertile valley just over the mountains you see in the distance. It is a land flowing with milk and honey as our God told us. He will remove his protection from us if you continue your complaints."

"You idiots, do you not see what has happened? God has already removed his protection. Our children are dying at this very moment," the wife of a chief shouted. Her husband, unaware that she had followed him, restrained her and ordered her to leave.

"Where is your faith?" Caleb shouted. "If we advance from this place, the Lord will be with us. The Canaanites and the Amalekites will fall before us like locusts in winter."

An elderly white-haired man pointed his finger at Moses. "Where are the other spies you sent? Why are they not here? They told us that the people of Canaan live in walled cities and that giants dwell in the land. They will put our young men to the sword and make slaves of our women and children. We must return to—." The old man suddenly gasped and clutched his throat. Before anyone could reach him, he collapsed. Reuben placed his ear to the man's chest and signaled with his thumb down that the man was dead.

Moses pointed to the body. "See how the anger of the Lord has come upon us. God whispers in my ear at this very moment saying, 'How long will these people complain against me? How many must die by my hand?' There lies the proof of his power and anger."

Those assembled began dispersing. Panic spread throughout the encampment when a rumor circulated that ten men had been killed by the hand of God. The chiefs of the twelve tribes returned to Moses an hour later. Pagial, chief of the tribe of Asher, had been chosen as their spokesman. They found Moses resting with his head on the table. When he sat up, all were shocked to see him totally dispirited, not the confident leader who had brought them out of Egypt.

137

"We know our lack of faith has caused us to sin. Speak to the Lord and tell him we are ready to fight for the land he has promised us."

"It is too late," Moses said lethargically. "God has ordered us back to the Red Sea. He said this wicked generation must dwell in the wilderness of the Sinai for forty years. None twenty or older will live to see the promised land, save Caleb, the son of Jephuneh, and Joshua, the son of Nun."

Aaron stepped forward and raised his staff, "Did not our God make me the priest unto our people? He did not tell me to return to the Red Sea, for the wilderness is a desert and beyond is Egypt and bondage. He wants us to advance into Canaan."

Pagial turned to the chiefs and shouted, "Hear the words of Aaron. Moses has lost his nerve. Let us show the Lord our faith by marching to the promised land and taking what is rightfully ours. Who stands with me?" A mighty roar filled the tent as the chiefs raised their standards. Moses slumped in his chair with the realization that he had just been stripped of his power.

"Do not do this," Moses warned. "Without God to lead you, the Canaanites will put you to the sword."

Pagial raised his sword, with the knowledge that he was now in command. "You no longer speak for us. We have defeated the Amalekites. Beyond the hills of our encampment is the promised land," Pagial shouted passionately, as he walked among his fellow chieftains. "Follow my lead and we will soon bathe in sparkling streams. Go arm yourselves and sound the trumpets of war. This night we march to the land given to our forefather, Abraham." As the chiefs and elders filed out of the tent, only Joshua and Caleb remained.

"Moses, we have no choice but to join the men of our tribes," Joshua said.

Moses gestured for them to leave. "Go, and may the Lord's anger be cooled against those who betrayed me."

When Moses stumbled into his wives' tent, he found only Shina waiting for him. "Where is Zipporah? Why is she not here with my sons?"

"Zipporah and Miriam have gone to the place set aside for lepers. Jacob went to protect them," Shina whispered. "Your sons are in the care of a midwife. Let me tend to you, my Lord."

Too distressed to care anymore, Moses removed his garments and allowed her to bathe him. He closed his eyes and thought of Zipporah as Shina removed her gown and came into his arms.

Zipporah and Miriam burned the rags they had removed from sick and dying children. Jacob stood guard, keeping the starving lepers at a safe distance. They began digging shallow graves for the children who had died that morning. When Zipporah almost collapsed from the heat, Jacob took the shovel from her hand.

"Zipporah, you will kill yourself if you are not careful," he said, handing her a container of water. "Go rest while I finish digging this grave."

"It might be more merciful if I died. Look around us," Zipporah said, pointing to women and children lying on the ground. "They are all dying. There is no water or food for them. They have lost the will to live."

Miriam straightened and rested her back. "Enough of your complaining. We must not lose faith at a time like this."

"Faith!" Zipporah said. "When I see such pain and suffering I wonder if I have any faith left."

Jacob took Zipporah's arm and dragged her to the shade of a boulder. "Don't speak of losing faith, Zipporah. It's not like you. Allow me to share my food with you. If you don't eat, you'll get sick," he said, reaching into his leather packet for a loaf of bread. "This is not the time to say this, but I must confess that I have admired you since the days we were at Mount Sinai." Without looking at him, she took the bread.

A ragged man stumbled toward her with his hand extended. Zipporah felt sick when she saw the gaping sore that had eaten away half his face.

"I am dying," he gasped. She broke the bread and shared it with him.

"Why do you waste food when you need it?" Jacob asked. "He will be dead within a few hours."

"I share because he is my brother," she said without hesitation.

"Can you share a small part of your heart with me?" he asked. She smiled faintly, took the shovel from his hand and returned to the gravesite.

CHAPTER 23

Then the Amalekites came down, and the Canaanites which dwelt
in that hill, and smote them, and discomfited them, even unto Hormah.
Numbers 14:45

Pagial informed Joshua that he would serve as his own commander and Korah, of the tribe of Levi, would be his second-in-command. He knew Korah had priestly ambitions. To gain his support he promised him the position of high priest. He did not trust Joshua or Joseph, knowing of their devotion to Moses. The messenger sent to inform Jacob that he had been demoted was ambushed and killed before he reached the leper camp.

Pagial reviewed the thirty-six thousand warriors under his command, then led them on a night march to the border of Canaan. It was dawn when they reached the hill overlooking the town of Hormah, just inside the border. The fresh air, green fields and clear running stream were a stark contrast to the semi-barren land that surrounded the Kadesh-barnea oasis.

Pagial rode to the top of a hill and raised his standard. "Men of Israel, before you lie the rich lands of Canaan," he shouted. "Look down upon the green pasture with its river and sweet springs. Beyond this town are the cities that will soon be ours. Here is the land of milk and honey promised us by our God. Victory will be ours because God marches with us. Are you ready to do battle as God commands?"

A mighty roar echoed throughout the hills as the warriors broke ranks and surged toward the town, motivated by the prospects of water and food. He shouted for his chieftains to maintain order, but to no avail.

When the warriors entered the town, they found it deserted. Men threw aside their swords and shields and looted the stone dwellings, taking everything of value. Others went to the stream and bathed themselves. By the time Pagial arrived, his men had broken into wine cellars and were quarreling over the distribution of the wine casks. Some grumbled when they discovered the women of the village had left.

Joshua rode to Pagial's side and shouted, "You must maintain discipline. Look at them. This is no army. It's a mob. We must prepare for battle. I'm sure the Canaanites know we are here. They may be watching us from those hills."

"Take twenty men and scout the area," Pagial shouted. "By the time you return order will be restored."

"Not if our troops keep gorging themselves on drink," Joshua said, turning his horse and riding off. Pagial seethed with rage, having been chastised by

Joshua within hearing distance of his officers. He would see to it that Joshua was placed in the forward ranks when the battle began.

By afternoon the chiefs succeeded in getting the infantry into battle formation. The tribes of Asher, Simeon, Levi and Naphtali were assigned to the front line. Following close behind were the archers, consisting of the tribes of Zebulon, Joseph, Benjamin and Dan. The tribes of Reuben, Issachar, Gad and Judah formed a third line of defense. Pagial remained in the rear with the three hundred cavalrymen.

When Pagial saw Joshua returning with his scouts, he rode out to meet him. "What word to you bring?" he shouted.

"The army of the Amalekites is marching out of those hills to meet us," Joshua said.

"What of the Canaanites?" Pagial asked.

"I saw only the standards of the Amalekites. Are the men ready for battle?"

"They are ready. But you will leave your horse here and take command of the front line," Pagial said. Joshua saluted by placing his fist to his chest. He dismounted without questioning the order.

Pagial signaled for the rams' horns to sound as stragglers rushed to their tribal standards. The twelve formations marched through a wheat field beyond the town. Pagial led the three hundred cavalrymen to a nearby hill. They heard the rumble of drums. When the Amalekites came into view, he ordered the forward units of the infantry to advance. With the blast of horns, warriors pounded their swords on their shields as Joshua and Caleb led them toward the Amalekite line. The mile-wide column of Amalekite warriors paused and knelt. Archers in their rear moved into position behind them. Joshua could see King Amalek on his horse with his arm raised. Along the Amalekite battle line the green and blue flags of the Amalekites waved briskly in the wind.

Several youths, eager to prove their courage, broke ranks and charged toward the Amalekite warriors. When they were within a few hundred yards, the Amalekite archers released their arrows that darkened the sky like a thunder-cloud. The Hebrew warriors raised their shields, effectively warding off the first shower of missiles. Joshua signaled his warriors in the front line to drop to the ground, allowing the archers in the rear to effectively fire their arrows at close range. A blood curdling battle cry escaped Joshua's lips as he led his men into the Amalekites' line of defense. The swipe of his sword severed the heads of the first two men who opposed him. The sounds of screaming men and clashing armor echoed throughout the valley. When the Amalekite line broke, Amalek sent more warriors into the breach. Pagial hesitated when Joshua signaled with his standard that he needed reinforcements. Only when a scout mistakenly reported that Joshua had been killed did he order more troops to advance.

Under a blazing noonday sun, more than sixty thousand warriors fought in bloody hand-to-hand combat. With bodies slashed and bleeding, men lost their footing in the slippery wheat field. Joshua never tired and remained in the thick of battle. His undaunted courage inspired his warriors to fight harder. The carnage ended with the sound of rams' horns calling the Amalekites to retreat.

"They're running. We've beaten them," Caleb cried at the sight of the fleeing Amalekites. "They are retreating toward the hills east of the battlefield."

Pagial led the cavalry around his right flank, hoping to cut off the Amalekite's line of retreat. His force clashed with the Amalekite cavalry; and after a brief skirmish, the battle ended in a stalemate. He watched Amalek escape with his army intact. When Pagial rode among his victorious troops, he saw Joshua giving aid to the wounded and dying. A young boy walked toward Joshua holding his own intestines. He staggered a few steps then collapsed at Joshua's feet. Joshua lifted the youth's body and carried it off the battlefield.

"I congratulate you," Pagial said, nonchalantly. "Take your scouts and follow the Amalekites closely. I want to know Amalek's every move."

Joshua made no reply. He mounted a horse and rode beyond the battlefield. From a position a few miles from Hormah, he watched as the last of the Amalekites retreated to the hills. Just as he turned his horse, he heard the sounds of distant trumpets and drums. An uneasy feeling prickled down his spine as he rose in his saddle and shielded his eyes. To his horror a second army was marching toward them from the north. There were hundreds of battle chariots driven by men waving the banners of the Canaanites. The Amalekites turned and cheered as their allies advanced. He realized the first battle was only the prelude to the real battle for Canaan. They had stepped into a trap.

Joshua galloped back, waving his arms and shouting the alarm. Pagial screamed orders for the warriors to form their ranks. As weary men rushed to their battle stations, they heard the thunder of chariots charging in their direction. Those in the forward ranks released their arrows but with little effect. Many had no chance as the deadly lances of the charioteers cut through their ranks like sickles through stalks of ripened wheat. Men stumbled over each other trying to escape the crush of wheels. Many were sliced to death from deadly twirling blades that extended from the chariot's axles. Pagial led his cavalry into the retreating mob in a futile effort to rally his warriors. Joshua could only watch as Pagial's horse stumbled over the bodies of his own men. The wheels of a chariot mangled both rider and horse.

With the death of their commander, a loud cry rose up from the ranks of the Hebrew warriors. Many threw down their weapons and ran for their lives. Joshua took command and led the retreat into the town of Hormah. As the dispirited men swarmed through the narrow streets, he shouted orders for the warriors of his own sub-tribe of Ephraim to remain and fight a rear guard action.

Joshua counted on giving the main body of troops time to escape into the foothills where the narrow trail and steep gorges could be easily defended. The strategy worked. The narrow streets rendered the chariots useless.

With Joshua inspiring them with his bravery, the warriors of Ephraim battled the Canaanites in the streets of the town until nightfall. When the Canaanites retreated to regroup, Joshua ordered his men out of the town under cover of darkness. They waited at the first mountain pass, but the Canaanites seemed content not to pursue them beyond the border of Canaan.

It was dawn when a courier arrived with the first reports of the defeat. Moses did not grieve over the death of Pagial, only for the young men who would not return. His hated nemesis had seized power and marched to Canaan in direct defiance of the orders of God. In a solemn mood, he read the dispatches to the assembled elders. Reuben rose and stood beside Moses.

"We were all blind to God's truth when we urged our young men to follow Pagial. God remained here with Moses. We must repent and turn again to him for leadership," Reuben said, his voice quivering. "Let every elder stand and pledge our support to him." One by one, the men rose to their feet and pledged with the lifting of their standards. Aaron sat with his head bowed, unable to look into Moses' eyes.

"Make your peace with God, not me," Moses said, struggling to control his anger. "I have asked God not to destroy Israel, but to punish me. He has ordered us into the wilderness by way of Edom."

"Will the king of Edom allow us to pass through his land?" Reuben asked.

"The king holds the grudge, not his people. I will offer to pay him to use his highway when we reach his borders."

A young man charged into the tent waving his arms and shouting, "The Amalekites have broken into the camp. Defend yourselves." Men grabbed their swords and rushed outside only to be met by a panicky mass of screaming women and children running in all directions. At the northern end of the encampment, Moses could see fires lighting the night sky as precious supplies went up in flames. Men rallied around him as he ran toward the fires. They heard the thunder of hoofbeats and saw several dozen horsemen approaching. When the lead rider passed, Moses brushed his lance aside with his sword and cut the hindquarter of the horse, throwing the rider to the ground. The other riders slowed their horses to avoid their fallen comrade. The Amalekite warriors found themselves engulfed in a sea of enraged men who pulled them from their saddles and hacked them to death.

Moses found his own tent in flames. As he frantically searched for Shina, all he found in the ashes was the silver bracelet he had given her. He remembered that Zipporah and Miriam had gone to the leper camp and had left the children with a midwife. The thought of his wives and his sister in the hands of Amalek was too horrible to contemplate. He was relieved when told his sons were safe.

As morning dawned, the warriors began straggling back into the encampment. Moses ordered fifty horsemen to ride with him to the leper camp. When they arrived, they found the bodies of more than a hundred men, women and children. Moses covered his face with a cloth as he searched for Zipporah and Miriam. There was no sign of them. When the scouting party returned to the encampment, Moses was escorted to a tent that had been pitched for him. On the table lay the remaining articles that had survived the fire. Among them were the two stone tablets he had brought down from Mount Sinai and the gold necklace he had also given Zipporah as a wedding present. Alone in the dark he listened to the cries of women and children. Certain that all the women in his life had perished, he sat and fingered the necklace. In his anguish, he fell to his knees and cried out, "This pain is more than I can bear. Let your punishment fall upon my head." At that moment he heard the angry rumble of distant thunder.

CHAPTER 24

And if you will not... hearken unto me, but walk contrary unto me; then will I walk contrary unto you also in fury; and I, even I, will chastise you seven times for your sins. And you shall eat the flesh of your sons, and the flesh of your daughters shall you eat...

Leviticus 26:28-29

...And the people abode in Kadesh; and Miriam died... and was buried there.

Numbers 20: 1

Zipporah knew by the position of the stars that midnight had not yet arrived. From the bluff above the leper camp, she saw a red glow in the night sky. It looked as though some smelting oven had spewed its melting ore across the distant heavens. She ran to the campfire where Miriam and Jacob rested.

"The night sky is red. What could it mean?" she asked nervously. Jacob ran to the bluff with Zipporah and Miriam following him.

"The encampment is under attack," Jacob said, pounding his fist in his palm. "What you see are the flames from our tents. There is a cave just above us. Hide yourselves there. If I do not return, may our God deliver you from this place of death." He kissed their cheeks then untied his horse.

"Tell my husband I pray for his safety," Zipporah said, stepping aside to avoid the hooves of the excited horse that kicked and whinnied nervously.

"Is there anything else you wish me to say?" Jacob asked, patting the horse's neck to calm it.

"Tell him I pray for the safety of our people."

A helpless feeling slithered down her spine as she watched Jacob ride down the steep ravine into the darkness. Taking Miriam's hand, they made their way to the leper camp. People were standing outside their crude shelters staring at the night sky. Miriam faltered and took several deep breaths, placing her hands to her chest.

"What's the matter?" Zipporah asked with alarm. "Do you feel sick?"

"Do not take heed of me. Speak to these people."

Zipporah shouted, "Take the women and children and hide yourselves in the hills. Mothers with babies follow us." But the assembled made no effort to move. Their vacant eyes and drawn faces showed no emotion.

"Tell us what is happening." Zipporah recognized the man she had shared food with the night before. "Is the world coming to an end? The sky is red with the fires of hell."

145

"The enemies of our people are upon us. If we do not protect ourselves, we will be killed," Miriam said hoarsely.

"We are the living dead. There is no strength left in us," the man replied. He turned and raised his arms, which had a calming effect on the lepers. "Let us remain here and prepare for the final judgment. It is better that we perish now than die slowly of this affliction."

To Zipporah's horror the people began dropping to their knees and prostrating themselves on the ground. Miriam whispered, "There is nothing more we can do here. We must go."

A woman holding a baby crawled toward them on her knees. Zipporah lifted her to her feet, carefully avoiding her sores. She could see the child was only weeks old.

"Take my baby with you," she pleaded. "She is clean. Do not leave her here to be eaten."

"What are you saying?" Zipporah asked, certain she had misunderstood her words.

"Some here eat the flesh of their children."

Miriam whispered to Zipporah, "There is nothing more we can do here. It is written that those who do not hearken unto the Lord will be chastised seven times for their sins. They will be reduced to 'eating the flesh of their sons and daughters.'"

Zipporah suddenly remembered she had read the passage in one of Moses' scrolls. She took the baby in her arms and held it tightly. What short of god would turn his own people into cannibals?

"These women are your servants, Lord. Keep them in your service," the mother cried.

Zipporah removed the rags from the child and could see by its hollow eyes and bloated belly that it was badly undernourished. Miriam, holding her hands to her chest, followed Zipporah up the steep incline to the entrance of the cave. Suddenly, they heard terrifying screams and shouting below. Zipporah looked back and saw fires burning. The leper's shelters had become an inferno. She thought she saw the face of Amalek in the flames.

Both women lowered their heads and made their way to the back of the cave where they remained silent for several hours. When Zipporah thought it was safe, she lit her clay lamp. She saw beads of perspiration covering Miriam's face.

"You are ill," Zipporah whispered.

Miriam did not respond and struggled to breathe. Both flinched at sounds near the entrance to the cave. Miriam motioned for Zipporah to follow her. They went deeper into the cave until the roof became too low to go further.

Zipporah set the lamp on the ground, removed her coat and wrapped it around the baby.

"I am in pain, my sister," Miriam muttered breathlessly.

Zipporah felt Miriam's head. "You have a fever."

"It was foolish of us to bring that child here. It is dying of hunger. If our enemies come, they will hear its cries then take us to Amalek."

"When that mother spoke to me, I heard the voice of God speaking through her. He told me to feed this little lamb," Zipporah whispered.

"With what? You have no milk to feed them."

"I place my trust in Elohim, the God I have loved all my life." Zipporah lifted her blouse.

"What are you doing?" Miriam asked, taking short breaths. "Your breasts are dry."

Zipporah sat cross-legged with her eyes closed. She placed her hands over her breasts, lifted her head and meditated. Gradually, she felt her breast enlarging and instinctively placed the child to her nipple and began nursing. The women laughed and cried as they enjoyed the miracle. After the feeding, Zipporah wrapped the baby in her wool shawl, cradled it in her arms and stretched out beside Miriam, alert to every sound. Was it her imagination, or had Miriam's breathing slowed?

"Miriam, what is happening?" she asked, as Miriam gasped for breath.

"My Lord is calling me," Miriam muttered.

Zipporah placed the baby aside and lifted Miriam's head onto her lap. "Why must your God call you at such an hour?" she cried bitterly.

"It is not for us to ask," Miriam said, her voice barely audible.

"But I must ask. My God is Elohim. He is slow to anger, and his love is everlasting. The God my husband follows nearly killed him. Now he wants to take you from me," Zipporah whispered between sobs.

Miriam closed her eyes. "Repent and fear the Lord before it is too late."

Zipporah stared at the ceiling of the cave and shouted, "Leave her alone. It's I you want. Take me." The baby began whimpering. Miriam coughed and her head slumped to one side.

"But I do fear your God. I have always feared him, even in my youth," Zipporah cried, her voice reverberating throughout the cave. "Don't leave me here alone! Please, don't leave me!" The oil lamp went out and the only sounds echoing off the walls were the weeping of Zipporah and the feeble cry of the baby.

Jacob reached the encampment later that morning, having been delayed by Amalekite horsemen who spotted him and gave chase. After a hard ride, he managed to elude his pursuers in the desert foothills. By the time he arrived at headquarters, most of Joshua's warriors had returned and formed a defensive perimeter around the encampment.   Feverish preparations were underway to abandon the Kadesh-barnea oasis.   There was concern that the Amalekites and Canaanites would join forces for a major attack.   When Jacob entered Moses' tent, he found his commander on his knees in prayer.   The elders and chiefs of the twelve tribes were seated nearby.   When Moses sat up, Jacob was shocked to see the strain on his face and the dark circles under his eyes.

"I have heard the voice of the Lord," Moses said.   "His anger is great against those who rebelled against his orders.   He has disinherited this generation and will smite the unfaithful with a great pestilence."   The tribal chiefs and elders stared at each other, not knowing what to make of his pronouncement.

"Can we hope to turn away the anger of our God?"   Reuben asked above a whisper.

"I have pleaded with him to forgive those who have offended him and offered myself as a ransom.   He told me that as truly as he lives, all the earth will one day be filled with his glory," Moses said, pounding his staff on the ground.   "This is the judgment of the Lord.   Those ringleaders who did not hearken unto his voice will perish.   The leaders who turned against me, both they and their families will be swallowed in the bowels of the earth."

"Has not enough blood been spilled already?"   Reuben shouted, as several of the chiefs stalked out in protest.

"What are we to do?"   Aaron asked, his hands shaking uncontrollably.

"For now, we will return to my adopted land, Midian.   There we will wait for God's command."

"Will we be welcomed in Midian?   When we came out of Egypt, the Midianites offered us sanctuary, but for only ninety days," Aaron said.

"I will ask Jethro to intercede on our behalf," Moses said, as he turned to the remaining tribal chiefs.   "Go to your tribes and prepare burnt offerings from the best of your flocks to atone for your sins.   Joshua and Caleb will seek out those who rebelled and carry out the judgment of the Lord."

The chiefs stared at each other as they filed out, leaving only Joshua and Jacob at Moses' side.

"Why do you stay?   Can you not see I grieve for my wives and sister?"

"I come from the leper camp bearing news of Zipporah and Miriam," Jacob said.

"But only the dead are there.   I went searching for them this morning.   There was no sign of life anywhere."

"They may be among the living.   I urged them to hide in one of the caves above the camp."

Moses' eyes lit up as he sprang to his feet. He strapped on his sword, ran outside and shouted to a guard to saddle his horse. As he prepared to mount, Jacob took hold of the reins.

"The Amalekites are waiting in ambush. Do not leave in haste. Allow me to lead a company of men to the place where I left them." Moses paused then nodded.

"Tell Joshua we go to the leper camp. Have him equip a hundred horsemen to accompany us."

It was dusk when the riders reached the desolate area. Moses felt his heart pounding as they rode through the remains. Winged scavengers, feasting on corpses, protested with raucous squawks as they scattered from the path of the horses. While the horsemen stood guard, Moses dismounted and followed Jacob up the steep incline to the mouth of the cave. Jacob cupped his hand to his mouth and shouted, "Miriam, Zipporah, where are you?"

Only his echo returned with its broken refrain. Jacob fashioned a torch from a dead branch by wrapping it with a cloth soaked in oil. He used his flint stone to light it. From the anxiety he saw on Moses' face, Jacob knew he still loved Zipporah despite all that had happened between them. As they moved deeper into the cave, they heard the feeble cries of an infant.

Walking with his head lowered to avoid the ceiling, Moses found Zipporah sitting on the ground with Miriam's head resting on her lap. Beside her lay the baby.

"Zipporah?" Moses whispered as he knelt beside her. She hummed a familiar tune and stroked Miriam's hair. When he touched Miriam's cold forehead, he knew she was dead.

"Don't touch her," Zipporah hissed, pushing his hand away. "Let her rest."

"Zipporah, don't you recognize me?" Moses said when she continued stroking Miriam's hair.

Jacob tapped Moses' shoulder. "With your permission, may I speak to her?" Moses took the torch and stepped back. Jacob knelt, placed his hand on Zipporah's shoulder and shook her gently. "Zipporah, I've returned as I promised." When she failed to respond, he placed his finger under her chin, lifting her head. "You are safe now," Jacob said. Her eyes blinked several times in recognition.

"You've come too late. God killed my sister as he almost killed my husband."

"Your husband is here. God brought him to you, Zipporah," Jacob said. Slowly and deliberately he lifted Miriam's body from her embrace. Moses stepped closer when she looked up at him. With difficulty she stood up and staggered toward him. Moses handed the torch to Jacob, swept her into his arms and kissed her cheek as he carried her to the mouth of the cave.

Jacob followed, carrying Miriam's body. Zipporah called out weakly, "Jacob, don't forget the baby. Don't let them eat the baby's flesh."

When they walked outside the cave, Jacob placed Miriam's body aside and waited until Moses had carried Zipporah to the waiting horsemen. He knew the child of a leper would not be allowed in the encampment. With a heavy heart, he took the baby to the edge of the bluff, muttered a prayer, then tossed the child onto the rocks below.

Zipporah and Moses stood with the elders and tribal chiefs beside Miriam's grave. Rams' horns sounded their final farewells. Zipporah did not hear the words of praise spoken by Aaron and the elders. Her grief was for the loss of both Miriam and Shina. At the end of the ceremony the elders watched as Moses took Zipporah's hand and led her toward his tent.

"Our children will remain with a midwife tonight. I need to be alone with you," Moses said.

Zipporah was pleased that they would share their grief together. But there was this nagging doubt of whether or not she still loved him. She held his arm while they walked through the crowd of mourners. When they passed twenty severed heads on the tips of spears buried in the ground, she turned away.

"Are they Amalekites?" she asked, gripping his arm tighter.

"No. You see the heads of the traitors who turned against me and betrayed our God," Moses replied. Zipporah continued shielding her eyes until they were well past the gruesome sight.

When they entered the tent, Zipporah slipped into her nightgown, collapsed on the bed and wept silently with her face buried in her pillow. When Moses removed his garment and placed his hand to her cheek, she moved to the far side of the bed. He pulled her into his arms and kissed her.

"Leave me alone in my grief," Zipporah said, struggling to free herself. "How can you even think of taking me on a night such as this?"

"I have been in the bowels of death for three days. In your arms I can blot out my pain."

"Do you not grieve for Miriam and Shina?" Zipporah whispered, turning her head to avoid his lips.

"I cannot restore the dead," he said wearily.

"And I cannot relieve your pain," Zipporah said, unable to conceal her smoldering resentment. "Has not God forbidden me to respond to your love?"

"Do not refuse me," Moses said. "Do as I command."

"You will not find release if my lips are cold," Zipporah said as she stood and tried to back away, only to have him grab her arm. Standing before him, she struggled to break his grip. "I am a daughter of Midian. I cannot bury my feelings in the barren desert the way some wives do."

She did not resist when he opened her gown and kissed the nipples of her breast.

"God made you a god like Pharaoh," she gasped, trying unsuccessfully to push his face away. "How can I return love to one who is both a man and a god."

He paused and smiled. "This night it is only your husband who holds you in his arms."

"If I could return your love freely I would gladly endure any punishment," Zipporah said bitterly. Despite herself, she pressed his face to her breast. "I will not deny you."

He hesitated, then raised his hands and interlocked his fingers between hers. Zipporah did not resist as he applied pressure, forcing her to kneel between his thighs. When their eyes met, she saw a familiar hunger in his eyes. Gone was the fear of his God. By flickering lamp light, his fingers massaged her scalp as she bent down and reenacted the Elephant-headed carpet scene.

"Through the pillows of Sur, my love has returned to me," he whispered.

In the buoyed moments that followed Zipporah knew she had broken his chain of fear, releasing the free-spirited Moses she loved, if only temporarily. She placed her hands to his chest, pressed him onto his back, and climbed on top of him. With their coupling, the mutual rhythm was reminiscent of the lapping waves washing over the beach at the Gulf of Aqaba. When he cried out, she laughed, remembering how his sounds had frightened the nesting sea gulls the night they first loved.

In the hour that followed, Zipporah rested in his arms. All the pent-up tension she had felt now faded, despite her lingering doubts. Did he love her after all? Could she forgive him for marrying Shina only months after they separated? She would try.

As dawn approached, Zipporah sensed his growing tension. She knew the full passion of the love they shared now frightened him. They sat up abruptly when thunder shook the earth beneath them, followed by the gentle sound of welcomed rain beating against their tent like slender cedar drumsticks.

"See. God is not angry with us, Moses. He is rejoicing in our happiness. His tears of joy are raining down on us."

CHAPTER 25

Remember what Amalek did to you... how he smote even those who were feeble behind thee, ...thou shall blot out the remembrance of Amalek from under heaven; you will not forget it.

Deuteronomy 25:17, 19

Moses stood before the Council of Elders and chiefs with Zipporah at his side. Reuben and Eleazar found it difficult to conceal their anger. The sight of Zipporah standing beside Moses infuriated them. Phinehas, standing guard at the entrance of the tent, showed no emotion as he stared at her.

Moses raised his staff for order. "Within the hour this encampment returns to Midian. It is there we will rest and regain our strength. From Midian, we will enter the wilderness as God has ordered us. I have sent a message by Joshua to King Zeeb of Edom, requesting that we be allowed to pass through his country, using his highway. If it becomes necessary to graze our flocks in his pastures, I have offered to pay for it. Joshua will bring his reply to Mount Hor, the place where the borders of Edom and Moab converge. It is there we will pitch our tents and rest."

Jacob stood and was recognized. "We must still deal with the Amalekites. Every day we sight their spies near our encampment. It is only a matter of time before Amalek orders them to attack us again. He has stolen your second wife, killed several of our women and children and burned some of our supplies. With a company of three hundred horsemen, I will put an end to this."

"What do you hope to accomplish against the power of Amalek?" Aaron shouted. "Has there not been enough blood spilled? I am sick of heroics. Let us leave this place and regain the favor and protection of our God." An undercurrent of muttering sounded among the tribal chiefs. Reuben glared at Zipporah as though she was somehow responsible for their predicament.

Moses pounded his staff for order. "My brother is tired and his faith is weak. We must not lose faith and go astray a third time," Moses shouted. "No more golden calves will be forged in this hour of peril. We will take the Ark of the Covenant before us as we move to Mount Hor. Jacob will take three hundred men of his choosing and protect us as we march."

Jacob stepped forward and kissed Moses' hand. "Thank you for placing your trust in me."

Zipporah took Gershom and Eli to the staging area and watched as Jacob and his men prepared to leave. She was pleased when he mounted his horse and rode over to them.

"I'm glad you came by," Jacob said, leaning over and tousling Gershom's hair.

"Take care of yourself. Don't take any foolish chances," Zipporah said.

"Do I hear concern for my safety?"

"You know I am concerned for your safety, as well as for all your men."

"You once said you will never rest as long as Amalek lives," he said grimly. "I hope to bring you his head."

"I wish no such trophy, only your safe return."

"It pleases me you have been reconciled with your husband."

"How can you be so sure?" Something in Jacob's expression told her he was lying.

"One had only to see your faces this morning."

Before Zipporah could respond, he turned his horse and waved for his men to follow him. She whispered a prayer as they rode into the rain-pelted desert. Afterwards, she tried to sort out her feeling for Jacob.

The night before, Zipporah had placed three wide-mouth jars outside her tent. When she returned and checked them, all were filled with rainwater. As she poured the precious water into bladder skins, a young woman approached her.

"May I speak with you?" the woman whispered shyly.

"Of course," Zipporah said, surprised that she would ask.

"My name is Cozbi. I am the daughter of Chief Zur."

Zipporah stared at her. "Chief Zur is your father? I was told a woman of Midian was here, but no one spoke of you being Chief Zur's daughter. How do you happen to come here?"

"I am betrothed to Zimri, the son of Salu, a prince of the Simeonites. I left my father's house after Zimri told me he loved me. We met when he came to my father's home to purchase weapons."

Zipporah could see she was extremely nervous. Moses had told her that the Simeonites prohibited marriage outside their tribe. "What do you wish to tell me?"

"I fear for your life and those of our people. You must be careful."

"Why so?" Zipporah asked, glancing over her shoulder.

"I overheard Zimri's father speaking with a group of men. They were plotting against our people. If Moses returns to Midian, the Hebrew chiefs have no intention of leaving," Cozbi whispered. "They also spoke of your husband being under your spell now that his second wife is no longer here. There are spies watching you day and night."

"Do you know their names?" Zipporah asked calmly.

"I cannot be certain. I think the elder, Reuben, and Aaron were present," Cozbi whispered.

"Have no fear. My husband will protect you," Zipporah said. "But what of you? Has a date been set for your wedding?"

"It has been postponed many times. My father would kill Zimri if he knew my lover had taken me to his bed. Zimri keeps making excuses. Now I am certain he will never marry me."

"I will speak to my husband about this," Zipporah said, trying to calm her.

Cozbi backed away. "No, no, please do not mention my name. I beg you." Cozbi turned and ran away. Zipporah felt sick. She knew this was not the time to speak to Moses of this. The journey to Mount Hor would take several arduous weeks. There would be an opportunity at the next encampment.

During the first days of the march, Jacob and his horsemen provided safe escort as the tribes moved slowly toward Mount Hor. Moses rode at the head of the column beside the Ark of the Covenant. The retreat was made easier by intermittent rains and cool breezes. Teams of oxen pulled wagons out of deep mud. On the evening of the seventh day, Jacob left the marchers and led his men into the desert toward Jebel-helal, the tent capital of the Amalekites. The warriors stopped short of their objective as Jacob rose up in his saddle and addressed them.

"Hear me, my brothers. King Amalek has brought his army against us twice and we have defeated him. By now his spies have informed him that Moses is leading our people to Mount Hor. I believe he will not attack us now but will wait to ambush us in the narrow mountain passes when we journey to Midian. This night we will strike first. Caleb will take fifty men and burn the village of Ger-nal that lies west of Jebel-helal. If Amalek's cavalry gives chase, we will move against his capital, using the element of surprise. Let the memory of Amalek never be forgotten. The beast has killed our women and children for the last time. Let the vengeance of the Lord be on the tips of our swords."

The Amalekite capital of Jebel-helal consisted of three thousand tents and a single stone structure that served as the temple of the fire god, Molech. The eight wells at the Jebel-helal oasis provided ample water for its population of ten thousand people.

Amalek, their divine king, held court in his elaborate tent to celebrate the exodus of the Hebrews from Kadesh-barnea. Seated under his table at his feet was his eunuch wearing a gold collar. The eleven-year-old youth had been castrated after he was captured during Amalek's first attack on the Hebrew camp. The chain attached to the collar was embedded in the arm rest of Amalek's chair. As Amalek watched the various troupes perform exotic dances he reflected on how close he had come to capturing Zipporah, the one woman he vowed to have. He hated her above all women. It had become an obsession after he learned she had killed his youngest son while defending Moses. Aroused by the thought of her, he yanked the chain, signaling the youth to crawl closer and give him pleasure while he ate. While gorging himself, Amalek stroked the youth's head and recalled the events that led to the sacrifice of Moses' second wife on the altar of his god.

After the opening battle for Canaan, he had ordered his cavalry on a raid that had carried them deep into the Hebrew encampment. His officers had been given specific instructions to kill Moses and capture Zipporah, but they returned with the dark-skinned woman instead. Enticed by her beauty, he gave instructions to his wives to prepare her for his evening's entertainment. If she pleased him, he would add her to his harem.

Amalek's wives brought Shina to his bedchamber and removed her gown. He pointed to his organ and motioned for her to kneel and satisfy him with her mouth. She refused and announced proudly that she was the second wife of Moses, mistakenly believing he would respect her high position. Amalek demanded to know where he could find Zipporah. Shina shook her head and refused to speak. She screamed when the wives held her hand and stuck pins under her fingernails. In desperation, she finally blurted out that Zipporah and Miriam were last seen heading for the leper camp. Amalek called for his guards and instructed them to take a company of horsemen to the leper camp and find Zipporah. Any man who captured her would be rewarded with gold.

While waiting for their return, Amalek recalled how Zipporah had humiliated him at the Ezon oasis. With his passion boiling, he knew only Zipporah could satisfy him. He ordered his wives to bathe and dress Shina. At daybreak, he would sacrifice both women to his god.

It was dawn when his warriors returned empty-handed. In a drunken rage, Amalek cursed his captain and ordered him to leave. He woke Shina and dragged her to the Amalekite temple. The beating of brass gongs drowned out her piercing screams as priests placed her on the altar. Above her loomed the hideous stone head of the fire god, Molech. The massive head rose five times the height of the men. Elephant tusks hung from the roof of its mouth and fires belched from its gaping lower jaw. The wooden altar was carved in the shape of a tongue. The priest anointed Shina's body with sweet oils and forced her to drink a bitter substance. When the drug calmed her, the high priest called for Amalek. He removed the patch from his eye and climbed on the altar. His bulging eyeball rotated in its socket when he mounted her and paid homage to his pagan god. With the offering of his seed, the high priest sprinkled desert flowers over Shina's body to insure Amalek's gift would bear fruit in the afterlife.

With the elevation of the altar, the bride felt no pain as she slid into the flaming jaws of Molech.

Though Amalek savored the remembrance of his offering, he knew he would never be satisfied as long as Zipporah remained beyond his reach. Even as he watched his dancers' twirling acrobatics, he envisioned the day he would offer her as the bride of Molech. He would make sure the ritual lasted until he was certain she carried his child. His thoughts were interrupted when chieftains rushed to his side and prostrated themselves before him.

"My king, word has come that the village at Ger-nal is burning. All the people have been put to the sword by Hebrew infidels."

"Hunt them down! Take as many men as you need," Amalek roared. "Return me the head of Moses, but spare the woman, Zipporah. She must be brought to me alive."

Amalek retired to his sleeping quarters, dragging his weeping eunuch behind him.

Jacob watched from the hillside as a large body of Amalekite horsemen left the capital and headed for the village of Ger-nal. He gave the command to attack and led his horsemen into the capital. Their flaming torches turned the tents into infernos, whipped by desert winds. In the panic that ensued, his warriors rode through the screaming masses, putting to the sword all who challenged them. Three of Amalek's elite guards thrust their lances at Jacob only to lose their heads to the swiftness of his sword. He recognized Amalek's standard posted in front of an elaborately decorated tent. Riding at a full gallop, Jacob began cutting the tent's cords.

Inside Amalek's tent, his son yelled in his ear and shook him. "Wake up, father. The Hebrews are inside the city gate." Amalek staggered from his bed and fumbled for his sword. He heard the thundering hooves of horses, followed by shouts and the clash of arms. It enraged him to think that Moses was inside his capital. Before he could make his way outside, the tent collapsed over him. When he crawled from under the canvas, he found himself in the middle of warriors on horseback fighting savagely at close quarters. The sweltering heat from burning tents left Amalek confused. He stood swinging his sword in all directions. In the red glare, he cursed when he saw a tall rider galloping in his direction.

Jacob turned his horse and rode toward his target. With one swipe of his sword, Amalek's severed head fell to the ground. The headless body stood motionless for a second. With blood spurting from the neck, the body dropped to its knees and pitched forward in the dust. Jacob turned his horse and plunged the tip of his sword into the gaping mouth, then held the head up for all to see. The grotesque sight, with one eye protruding from its socket, brought a loud cry from the Amalekites who turned and fled.

Jacob rode to the temple, hoping to find Shina alive. When he threatened the high priest with death, the man pointed to the mouth of the stone head. "She is the bride of Molech."

Jacob forced the priest to place his head on the altar. With one blow of his sword, he severed the head and tossed it into the flaming jaws. After stripping the temple of its gold and silver, he set fire to its curtains and ordered his men to retreat.

A naked youth ran to him, screaming for help. When he realized the boy was Hebrew he grabbed his arms and slung him onto his saddle.

After riding into the desert they paused long enough to watch the flames light the night sky over Jebel-halel. Jacob covered the youth's body with his cloak.

"Never forget this night, you men of Israel. The treachery of Amalek and his pagan god have been avenged. The power of our God has spoken through our swords this night."

Loud cheers echoed across the desert plains as Jacob led his men toward the encampment.

CHAPTER 26

And the Lord said to Moses, "Take Aaron and Eleazar his son and
bring them up unto Mount Hor, and strip him of his garments and put
them upon Eleazar his son" ...and Aaron died there on the mount...

Numbers 20:25-28

The retreat from Kadesh-barnea to the border of Moab took thirty-one days.
When Jacob returned and reported the death of Amalek, wild jubilation broke out
along the line of march. Moses ordered the congregation to halt for prayers.
Jacob presented the council with the treasure stripped from Amalek's temple. He
was proclaimed a hero and promoted second-in-command to Joshua.

Zipporah saw Jacob only at a distance and it was not until the tents were
pitched at the base of Mount Hor that they met. She and her sons stood waiting
their turn to bathe in a stream, along with several thousand women and children.
For the first time in months, there was enough water for both drinking and
bathing. When guards tried to put her ahead of other women and children, once
again she restrained them, insisting she wait her turn.

Joshua had designated sections of the stream for men and women to bathe
with their children. Those needing to defecate were sent to an area outside the
encampment. All were required to carry a spade with them. After defecating,
they were instructed to dig a hole and cover the excrement. Any person caught
disobeying the decree would be whipped. Second offenders would be stoned on
the spot.

Zipporah was so relieved to be out of the desert she dropped to her knees and
ran her hands over the carpet of grass. She pulled several blades and pressed
them to her face. After months of stagnant air, flies and intolerable odors, the
sheer joy of the green earth brought tears to her eyes.

"Why is it that every time I see you, you look more beautiful?" Jacob said as
he stood watching her. Gershom leaped into his arms and hugged his neck. "I
see your children are no longer hungry. What are you feeding them?"

Zipporah quickly stood and brushed grass from her skirt. "Grapes, figs,
vegetables and honey. Market women from the villages of Moab are coming
each morning to sell us their fruits and vegetables." She offered him a stem filled
with glistening blue grapes. "I hoped I would see you," she said shyly. "That
rainy morning you led your men into the desert, I prayed for your safe return.
Moses told me he has made you one of his top commanders. Congratulations."

"I have something for you." Jacob extended his closed fist. She hesitated,
uncertain if she should accept it.

"You deserve it," he said, placing a gold earring in her palm. Zipporah dropped it as though it were a poisonous insect. How could she ever forget that single gold ring Amalek wore in his ear that horrible day at the Ezon wells.

Zipporah shuddered. "I could never accept any trophy from the body of that man," she said.

Jacob picked it up and placed it in his pouch. "I thought you would be pleased," he said. "You didn't want his head. The ring is a much better trophy."

Gershom pulled the hem of Jacob's coat. "May I speak?"

"Of course you may," Jacob said, running his hands through Gershom's hair.

"Is it true that you cut off his head with your sword?"

Zipporah placed her hands over Gershom's ears and shook her head, pleading with Jacob not to answer.

"Do not shield your son from the truth. This is a violent world, Zipporah. He must learn to survive among evil men and gods," he said, placing his arms around Gershom.

"He will know soon enough. Let us speak of other things."

"Such as the news I received from your husband?"

"What do you mean?"

"This morning Moses took Aaron and Eleazar to the summit of Mount Hor. He told me Aaron's faith is weak. His brother has undermined his leadership once too often. He plans to strip Aaron of his authority and place the garments of priesthood on the shoulders of Eleazar."

Zipporah frowned, unaware of Moses' decision. On their first night at Mount Hor, she had spent the night with Moses but he did not mention it. After bathing his feet and resting in his arms, she had told him of her conversation with Cozbi but he had seemed preoccupied. She had not mentioned that Reuben was among those overheard plotting against Midian. Did Jacob's friendship mean that much to her? As for Eleazar, she distrusted him more than Aaron. On more than one occasion she had caught him staring at her. She had seen that look in the eyes of other men.

"When my husband returns, I hope you will dine with us some evenings," she said avoiding his gaze.

"I have never forgotten that duck you served me when we were at Mount Sinai. It was delicious," he said, looking at the position of the sun. "As much as I hate to leave, I must attend a meeting of the chiefs that is about to start." When he left, she realized his friendship was precious to her. He was no longer just the son of Reuben, the elder, but her protector and a friend she felt she could trust. If only he could have stayed longer. A woman signaled that it was her turn to bathe the children.

Zipporah jerked, finding herself awake at the sound of wailing. She dressed and rushed outside where she found a group of women beating their breasts and screaming. Her heart skipped, fearing something tragic had happened to Moses.

"Why do you weep?" Zipporah asked a young woman.

"Have you not heard? Moses has returned from Mount Hor with the body of his brother, Aaron. I fear it is a sign that our God is still angry with us. In his anger he may kill us all. Last night I found both my children sick with fever. Now one is dead."

Shaken, Zipporah made her way through the crowd of mourners to Moses' headquarters. Phinehas was standing guard at the entrance. His dark eyes showed no emotion as he pulled back the flap and nodded for her to enter. When she stepped inside, the elders and chiefs moved aside to make room for her. She felt a chill when she saw Eleazar wearing Aaron's purple robe. In the center of the tent lay the body of Aaron, covered with the standard of the Levi. She felt eyes following her as she walked to Moses' side and took his hand. Together, they knelt beside the body. She saw the face of a man who looked at peace with himself. She remembered Miriam's words concerning the gentle side of Aaron's nature. It saddened her that he would not see his promised land. She and Moses rose and stood vigil over the body for the remainder of the day. As the sun set behind Mount Hor, Zipporah followed Moses to his tent.

"God spoke to me in a dream, Zipporah," Moses said, collapsing on his bench. "He told me to remove the cloak of priesthood from Aaron because his faith had grown weak. Twice he betrayed me."

"Did God kill him?" she asked, trying to suppress her fear.

"When we reached the summit of Mount Hor, I told my brother what the Lord had commanded of me. When I removed his robe and placed it on his son he became filled with rage. During the night he died in his sleep. It was the will of God. I love my brother and sister, now they are no longer in this world."

She placed her hand to his cheek and wiped his tears. For the next hour she lay in his arms but neither slept. Suddenly he sat up on one elbow. "Within weeks the encampment must return to Midian," he whispered. "I will need your father's help if we are to survive. Will you go to Jethro and speak to him on our behalf?" Zipporah felt her fear change to joy.

"Whatever you ask I will gladly do," she replied without hesitation. "But how will I return to my father?"

"Jacob and a company of his men will leave for Midian before dawn. You will travel with them. Convince Jethro to help us, then go to Ezion-geber and speak to the chiefs on our behalf," Moses said wearily. "Tomorrow I will meet with the elders and chiefs. I have a premonition that King Zeeb will deny us permission to pass through Edom into Midian. To avoid Edom, our people will have to travel once again through the mountains of the Amalekites."

160

"What of our sons? I was told there is sickness in the camp."

"Have faith, Zipporah. There must be no delay during this journey. Our sons will remain under my protective care," Moses said. Zipporah was overjoyed that he trusted her to help carry out such an important mission, but it was overshadowed by her concern for their children's safety. And again she would be traveling with Jacob. She tried to suppress her joy, remembering she was now a devoted wife.

Joshua returned from the capital of Edom and gave Moses the sealed scroll from King Zeeb. After breaking the seal and reading it, Moses called a meeting of the Council of Chiefs. From his grave countenance, the chiefs prepared themselves for the worst.

"King Zeeb has denied us passage along his highway. Although we offered to pay him gold if our flocks grazed in his pastures, he refused to consider any offer. His army may be at the border as we speak." Angry shouts and threats filled the tent.

"Let us fight our way through Edom," Reuben said. "The Lord our God has returned his favor to us. We can defeat the Edomites and make them serve us."

"We do not have enough arms for battle," Joshua replied. "Many men threw down their weapons when we retreated from Canaan."

"Do not doubt yourself," Reuben countered. "Was not God with my son when he took three hundred warriors and put Amalek to the sword?" Chiefs argued and banged their cups on the table.

"Let there be silence," Moses shouted, raising his staff for order. "Last night Jacob and his men left for Midian. My wife travels with them. I have sent a message to Jethro, asking him to appeal to the Midian chiefs on our behalf."

"In the meantime what are we to do, sit here like dumb sheep?" Chief Salu shouted.

"We will put our trust in the Lord and move our people on faith. God has forbidden us to fight the people of Edom. They are the children of Esau. The lands of Edom were set aside for them by our God."

"If we cannot pass through Edom, what route shall we take?" Salu said. "All of the mountain trails are in the lands of the Amalekites. They will surely ambush us to avenge the death of Amalek."

"It is a risk we have to take. I received a report that sickness is spreading among our people," Moses said as he motioned for Salu to take his seat. "Joshua has scouted a route that will take us through a mountain pass in the Wilderness of Paran. The Amalekites have seen the power of our God. I do not think they will face us in an open battle any time soon. Now go and prepare your people for the march."

When the meeting ended, Moses took Joshua aside and handed him a scroll. "This is a copy of the message Jacob will deliver to my father-in-law," he said quietly. "I sent Zipporah with him because she is respected by the Midian chiefs. She did not hesitate to risk her life for our people."

"Jacob will protect her with his life," Joshua said. "Speak to me of this sickness spreading among our people. Is this the beginning of the punishment you spoke of when we were at Kadesh-barnea?"

Moses sighed and shrugged his shoulders.

CHAPTER 27

...And Israel abode in Shittim, and the young men of Israel became (sexually permissive) with the women of Moab...And the Lord said unto Moses, "Take all the heads of the fornicators and hang them up before the Lord against the sun that the fierce anger of the Lord may be turned away from Israel.."

Numbers 25:1, 4

When Moses announced that the congregation would travel to Midian through mountain passes controlled by the Amalekites, a great outcry arose. As word spread throughout the encampment, men rioted and threw stones at Moses' tent. A mob formed and broke into storage tents, carrying off precious food supplies that had been purchased for the journey. Several of the sub-chiefs inflamed the mob by complaining that Moses had brought them out of the wilderness and, with Aaron dead, was now forcing them back into the desert without adequate food or water. Moses ordered his warriors to quell the disturbance and by the end of the day, more than two hundred rioters lay dead.

With order restored, Moses retired to the privacy of his tent and wept. For the third time he had found it necessary to spill the blood of his people. If only Zipporah were here to comfort him. It would be weeks before he heard from Jacob, and for the first time he doubted the wisdom of risking her life. But what choice did he have? If anyone could convince Jethro of the gravity of their situation, it was Zipporah. As he contemplated his next move, Eleazar entered the tent and sat beside him.

"Moses, there is an urgent matter that I must speak about."

"What new crisis is upon us now?"

"Since we arrived at Mount Hor, women from the town of Shittim, just inside the border of Moab, came each day to sell us their produce. Some of our young men have been following them back where they spend their nights whoring with the village girls. Some go with these women to worship their god, Baal-peor. Others have chosen to remain with the infidels and have sent word to their parents that they will never return. I have heard from God in my dreams. He demands we punish those who have turned their backs to him."

"Such behavior cannot be tolerated," Moses said, pounding his fist on the table. "Post a proclamation stating that all who are found guilty of desertion will be brought back and stoned. Their heads will be placed on stakes for our Lord to see. Let us hope the anger of God will not increase against us."

163

"What of the infidels among us who do not worship our God?" Eleazar asked.

"Do you have evidence of this?"

"There are men who are married to foreign women. Others have concubines. These women are from the lands of Egypt, Nubia, Ethiopia and Midian. It is whispered that they worship the gods of their wives to please them."

"Do you know of any women from Midian who are guilty of this crime?" Moses asked coolly, suspecting that Eleazar harbored a secret prejudice toward Zipporah. He hoped he had not made a mistake by appointing him the high priest of Israel.

"It is reported that the woman, Cozbi, daughter of the Midian chief, Zur, has caused Zimri to worship the false gods of Midian. They pollute our people with their nightly orgies," Eleazar said, knowing he was treading on dangerous ground.

"Think before you speak. My father-in-law is the Priest of Midian and a true servant of the God of Abraham," Moses replied sternly.

"Hear me, Moses. It will please our God if we weed out all infidels not of our race and tribes."

"Cozbi is the daughter of Zur," Moses said, concerned that any action taken against the woman could jeopardize his request for aid. "No harm must come to her. I will handle the matter. Is that understood?"

"As you wish." Eleazar bowed twice and backed out of the tent. Moses suddenly realized that this son of Aaron could pose a dangerous threat to his leadership.

Eleazar left the encampment on horseback at midnight. He rode through a dense fog, arriving an hour later at a cave at the base of Mount Hor. He lit a torch and waited at the entrance, concerned that those whom he invited would not find it. Within the hour he heard the sounds of hoof beats.

"Eleazar, we are here," Reuben called out above a whisper.

Eleazar responded by waving his torch. The three riders dismounted and hurried inside the cave. Its ceiling was low and all bowed their heads while moving through the narrow tunnel. The walls were decorated with drawings of wild animals. The realistic pictures of deer, elephants and water buffalo had been painted with rustic earth colors and charcoal, giving evidence that some ancient people had used the cave as a dwelling place. Eleazar escorted them to a chamber where six flat stones were arranged in a circle.

Eleazar embraced Reuben and kissed his cheeks. "I have brought Shelumiel, chief of the tribe of Simeon, and Nahshon, chief of the tribe of Judah," Reuben said.

"What of Sulu? Was he not present when you met with my father?" Eleazar said.

"We did not invite Sulu because of his son, Zimri. The son refuses to rid himself of the Midian woman, Cozbi. We are certain she was the one who informed Moses' wife of our plans," Reuben said.

"The death of Aaron rests on the heads of both women. They must not be allowed to undermine the will of God," Nahshon said.

"Eleazar, the people continue to lose confidence in Moses' leadership. They grow more resentful every day because of the reprisals he has taken against those who revolted," Shelumiel said. "We must restore strong leadership to this congregation or we perish."

"No matter what plan is adopted, we must first convince the people that God is with us," Eleazar said. "That will be my responsibility."

"Of course, but it will not be easy," Reuben said. "Moses has told the congregation that we must dwell in the wilderness of Sinai. That means occupying the lands of the Amalekites. Our people cannot survive in that damnable desert. Besides, the tribal chiefs know the Amalekites are still in league with the Canaanites. Moses permitted my son to take Zipporah to Ezion-geber to convince the Chiefs of Midian to grant us sanctuary. When we reach the fertile lands of Midian, it is there we will remain, with or without their approval. For that reason we must avoid a war with our Edomite cousins at all cost."

"But are not the Midianites also our cousins and our allies? How will we deal with Moses when the time comes to seize the lands of Midian?" Shelumiel asked. "It was Jethro who came to our aid and advised Moses on the appointment of our current system of judges."

"Jethro was invited to join us. He refused the offer of God to be one of us," Reuben said. "He and his people have lost favor with our God."

"I now wear the robe of the high priest," Eleazar said smiling. "The season of God's choosing is at hand. God said to me that when Rebecca, the wife of Isaac, carried twins in her womb, he told her, 'Two nations are in your womb, and two peoples born to you will be divided; the one will be stronger than the other, the elder will serve the younger.' This is why centuries ago it was predestined that Jacob would trick Esau out of his birthright. Both Midian and Edom will be our stepping stone to the Promised Land. Its people will bow down and serve us."

"I am proud of you," Reuben said, slapping Eleazar's shoulder. "You have passed the first test of your priesthood. I will see that your words are recorded in our chronicles."

Eleazar gritted his teeth. "But first, we must rid ourselves of the whores that have polluted our holy race. The first among them is Zipporah."

"Do not let hate consume you, Eleazar. Mistakes are often made when hate is allowed to cloud one's judgment," Reuben said.

Jacob, Zipporah, and a company of eight cavalrymen reached the plain of Elate, just inside the border of Midian. After riding two nights through treacherous mountain passes, the sight of trees, green fields, and clear water from a mountain stream brought cheers from their parched throats.

Zipporah's riding skills impressed Jacob. He had feared she would tire and delay them, but she rode with the skills of a trained cavalryman. Was there nothing this remarkable woman was incapable of doing? The sun was approaching its zenith when Jacob made the decision to rest beside a shallow stream. He knew they were only a half-day's ride from Jethro's compound. Two of the men went hunting and returned with a young spring buck. Zipporah helped them skin and prepare the carcass, while others dug a fire pit and lined it with stones. She tied strips of meat to stakes and roasted them over an open fire.

Zipporah told Jacob she wanted to bathe before eating. She rode her horse to a cluster of shrubs situated near the bank of the stream. After undressing in the shade of a tamarisk tree, she waded into the water. After the refreshing bath, she dressed and sat on the bank taking in the scenery. Jacob called to her and brought over a platter with meat, cheese and wild berries. "May I sit with you?"

"Of course," Zipporah said, smiling. "We are not far from my home. I know this place well."

"It's good to see you smiling," Jacob said, watching her enjoy the food. "You've missed your family these past months, haven't you?"

"Yes. My heart rejoices, being this close to home. If only my sons were here with me."

"Do you think your father will convince the Midian chiefs to support us again?"

"We must convince him first," Zipporah said with concern. "I'm sure by now he has heard that God no longer listens to the cries of your people. If God has abandoned Israel, what can my people do?"

"God has said that this generation will not enter the land given to Abraham. However, the sons of Israel will grow to manhood and carry out God's plan," Jacob said as he offered Zipporah more cheese. "Your people have showered us with their kindness. I hope they will continue to do so."

"Are my people expected to show greater kindness than God?" She could see her question upset him.

He sighed. "How can you ask such a question? Do you not fear God, Zipporah?"

"Yes, I fear him. Your father convinced me that your God tried to kill Moses."

166

"If God wanted to kill him, he would have done so. There is something I must tell you. I never believed our God tried to kill him. I have not allowed myself to speak of it until this moment."

"Why do you say it now?" Zipporah said, surprised by his words.

"Did Moses ever speak to you of the Egyptian god of flame, who comes from Hat-Ptah-ka?"

"Yes, before we married. He is one of the forty-three Egyptian gods who judges the dead in the great Temple of Double Right and Truth. I once suspected the son of Hat-Ptah-ka injured my husband."

"I can only tell you what I witnessed the night Moses was struck down. I was in the garden only a short distance from where he was standing when the storm began."

"You were there?" Zipporah asked, gripping his hand. "Tell me what happened. I will never forget that night. The drums of heaven sounded, followed by a flash of light that frightened me."

"Moses was standing under a tree with two elders when I saw a terrible sight. A finger of blue fire came from the sky and struck the tree, knocking Moses and the elders to the ground. My father never told Moses that one of the elders standing beside him died. When Moses recovered, they only told him that our God tried to kill him."

"But why would they not tell him the truth?" Zipporah asked with astonishment.

"My father and the elders wanted Moses to get rid of you. They consider you and your people the scum of the earth. In their false pride, they could not accept a woman of Midian as the wife of Moses. They convinced him that he was being punished for not having his sons circumcised, and they blamed you. They got what they wanted when Moses sent you to your home."

"Why are you telling me this now?"

"I have lived with this lie much too long. I just thought you should know."

She drank in the earnestness on his face and suddenly lost her appetite. After dipping the plate in the stream she turned to him and smiled. "When we first met, I hated you. Now I love you for your courage, your honesty and... your faithfulness to my husband."

Jacob laughed. "Would you consider it unfaithful of me if I told you I have dreamed of loving you?" he said. "Is that a sin?"

"In the eyes of your God it is. However, I do not believe dreams are sinful. It would only be a sin if you force your dreams upon me," Zipporah whispered shyly. "I too will confess that when I was separated from Moses, I dreamed of you."

Jacob's face brightened. "You honor me with your truthfulness."

"Let us speak of this no longer," she pleaded. "Let faithfulness be the cornerstone of our love for each other." Zipporah watched as he stood up and extended his hand to her. When he pulled her to her feet, she knew he was resisting the urge to kiss her. She saw the joy in his eyes when she rose on tiptoes and kissed his cheek, then held his arm as they walked across the meadow to where the horses grazed.

CHAPTER 28

And Moses made a serpent of brass and put it upon a pole, and it came to pass, that if a serpent had bitten any man, when he looked upon it, he lived.

Numbers 21:9

Jacob sat at Jethro's table waiting patiently as the family celebrated Zipporah's surprise return. His eardrums still rang from her sister's piercing screams of greeting. The husbands of Leah, Anah and Naomi were also seated at the evening meal.

For Zipporah, the marriage of Naomi came as a pleasant surprise. Everyone in the family feared no man would want her after learning she had been violated by Amalek and his men. When she had last seen Naomi, her sister had difficulty looking into the eyes of men. Her husband was a shepherd from a neighboring village. At Leah's wedding he took Naomi aside and confessed he had loved her since they played together as children. It took six persistent months to convince her he was sincere.

Jacob was impressed by how much Timna had grown. Although eight years younger than Zipporah, she had the same captivating eyes and natural smile. For three hours he listened to the giggling and whispering of the sisters. It ended when Zipporah turned to Jethro and pulled his sleeve.

"Father, Jacob has an urgent message for you. We should not keep him waiting."

"Your mother has made a special cake with dates," Jethro said proudly. "We will enjoy it with a cup of my best wine. Only after we have eaten will we go to my study for talks."

Jacob had to admit the cake and three cups of vintage wine were just what he needed to ease his tension. An hour passed before Jethro closed the evening with prayer and motioned for Jacob and Zipporah to follow him to his study. Jacob handed Jethro the scrolls after he lit a clay lamp. When Jethro finished reading the message, he reflected without speaking. Zipporah cleared her throat.

Jethro shook his head sadly. "I warned Moses that his people should rest with us before attempting to enter the land of Canaan. Why has God turned his back on the suffering of your people? What great sin have they committed?"

"The faith of our people was weak. Our God knew we were not ready to enter Canaan. He ordered us to return to the Red Sea," Jacob said quietly. "The chiefs turned against Moses and tried to conquer the promised land without him. Our army was defeated and driven back."

169

"Disobedience is a terrible sin," Jethro said. "Moses writes that God has now ordered your people into the wilderness to renew their faith. He wants to return to Midian so your people can recover from their defeat. Midian is not a wilderness."

"The chiefs are convinced we are too weak to enter the Sinai wilderness. We need time to regain our strength."

"Did not God deliver your people from Egypt? If they keep their faith, God will provide for them."

Jacob stared at Jethro, fearing his mission had failed. "At this moment Moses is leading a retreat through the mountains of the Amalekites. Many of our people are sick and dying. We beg you to plead our cause before the chiefs of Midian. Ask them not to turn their back on us as the Edomites did."

"Father, our people need help now," Zipporah said fervently. "Ask the chiefs to send a relief caravan to aid them and let them rest in our land. Every day we delay means more deaths. I fear not only for Moses' people but for my sons and all the children."

Jethro's face softened as he reached out and took Zipporah's hand. "It will be done, daughter. Go rest, for tomorrow we leave for Ezion-geber." Jethro turned to Jacob. "I will speak to the Chiefs and sub-chiefs of our Midian confederation and ask them to allow your people to rest in the valley of Horeb until they regain their strength. However, your leaders must understand that our lands cannot support your people and ours. The land of the Amalekites stretches throughout the Wilderness of Zin. It is there they must dwell until God calls them."

When Zipporah entered the tent where her sisters slept, she found Timna waiting for her. She handed Timna a rock shaped like a seashell. "I found this in the desert. It must be very old, for the shell has turned to stone." Zipporah said.

"Thank you. It's beautiful," Timna said, running her finger over its curved surface. "I have missed you so much. You are the only sister that I could share my secrets with."

"And what secrets do you want to share with me?"

"Well, last month I became a woman."

"That's wonderful. But surely our mother and sister know of this?"

"They do. But I'm scared of what will happen when I marry," Timna whispered. "I heard Anah and Leah talking about their wedding nights. Anah said it felt like her husband was splitting her open. And Leah said she bled for a long time. I don't want to be split open. I might bleed to death."

Zipporah smiled and patted her hand. "I will tell you a secret. On my wedding night, Moses was very gentle with me. First, he kissed my body in a special way and when he finally took me in his arms, it was not too painful.

Soon all our nights were filled with joy. I love feeling his organ inside me, and some day, after you meet the right man, you will too. But you must insist that the man you marry loves you with all his heart. Tell father you will never marry a man you do not love."

"I hate the stupid boys that live in the next valley. I would never marry any of them," Timna whispered. "You will never guess what I saw them doing?"

"What were they doing, little sister?" Zipporah asked, trying to look serious.

"While I was tending the sheep, I heard a noise coming from behind some bushes. That's when I saw some boys holding one of our ewes. Another was humping her from behind. It must have hurt the poor thing, the way she was crying. When I yelled for them to stop, the boy pulled out his organ and waved it at me. It was *huge*." Timna gestured with her hands.

"And what did you do then?" Zipporah said, remembering the black boy who had left his carpet.

"When he came running toward me, I hit him between his legs with my staff."

Zipporah laughed and hugged Timna. "You are truly my sister."

Moses halted the advance column of warriors before the approach to the narrow mountain pass. Joshua surveyed the menacing canyon walls that loomed above them. Once they entered the pass they would be again in the land of the Amalekites.

"The Amalekites may try to ambush us from those cliffs," Caleb said. "We will have no defense if they roll stones and cause an avalanche."

"It would take only a few hundred of our enemies to block this pass," Joshua said.

"Joshua, take a company of men to the mountain summit. Clear it of any Amalekites you may find there," Moses said.

"I will leave at once. However, I beg you not to enter the pass until dawn tomorrow."

"No. We cannot wait. One day's delay will greatly diminish our meager water supply."

Moses raised his arms, called for the horns to sound and signaled for the eight men carrying the Ark of the Covenant to follow him. Soon the multitude began moving slowly toward the entrance of the canyon. As the march proceeded, Eleazar reported to Moses that several hundred young men had deserted and remained in the land of Moab.

"I met King Balak's son when I first came to Midian. Prince Elam dined at Jethro's table. I will send a message to him requesting that they be sent back," Moses said.

"It's too late. King Balak has granted them sanctuary."

171

"At the time of the Lord's choosing, his punishment will fall on their heads."

"My son has remained in Moab to seek out and punish them. May it please our God."

It angered Moses that Eleazar had taken it upon himself to send Phinehas without consulting him. Zipporah had warned of his erratic behavior. He could only hope that Phinehas' actions would not cause strife between Israel and Moab. He had enough problems with the Edomites.

As the congregation made its way through the gorge, the sounds of thirsty sheep and goats echoed off the craggy mountain slopes with one continuous groan. Delays were frequent at points where the trail narrowed. Shepherds desperately searched for young lambs to protect them from being crushed by older sheep trying to squeeze through the gorge.

It was dark when Moses heard screams and shouting. He ordered his men to place the Ark in a safe location as he mounted his horse and rode through the panicky crowd.

"Serpents, thousands of poisonous serpents are raining down on us! It is a sign from God," women screamed. Moses' horse reared up when a viper bit its leg, throwing him to the ground. Several men killed the snake with their flaming torches. By daylight more than two thousand snakes had been killed but not before scores of persons had been bitten, resulting in more than sixty deaths.

Eleazar found Moses treating a cut on his knee. "It is clear this is the work of the Amalekites. They came in the night and released the snakes at the mouth of the narrow gorge," Eleazar said.

"However, the people are convinced that God is punishing them. Already some are turning back."

Groups of people milled about in clusters and began clamoring to return to Mount Hor. Moses collapsed against a rock and stared at the summit for some sign of Joshua. Beads of perspiration covered his face. "Go to a blacksmith and have him fashion a brass serpent and attach it to a rod," Moses said.

"A brass serpent? What will you do with it?" Eleazar asked with alarm. "You told the people not to make any graven images!"

"Are you questioning my authority?" Moses shouted. "Just do as I tell you."

Visibly shaken, Eleazar bowed and backed away. When he returned with the blacksmith at midday, he handed Moses the rod with the brass snake coiled on one end of it. Moses climbed on a rock and called those within hearing distance to gather around him. He looked down at the several thousand people who pressed to get closer. "The fiery serpents that have fallen from the sky are a punishment for your sins. The Lord has grown weary of your complaining. He is angry because many of your sons have deserted him for lesser gods. If you restore your faith and obey him, God will remove the serpents and cure you," Moses said, holding the rod above his head. "Here is the serpent that the Lord

172

ordered me to place before you. All who have been bitten and who touch this serpent, will be cured."

Moses held out the rod as men pushed and shoved to touch the brass object. He ordered them back, allowing women and children to touch it first. Eleazar and Reuben were amazed when those who touched it shouted that they were cured. Hours later, Moses collapsed in the shade of a boulder.

Caleb knelt before him. "Moses, look to the summit. Joshua has placed our standard above the encampment."

As the elders gathered around Moses, Reuben reported there were no additional deaths from serpent bites but a deadly fever spreading among the people had resulted in more than four hundred deaths. For the first time, the word *"plague"* was being whispered.

Three weeks later, the multitude emerged from the mountain into the valley of Elath. The sight of water and green fields caused a stampede as thirsty people and animals competed for places to drink at a stream. By the end of three weeks, two thousand men, women and children had died.

Moses sat beside a campfire totally exhausted. His knee was swollen and his body was extremely warm. Caleb ran to him shouting that riders were approaching. His heart raced when he saw Jacob and Zipporah riding at the head of a column of thirty men on horseback. Zipporah leaped from her horse and ran the short distance into his arms and kissed him. She leaned back and looked into his eyes.

"Are you sick?" She touched his forehead. "Your head is burning with fever."

"I'm just tired," Moses replied and turned to Jacob. "What word do you bring us?"

"The Midian chiefs have given us permission to pitch our tents in the valley of Horeb. We may remain for six months," Jacob said, staring at Moses. "You don't look well, my Lord."

"Do not be concerned for me," Moses said. He staggered then wiped the sweat from his face. "Help my people. They are dying." His eyes rolled back in his head as he collapsed to the ground. Zipporah screamed and knelt beside him, placing his head in her lap. "Is God punishing him again?" she cried.

"It's the fever," Jacob whispered.

"Jacob, we must move Moses to my father's house," Zipporah cried frantically. "Fathers' prayers will save him."

Over the protest of Reuben and the elders, Jacob made arrangements to carry out her request.

Eleazar took Reuben aside. "Do not protest too loudly. If he dies, our plan for the conquest of Midian can begin without interference."

CHAPTER 29

> Phinehas took a javelin and went after the man of Israel and into the tent, and thrust...the man of Israel and the woman (Cobzi) through the belly...so the plague was stayed from the children of Israel.
>
> Numbers 25:7-8

The stretcher bearers brought Moses into Jethro's temple and placed him on a cot in the study. Zipporah wiped her husband's face with damp cloths as Jacob and Jethro watched anxiously. For seven days Moses drifted in and out of a coma. She remained at his side caring for his every need, leaving only to bathe and relieve herself.

Though exhausted, Zipporah found comfort in Jethro's prayers. She knelt beside him.

"O Lord, who speaks to us, not from the peaks of mountains or from the depths of deep wells, but in the valleys of our own hearts, hear now my prayer," Jethro whispered. "Grant your servant, Moses, continued life so that he may lead his people, Israel. Let your mercy flow over the valley of Horeb and cleanse the people. Drive the gods of pestilence from our land."

She clenched her teeth, convinced that Moses' God was punishing him again. At that moment Moses opened his eyes.

"It is a miracle. Elohim has answered our prayers," Jethro shouted excitedly. Zipporah kissed Moses and gently restrained him when he tried to sit up.

"You must rest, my love. God has given you back to us," she said, stroking his face.

"Where am I?" Moses said hoarsely.

"Zipporah brought you home. You are in the House of the Lord," Jethro said, dragging his stool closer to Moses. "You must not concern yourself with earthly matters until you regain your strength."

"Jacob, give me a report," Moses said, gesturing for him to come closer. "How long have I been here? What is the situation among my people?"

Jacob glanced at Zipporah and shrugged his shoulders. "We have camped in the valley of Horeb, as you ordered. It has become a place of death."

Zipporah pushed Jacob aside and placed her hands to Moses' lips. "Listen to father. You must not concern yourself with such matters. Rest for the people's sake. For seven days you have been near death. You need more rest."

"Seven days?" Moses replied, bewildered by her words. "Where are my priest, Eleazar, and my senior elder, Reuben?"

"They have gone to the mountain of God to beg for mercy. The anger of God is great. His punishment has taken the lives of more than twenty-four thousand souls," Jacob said.

"Twenty-four thousand?" Moses whispered, overwhelmed by the magnitude of the disaster. His breathing became erratic as he slumped back on his pillow with only the whites of his eyes showing.

Zipporah screamed as Jacob tried to calm her. When Moses groaned she cried, "Why did you have to speak of this now? Can't you see he needs rest? Your words are killing him."

Jethro intervened and ordered Jacob from the room. "It is best that you leave us for now."

Zipporah feverishly kissed Moses' cheeks. "God, turn your anger upon me and spare my husband. I am the one who doubted you." She placed her head on Moses' chest, then felt his hand stroke her hair. Through blurred eyes she looked at his face that seemed to glow. A strange light was illuminating the room. Zipporah ran to the window. For the second time she saw the mysterious sight of pastel lights blanketing the sky. The delicate pink clouds were shaped like a reed fan that streamed upward from a single point on the horizon. The breath of a temperate breeze kissed her tortured face.

"Elohim," Zipporah whispered. She went back to Moses and dropped on her knees beside him. "Our God is with us."

When Cozbi entered the tent of Zimri, he removed his garment and motioned for her to come closer. When she hesitated, he pulled her to him and tried to kiss her.

"What has come over you?" Zimri asked, as Cozbi struggled to free herself.

"I left my father's house because I believed you loved me," she cried, wiping her mouth on her sleeve. "You promised to marry me, yet you refuse to set a date. Now we have returned to the land of my father. What will happen if he learns I am nothing but your concubine?"

"Concubine?" Zimri said scornfully. "You are not my concubine. If I desired one, she would be of my tribe. That is the law of our people."

"Then what am I to you?"

"My love slave," he said, laughing, and tightening his arms around her waist. "You should consider it an honor."

Cozbi wailed then raked her fingernails across his face, drawing blood. Zimri slapped her. "Listen to me. I am of the tribe of Simeon. I have been forbidden to marry outside my tribe."

"You knew that all along. You tricked me with your lies, telling me you loved me. When Zipporah learns of this, you will be punished."

"You have spoken to Moses' wife about us?" Zimri asked, his voice trembling with rage.

"Yes," Cozbi said, backing away. "And I'll do it again."

"So, I should have known it was you who spied on my father when he spoke to Aaron! You betrayed me. From this day forward I will keep you caged." Zimri ripped her gown from her body, wrestled her to his bed and pinned her underneath him.

"I hate you!" Cozbi cried. She spit in his face as he tried to kiss her.

Zimri struck her jaw with his fist, stunning her. She gasped as he penetrated her and satisfied himself. Suddenly, through her tears she saw a dark figure emerge from behind the curtain and move toward them with a javelin raised over his head. Cozbi tried to scream but no sound came from her paralyzed throat. She heard Zimri gasp, then a searing pain ripped through her belly as the javelin passed through both their bodies. The intruder stepped back and watched as Cozbi's body twitched beneath her dying lover.

"I have removed those who have offended you, my Lord," the assassin said as he surveyed the scene. "I pray that your anger will now be lifted from our people."

Eleazar led Reuben and Chief Nahshom to the stone altar on the Mountain of God. Reuben placed flowers at the base of the twisted stump that had sprouted new growth.

"The bush is waking with new life," Eleazar said triumphantly. "It was here Moses first saw the form of God. We will appeal to him to forgive our sins and remove the plague."

They saw a figure coming up the steep incline. He removed his cape and knelt before Eleazar.

"Phinehas, my son. What news have you brought us?" Eleazar asked.

"The deed has been done," Phinehas said without emotion.

"You are certain Zimri and the woman, Cozbi, have answered for their sins?"

Phinehas smiled as he showed Cozbi's severed ears to Eleazar. After removing the gold earrings, he tossed the ears at the base of the bush.

"And what of Zipporah's cousin, Rehob? The one who came among us dressed as a woman," Eleazar said.

"He and his Hebrew lover have been placed in a stockade and await your judgment. When they resisted arrest, I punished them," Phinehas said. Eleazar did not ask what punishment had been inflicted by his son. He had discovered a cruel streak in his nature when he was only eight. It was the year he had found him cutting out the heart of a live cat. Four years later he had molested a child, and Eleazar paid her poor widowed mother silver coins to remain silent.

"God will grant you the covenant of his peace," Eleazar said proudly. "The woman of Midian has been slain by the hands of Phinehas. Tomorrow I will pass judgment on Rehob, for he slept with a man of Israel. Both will be stoned for their sin. When word of our justice reaches the ears of the Chiefs of Midian, there will be a great outcry. Their protest will be our excuse for war."

Phinehas showed no emotion. After arresting Rehob and his partner, he had beaten and raped both of them. He had no fear of Rehob protesting, for it would be his word against that of a despised Midianite 'pervert.'

"I do not condone murder," Nahshom said with disgust. "Was Moses consulted before you instructed Phinehas to kill Cozbi and arrest a member of Jethro's family?"

"This was not murder, but the beginning of a holy war. Moses is sick and does not have the strength or the stomach to lead our people," Eleazar said angrily. "It is up to us to prepare the way of the Lord."

"This is not a time for weakness, Nahshom," Reuben said. "The hour is at hand for men of faith to take up the standard of our Lord. If you cannot see God's hand in all this, depart from us."

CHAPTER 30

If a man commits a sexual act with a man, both of them have committed an abomination; they will surely be put to death.

Leviticus 20:13

Joshua and Jacob rode at the head of a caravan traveling to Ezion-geber. The members of the camel team had been authorized by Reuben to purchase medical supplies and grain. They entered the city gate and headed down the narrow streets toward the marketplace. Jacob noticed that the people who crowded the bazaar stopped what they were doing and stared at them. Where were the friendly faces that had usually greeted them in the past? Their silence sent chills through him. When they entered the plaza, eight armed guards were waiting.

"What is happening here?" Joshua asked. "Why do the people seem hostile toward us?" The captain made no reply and motioned for Joshua and Jacob to dismount and follow him.

"Where are you taking us?"

"Chief Kaleb ordered us to bring you to the Palace of the Seven Chiefs," the captain said indignantly, jamming his staff into Joshua's back to hurry him along. Both men remained silent as they marched to the meeting hall. Seated at the table were the Midian chiefs, Kaleb and Zur. Chief Kaleb ordered them to kneel. They quickly obeyed.

"Why have you brought us here?" Joshua asked.

"Don't you know?" Chief Kaleb replied as he leaned forward, staring at him coldly.

"Has the plague spread beyond the valley of Horeb and now infected your people?" Jacob asked.

Chief Zur sprang to his feet and pounded the table with his fist. "I have received word that my daughter has been murdered. She left my home with that lying Simeonite," he shouted. "My spies tell me it was on the direct orders of Moses' priest, Eleazar. Surely Moses knew of this."

Jacob and Joshua glanced at each other, shocked beyond belief. "Moses has been seriously ill for eight days. Even now he is recovering at Jethro's house," Jacob said.

Chief Kaleb raised his hand. "You say Moses is at the house of Jethro? Who rules in his absences?"

"Reuben sits in Moses' chair," Joshua said. "He is our chief elder."

"Moses is recovering," Jacob said, fearing they would not be allowed to leave. "He will resume command soon, and when he does he will find and punish those guilty of this crime."

"Your warriors also carried off a citizen of Midian. His family was beaten when they resisted," Kaleb shouted, slamming his fist on the table.

"We know nothing of this," Joshua said, bewildered. "Who is the man?"

"He is Rehob, the nephew of our priest, Jethro. See to it that no harm comes to him," Kaleb said, pointing his finger at Joshua. "If he has broken any law, he will be judged by his own people, not yours. Have I made myself clear?" Joshua nodded, trying to maintain his calm. He knew there was only one reason Rehob would have been seized.

"The anger of our people is great," Zur said. "They are calling us to drive your people out of Midian. Your leaders have shown no gratitude for the generous hospitality we have extended to them. The Council of Midian Chiefs will meet within seven days. We will expect Moses to be present to explain why we should not drive your people into the wilderness. We have been told that your God ordered you to go there."

"Will we be permitted to buy grain and supplies for those who are sick?"

Chief Kaleb stroked his beard. "Yes, but be out of our capital before dark. I cannot guarantee your safety. I will see that the supplies are sent to your encampment. Now be gone."

Jacob and Joshua did not speak as they were escorted back to the marketplace by armed guards. At the plaza they were met with a barrage of eggs and spoiled vegetables.

"These are the men who killed the daughter of Chief Zur! Stone them," a merchant shouted. Jacob and Joshua ducked as stones flew in their direction, striking a guard. A camel panicked and ran into the crowd only to be pelted with paving stones and turned back. More guards arrived and drove the mob back with whips, allowing the members of the caravan to finally leave the plaza. Joshua shouted for the drivers to follow the guards. As Joshua guided them toward the city gate, hundreds of people shouted obscenities and threw objects from windows. Young boys with slings pelted the camels with stones.

"Leave our land, ungrateful infidels. Your god is a man of war," shouted one woman. A jar containing excrement smashed against the head of a camel driver, knocking him to the ground. Outside the city gate the guards made threatening gestures before allowing them to begin the return trip to the encampment.

"What madness has befallen us?" Jacob asked, wiping splattered melons from his garment. "Why were we not told of Cozbi's death and the arrest of Jethro's nephew?"

"I think it wise not to ask questions. We are soldiers. Ours is only to obey," Joshua said, seething with rage.

"But on whose orders? I can only hope we are not too late to save Rehob," Jacob said, fearing the worst.

Zipporah woke, having slept in a chair with her head resting on Moses' bed. She touched his forehead. "You are still warm but the high fever has passed," she said, smiling. "Soon you will be able to return to your chair of leadership."

"I should go now," Moses said, clearing his parched throat.

"I beg you. Please remain here until you have fully recovered." Zipporah placed a cup of water to his lips. He took a sip and placed the cup aside.

"I have been gone far too long," Moses said. "The hour grows critical for Israel."

"You cannot help your people if you are sick. Father has just received word that the plague has slowed. The anger of the Lord has cooled. Now eat this stew I have prepared for you."

"Your kindness will be measured by our God," Moses said, patting her hand. "What of our sons? Are they safe?"

"They are in the care of my sisters. Father has kept you in isolation, fearing the fever." Zipporah forced herself to smile. She found it unconscionable that God could destroy twenty-four thousand of his own people because they complained about the hardships imposed upon them. But of course, he is a vindictive God whose punishment extends to the second and third generation of those who oppose him.

The door of the study opened. Timna appeared looking fearful, and motioned for Zipporah to step outside.

"Eat and rest. I will return soon," Zipporah said. She tiptoed from the room and found Timna waiting outside the temple door. "Timna, what's the matter? Is a member of the family sick?"

"Something terrible has happened," Timna cried hysterically. "Rehob's family came to us this morning. They said Hebrew warriors slipped into their compound during the night and took Rehob and his companion away, but not before beating them savagely. When Rehob's brothers came to their aid, they were beaten. Our uncle, Eber, tried to fight them off but they broke his arm and knocked out his teeth. They burned Rehob's tent and all of his possessions."

"What treachery is this?" Zipporah screamed.

"That's not all. Cozbi, the daughter of Chief Zur, has been murdered. I fear the same will happen to our dear cousin."

Zipporah tried to stifle her cry. "Does father know of this?" she whispered.

"Yes. He is giving comfort to Rehob's family."

Zipporah tried to think clearly. She remembered Cozbi's prediction. "Quick, saddle two horses. We will ride to Moses' headquarters and demand the release of Rehob. I know this is the work of Reuben and Eleazar. They will do everything in their power to undermine Moses' leadership and cause strife between our peoples."

"Shouldn't we tell Moses what has happened?"

Zipporah hesitated as she paced back and forth. "No, not now. It could only make his illness worse. If he leaves his bed, the fever could return and kill him."

When Timna ran to the stalls, Zipporah rushed to her husband's bedside. She calmly leaned over him and kissed his cheek. "I will be gone until late afternoon." She took a cloth and washed his hands and face.

"Your hands are trembling."

"My hands rejoice that you are recovering."

He smiled, laid back and closed his eyes. She tiptoed out of the room and ran to the corral where she found Timna struggling to place a saddle on one of the horses. Zipporah calmed the horse by offering it a clump of grass. They mounted and rode toward the valley of Horeb.

At the command tent they deliberately brushed past the guards and found themselves standing before the Council of Elders and Chiefs. Jacob started toward her, but was restrained by Joshua.

When the guards blocked them from coming further, Reuben raised his hand and permitted Zipporah to approach.

"Do you bring us news of Moses?" Reuben asked arrogantly. "Has he died?"

"No, he is not dead. He grows stronger each day," Zipporah replied, trying to control her temper. "Last night your warriors came to our valley and took my cousin hostage. We demand to know what you have done with him."

"You demand?" Eleazar said. He rose to his feet and approached her. "But of course, you are a woman of Midian. You have no respect for your elders or the laws given to us by our God."

"You liar," Zipporah hissed. "What have you done with Rehob?" The elders and chiefs sprang to their feet in an uproar. How dare a woman speak in such a manner. Reuben raised his hand for order.

"Your cousin broke our laws. Is it not written by Moses' own hand that man shall not have carnal knowledge with man as he would with a woman? Did our God not decree that no prostitutes are permitted in Israel, neither men or women? Your cousin was a male prostitute," Eleazar said. "For this abomination we have tried both him and the Hebrew man he enticed to his bed. They were both found guilty."

"Lies, lies! What have you done with him?" Zipporah screamed.

"Have you not read the judgment written by your husband's own hand?" Eleazar said calmly. "It is said that you are well-versed in our laws. The punishment by stoning was carried out this morning."

Zipporah's piercing scream caused several elders to cover their ears. She dropped to her knees and pounded her fist on the ground. Timna tried to pull her to her feet. Zipporah slowly rose and pointed her finger in Eleazar's face. "I know you ordered Cozbi's murder. When my husband learns of this, you will be punished."

The elders rose to their feet and demanded she be removed. Eleazar raised his hands for order. "Zipporah, woman of Midian, it is written that men and women will not commit adultery. Cozbi and her lover sinned in the sight of God."

"Murderer!" she screamed, as Timna tried to restrain her. "You are judge and executioner! Cozbi's blood and that of Rehob will stain your filthy tongue forever."

Eleazar's ruddy face turned a darker red. He raised his staff and turned to the elders. "You have heard the words of this infidel," he shouted. "She is the reason our God turned his anger on us. Moses has been corrupted by her lies. This woman and her people worship the god, Baal-Peor."

"How can such filthy lies pour from your lips?" she said as guards restrained her. "My husband will learn of your treason. You do these things to make strife between our peoples."

"Jacob, remove these women from our sight before the wrath of God descends upon this place," Reuben shouted.

Jacob rushed to Zipporah. "Come with me," he pleaded, but Zipporah shook him off. Taking Timna's arm she hurried outside and did not notice Phinehas leering at her.

"You have made matters worse by coming here," Jacob said, following her.

"Just take me to the place where they stoned Rehob."

Jacob hesitated, then led them to a field where a group of men stood before an open pit. Zipporah and Timna pushed their way through the crowd. Below were the bloody bodies of two men tied to a picket fence; their faces shattered. Timna screamed hysterically as Zipporah restrained her from jumping into the pit. Curiosity seekers laughed as Zipporah tried to calm her.

"Zipporah, allow me to remove the body and have it wrapped for burial," Jacob said.

A man stepped forward and threw a stone into the unrecognizable face of Rehob. In a fit of rage, Zipporah whipped her knife from its sheath and lunged at him. Jacob grabbed her arm and wrenched the knife from her hand. Timna picked up a stone and struck the offender in the middle of his back as he retreated into the crowd.

It was dark when they neared Jethro's compound with Rehob's body strapped to a donkey. Zipporah remained silent until she saw the fires from the outdoor cooking pit in the distance.

"Why is your god punishing us?" she whispered. "What have we done to deserve this?"

"I confess I do not understand the acts of God," Jacob said. "I was taught to obey and never question."

"Obey? Never question?" Zipporah said bitterly. "Moses obeyed Yahweh and led your people to the land of Canaan. Your god abandoned all of us in that wilderness and thousands died of starvation, thirst and the unbearable heat. When they protested, he punished them with the plague. Thousands of innocent men, woman and children have died. How can you never question?"

"Zipporah, do you believe in our God, Yahweh? Do you believe He brought us out of the land of Egypt and walks with Moses?" Jacob said.

She saw fear in his eyes and knew her answer would have a lasting impact on their relationship, and could possibly endanger her own life. "Do you remember my father's prayer when Moses was near death?"

"Yes. He prayed that God would heal Moses and from that moment the fever began leaving him."

"He said, 'O God, who does not dwell on the peaks of mountains or in the depths of deep wells, but in the valley of our hearts, hear our prayers,'" Zipporah said, guiding her horse closer to him. "The true God of Abraham is merciful and compassionate. He joins in our singing and in our dancing. When we rejoice, He rejoices with us. When we weep, He weeps with us. Now He is weeping for our beautiful Rehob whose bones were crushed by orders of your father and his god."

Jacob stared at her as though he was seeing her for the first time. "Do you not fear God?"

"Moses calls his god a 'Man of War.' I fear all gods of war. Of all the seeds of Abraham, he chose only your people. My people and all others are expendable. I do not want my sons to grow up thinking they are privileged because they are among the chosen few. False pride will destroy them."

"Now I know why the elders fear you."

"But what is there to fear, Jacob?" Zipporah asked passionately. "The God I love speaks to me from the vineyard of my heart. His name is Justice, not Jealous. He does not murder his own. Elohim, the God of Abraham, loves all of his children equally, Hebrews, Midianites, Edomites, Moabiates, Ammonites and yes, even the children of Canaan."

"Speak no more, for I am a man of war. Your words confuse me."

"Listen to your heart's song. You just may hear him whispering to you."

Jacob spurred his horse and rode ahead of her for the remainder of the trip. When they reached the center of the compound they found Jethro and Rehob's families seated together. Jacob unloaded the body and placed it on the ground. The sisters gathered around the body and wept.

Ruth pulled Zipporah aside and whispered, "Moses is not here. Eleazar and Reuben took him away over our protest. When your father tried to stop them, Eleazar's son beat him," Ruth cried. Zipporah ran to Jethro, dropped to her knees and hugged him.

"The hour is late," Jethro whispered through swollen lips. His hands trembled as he ran his finger across Zipporah's tear-stained cheeks. "The shadow of death has fallen over our land. Our God, Elohim, has ordered us to leave our home and flee into the mountains."

CHAPTER 31

And the Lord spoke unto Moses, saying, Strike the Midianites and destroy them; for they annoy you with their complaints regarding Cozbi, the daughter of the prince of Midian who was slain in the days of the plague for Peor's sake

Numbers 25:16-18

Four stretcher-bearers brought Moses before the Council of Elders. The night before, Eleazar and twenty warriors had slipped into Jethro's compound and entered his study. After informing Moses that the Midianites were arming for war against Israel, he dressed and went with them. Moses was unaware that Phinehas had struck Jethro when he told them that his son-in-law was in no condition to be moved. Jethro and his family were forced to remain quiet and not interfere.

By the time Moses reached his headquarters, he was too weak to enter. When the guards placed him before the council members, they pressed forward to see if he was in any condition to resume the mantle of leadership. They cheered when he rose from the stretcher and motioned for Reuben to relinquish his chair. Reuben, dressed in the purple robe of authority, assisted Moses to his seat.

Perspiration beaded on Moses' face as he motioned for the members to be seated. Eleazar stood before him and bowed. "Our God has restored his blessing upon our people. The plague has been lifted," he said. "God is no longer angry because some among us secretly worshiped the pagan god, Baal-Peor."

"What has happened during my absence?" Moses asked.

"Chief Kaleb has called the Midian chiefs to a council of war. The Midianites are preparing to drive us from the land by the sword. Their wailing against us has angered our God."

Moses beckoned for Joshua. "Eleazar tells me you have spoken to Chief Kaleb. Why are the chiefs angry with us?"

"When we went to the capital for supplies, Chiefs Kaleb and Zur sent for us. They are angry over the slaying of Zur's daughter and the arrest of your father-in-law's nephew, Rehob. Chief Kaleb has ordered you to appear before the council."

Nahshon shouted, "It's a trick. They will kill you, then send their army against us. We must prepare for battle and strike first." The clamor for a preemptive strike erupted among the chiefs and elders. Moses slammed his staff on the table with such force that no one dared speak.

"Who ordered the slaying of the daughter of Zur?" Moses shouted, glaring at Eleazar. "What have you done with Jethro's nephew, Rehob?"

Eleazar rose and stared at Moses defiantly. "The orders came from God who spoke to us on his holy mountain. The stain of Cozbi and Rehob has been removed from the congregation."

"We had no choice but to carry out the orders of God," Reuben added. "Because we did as our Lord commanded, the plague was lifted. However, the purging must be completed. God demands it."

All eyes riveted on Moses. As he searched their faces, he clearly understood his authority was being challenged. "What do you mean?" he said, wiping the beads of sweat from his face.

"Twice you have felt the punishment of God because of your Midianite wife!" Reuben shouted, his eyes bulging. "She came before this Council and denounced our God for the judgment we carried out in his name. She is a thorn in the side of Israel. Sit no longer blind to the truth concerning this woman, Moses. She is a witch who has blinded you from the truth with her beauty. God has ordered us not to let witches live. You told us yourself."

Moses wiped his face, then motioned for Jacob to approach. "You have been my faithful friend. Speak of the accusations spoken by my priest and your father."

Jacob knew his position as second in command was at risk. "My lord, Moses, I can say truthfully that Zipporah has been a loving and faithful wife all the days she has been at your side." A chorus of angry murmuring rippled through the tent.

"But does she believe in our God?" Eleazar cried. Moses raised his hand for silence.

"Until now she accepted our God as her God," Jacob said. "After she saw the broken body of Rehob...she told me she believes the true God of Abraham is not a 'Man of war.'" Moses' ears rang from the explosive curses that erupted. Stunned, he sank in his chair while Reuben called for order.

"Moses, you have heard the words of Jacob," Eleazar shouted. "Is this not proof that she stands between you and our God?"

Reuben leaned over Moses, "God has ordered us to slay the Midianites, *all of them*. None are to be spared. The decision is now in your hands." Moses tried to think clearly, but the rapid beating of his heart made it difficult to concentrate.

"Which will you choose? The woman of Midian or your own people," Eleazar said. "The chiefs of Midian are preparing for war as we speak."

With his eyes closed, Moses tried in vain to block them all out. He thought of Zipporah, but the image of her faded when he remembered the experience at the burning bush. He muttered half aloud, "If they will not believe, take water from the river and pour it upon the dry land, and the water from the river will become blood upon the dry land."

Impatient, the chiefs and elders began chanting and pounding on the table, "War, war, war." As the refrain grew louder, Moses opened his eyes and lifted his head upward as though in a trance.

To the relief of the chiefs and elders, he finally stood and spoke in a voice that thundered beyond the confines of the tent. "Arm yourselves for war against Midian. Gather unto me one thousand men from each of the twelve tribes. Let the trumpets sound the call to battle. Use the element of surprise and strike at the heart of Ezion-geber. As our God has ordered, cleanse the land of all Midianites."

The elders and chiefs ratified his declaration of war in one thunderous roar. Reuben nudged Eleazar and whispered, "We've won."

"Not until Zipporah's head is placed upon a stake for our God to see," Eleazar whispered.

Moses raised his staff for order. "Go to your tribes and have them put on the armor of God. Joshua and Jacob will remain here with me."

After the chiefs and elders departed, Joshua sat beside Moses. "You must return to your bed and rest. If you don't, the fever will return."

"I am giving you the authority to carry out my orders. Jacob will assist you. Strike throughout Midian at dawn. After you have seized the capital of Ezion-geber, return for me."

"What of your wife and family?" Jacob asked quietly.

"I have blotted Zipporah from my mind forever. She has spoken against Israel and my God," Moses said dispassionately. "Go to Jethro's compound and carry out the order. Take care that no harm comes to my sons. If possible, do not allow the family of Jethro to suffer long. Let the Lord's punishment be swift."

Jacob searched Moses' feverish eyes. If Moses had fully recovered would he have ordered the destruction of Midian and the execution of Jethro's family? Would he have spared Zipporah?

After Moses retired to his tent, Joshua assigned two women to attend to his needs. Satisfied Moses was resting, he issued orders for the commanders of the twelve tribes to reassemble. When all had gathered, Joshua said, "Ours will be a two-pronged attack. I will lead the main force against Ezion-geber before dawn. Jacob will take a second force and clear out the smaller towns and villages. If possible, keep your men under control. Men in the heat of battle will want to take women before killing them."

After the chiefs left, Jacob remained. "The killing of women and children offends me," Jacob said, remembering the pleasant hours he spent with Zipporah and her sisters.

"Have you lost your stomach for battle?" Joshua asked. "Do not forget. We are the vanguard of a new world order ordained by God. His government will be

187

headed by priests from the tribe of Levi. Israel will be a light to the whole world. If you can't carry out my orders, I will relieve you of command."

Jacob sighed. "That will not be necessary."

Zipporah stood beside her sons and watched her family drive the flock toward the mountains. Soon their journey would take them past the place where she first met Moses. At the last moment, she decided not to leave, but to wait for Moses' return. Over the protest of her mother and sisters, she had told them her place was at her husband's side. Jethro feared for Zipporah's life, but he was proud and respected her decision.

As the evening shadows crept across the pastures, she took the children to Jethro's temple.

After lighting two lamps she knelt and prayed silently. This temple was the place where she had learned of many gods. Had the God she loved abandoned them? Was her God powerless to confront the terrible powers of the warrior god, Yahweh Sabaoth? The thought sent chills through her.

"When will father come for us?" Gershom asked, snuggling close to her.

"I'm sure he will come soon," Zipporah replied. But what if his illness worsened? If Reuben remained in Moses' chair, she had reason to fear for her life.

Jethro had left one of his scrolls on the altar. Zipporah unrolled it. She smiled and placed her arms around her sons.

"What are you reading, Mother?" Gershom asked.

She read the words slowly, "Fear not, for you are of more value to me than many sparrows."

CHAPTER 32

And Moses sent them to war, a thousand of every tribe, them and
Phinehas, the son of Eleazar... And they warred against the Midianites,
as the Lord commanded Moses; and they slew all the males.

Numbers 31:6-7

The morning sun was finger-length above the horizon when Jacob led his
warriors to the village of Dar. From the hillside, they saw shepherds moving
their flocks of sheep and goats across the lush meadow. At a nearby stream,
women washed their clothing and children waded in the water, laughing and
throwing flat stones across its smooth surface. Smoke from outdoor ovens hung
like a gray mist over the village of mud-brick structures with thatched roofs.

Before the march to the village, Jacob had instructed his men not to take any
prisoners. When several of his captains protested privately, he told them the
order had come from God. However, he suspected the decision was a political
one formulated by his father and Eleazar during Moses' illness.

As he watched the faces of his warriors, Jacob knew it was more than the
prospect of battle that excited them. When he gave the order, curdling war cries
sounded and his warriors stampeded toward the stream. Women turned from
their daily chores, shielded their eyes and focused on the horde descending upon
them. Screams shattered the morning calm as the women grabbed their children
and ran toward the village. Older women were the first to be overrun and hacked
to death.

By the time Jacob arrived, men were stripping the garments from the women
and girls. Clusters of men fought among themselves over first rights to their
screaming victims. He came to his senses when he saw a child snatched from its
mother's arms and tossed into the stream. Jacob shouted orders for the warrior to
release the mother who was crying hysterically. When the man ignored him, he
drew his sword. Only then did the warrior step back from her. Jacob stared at
her bruised body, avoiding her pleading eyes. The warriors grumbled as he knelt
beside her, pulled back her head and slit her throat.

"The Lord demands that his justice be swift," he shouted. Others refused to
follow his example. Upon entering the village they were met by young boys
armed only with slings. Jacob's horse reared up after being pelted with a barrage
of stones. The youths scattered and ran into the wheat field while the warriors
entered houses searching for women and articles of value. When shrill screams
sounded, Jacob was too overcome with emotion to interfere. When the lust of the

warriors had run it course, the slain victims were dragged to a ravine, covered with brush and burned. A deathly silence fell over the village

The setting sun glowed as red as the embers in the ravine. Several young warriors dropped to their knees and wept as others ridiculed them. The sight of butchered women and children had sickened them. Jacob frantically washed his hands in the stream, but could not remove the imagined stain.

"What are your orders?" the captain asked.

"I will take eight men to the compound of Jethro, the Priest of Midian. It is not far from here," Jacob said. "You will be in charge while I am gone. Send your men into the fields, hunt down and slay the men of this village, then round up the sheep and goats. Burn the houses then take the flocks to the encampment. I will expect you back by dawn tomorrow."

"I do not envy what is required of you. I was with you when Moses' father-in-law came to Mount Sinai with supplies for our journey."

"Speak no more of it," Jacob said, placing his hand on the captain's shoulder. "We are warriors in the service of the one true God." Why did the words seem to stick in his throat like a fish bone?

It was dark, but the position of the stars told Jacob it would soon be daybreak. His heart raced as he led his party of eight warriors into Jethro's compound. The prospect of having Zipporah's destiny in his hands intrigued and frightened him. He prayed she would not be there. Upon their arrival, he was relieved to find the tents had been dismantled and removed. After examining the ashes in the outdoor fire pit, he concluded Jethro and his family had departed the previous night. Jacob selected several men to search the storage sheds for food and any remaining tools that might be useful.

When two warriors entered the house of worship, they smelled the sweet aroma of incense. After lighting the clay lamp on the altar, they saw a woman huddled in the far corner with two children sleeping beside her. Her head and face were covered. The first warrior, a bearded man of forty, walked over and snatched the shawl from her face. He smiled when he saw his prize. "Do as we tell you and we will spare your children," he whispered.

"I am the wife of Moses, and these are our sons," Zipporah said, fearful that the children would wake.

With sudden swiftness, he clamped his hand over her mouth and ordered his companion to hold her legs. They dragged her scratching and kicking to the stone altar and placed her face down on its flat surface, her feet dangling off the floor. Surprised by the strength of her resistance, they struggled to keep her quiet.

Zipporah bit the hand that covered her mouth and screamed. Gershom woke and cried out, "Leave my mother alone." He ran to the older man and began pounding on his back, only to be slapped aside. Jacob burst through the door and pushed the men away from her, kicking the older man in the pit of his stomach. The other warriors, attracted by the noise, entered the hall. They gathered around Zipporah as she held her crying children.

"Leave this woman to me," Jacob shouted, removing the frightened children from her arms. "Take the children outside and see that no harm comes to them. They are the sons of Moses." Gershom and Eli screamed in protest as the men picked them up and left the temple. Zipporah fell to her knees and wept.

"After you finish, let us have some of that," the last warrior said before shutting the temple door.

Jacob shoved Zipporah into Jethro's study then locked the door. "Did they hurt you?"

"Yes, but you prevented them from raping me," she said, rubbing her arm.

"Where is your family?"

"They heard the call of our God and fled into the mountains."

"And why didn't you take your sons and go with them?"

"I am the wife of Moses. My place is by his side."

"Surely you know Moses no longer considers you his wife. Your words, spoken before the Council of Elders, condemned you."

"I spoke the truth and you know it. I went to save Rehob. The elders had no right to judge a citizen of Midian. If Moses has turned against me, it is because your father and Eleazar have tricked him."

Jacob glanced at the empty shelves where Jethro's scrolls had been stored. Only the writing table and cot remained. Zipporah went to the cot, removed a knife from under a pillow and placed it on the table.

"What do you intend to do with that?" he asked.

"If you plan to kill me, do it now," she said. "I ask only one question: Did your father order you to kill my family?"

"I will not lie. Moses issued the order to cleanse this land of all Midianites." The words choked in his throat. "I came here on his orders."

Zipporah collapsed on the cot. "Only a god of war could have ordered a husband to kill his own wife and family," she cried bitterly. "Can you prevent your men from raping me? They act like a pack of wild dogs."

Jacob's eyes teared when he sat beside her. "Zipporah, I could never allow anyone to abuse you," he whispered passionately. When he touched her hand, she rose from the cot and rushed to the table.

"Obey your God," she cried, taking the knife and tossing it to him. "Do it quickly. I beg you."

Jacob slapped the knife aside, causing it to spin as it slid across the floor. "You will never die by these hands," he whispered adamantly. "But allow me to love you just this once."

"You want to use me?" she asked, astonished. "What happened to that faithfulness that was the cornerstone of our love?"

"How can you speak of faithfulness when Moses sent me here to kill you?" he asked bluntly.

Zipporah began shivering. When he placed his arms around her waist, she shook her head and whispered, "I can't."

"Don't make me take you against your will. I cannot help myself," Jacob cried passionately.

She stared into his feverish eyes and did not resist when he kissed her. She turned her head when he tried to kiss her again. "If I give myself to you, will you spare the women and children of Midian?"

Jacob reflected momentarily. He knew if he honored her request it could mean his death. She moved distractedly toward the window, trying to compose herself. Unsure what to say, he followed and stood behind her. He saw her trembling as she lifted her flaxen garment over her head and tossed it aside. When she turned and faced him, he knew she was placing her trust in their love. He stood mesmerized when she knelt, loosened the straps of his trousers and removed his swollen organ. He restrained her by stepping back.

"That's all I thought you wanted," she said, wiping her tears.

"Surely you know better," Jacob said. After removing his clothing, he picked her up and placed her on the cot. When she placed her arms around his neck, he rejoiced. After looked into her eyes for a while, he kissed her lips then gently took the nipple of her breast into his mouth. Suddenly, he sat up and began coughing violently.

Frightened, Zipporah moved against the wall and covered herself as his coughing spasms grew worse. When he finally regained his breath, he sank to his knees with his back toward her. The only sound she heard was his heavy breathing. He rose slowly, walked to the corner of the room and picked up the knife. After making an incision in the palm of his hand, he took her garment and smeared his blood down the front of it.

"What is happening?" Zipporah whispered, mystified.

"One day you may know," he said, after clearing his throat. "I will take this garment and show it to my men as proof that you have been slain. After we leave, go find your family. I will take your sons to their father."

"Why are you doing this?"

"Don't you know by now?" he said earnestly. "I will not sacrifice you on the altar of my God and I am prepared to pay the price. No more women and children will be slain by my order or by these hands." He walked to the door and paused. "You are the only woman I have ever loved."

Zipporah sprang from the cot, ran into his arms and kissed his lips and face. "Tell my sons their mother will always love them." When he closed the door, she threw herself on the cot and buried her face in the pillow to stifle her cries.

CHAPTER 33

And the people of Israel took all the women of Midian captives, and their little ones, and took the spoil of all their cattle, and all their flocks, and all their goods. And they burnt all their cities wherein they dwelt...

Numbers 31:9-10

The triumphal march of the Hebrew army to Ezion-geber proved an emotional one for Moses. When his commanders showed him mounds containing the bodies of men, women and children, it sickened him. At the bluff overlooking the capital, he saw smoke billowing from the shells of burned out dwellings. The insufferable odor of death flowed up the·bluff, filling his nostrils. He cleared his throat and spat, but the stench remained.

Moses tried to blot out the memory of Zipporah. Were her ashes and those of her family in one of those mounds? Was God satisfied that he had carried out his command to exterminate the Midianites? He wished the hand of God had stayed the order and spared Jethro's family, as he had spared Abraham's son when dawn was young. "God, cleanse the thought from my mind," he whispered.

A scout arrived with a report from Jacob stating that all the villages and towns had been burned and the rich pasture-lands north of the capital were now cleansed. Moses issued orders for the Hebrews to move from their plague-infected camps and occupy the fertile plains of northern Midian.

Moses rode to the palace grounds and was relieved to see that his commanders had spared the building, inflicting only minimal damage. He found Joshua conferring with the chieftains in the main hall. The chiefs and elders rose and cheered when he entered. It was in this room that he first met the kings and chiefs of the four related nations.

Joshua bowed. "Welcome Moses. We are pleased to report that all resistance inside this city has ended."

Moses motioned for his council to take their seats. "Give your report."

"When we arrived at the walls of the city, our men surprised the guards and overtook them before they could give the alarm. By the time their warriors discovered us, our men were inside the city gates. The battle raged all night and well into the next day. We broke into the palace grounds and slew the chiefs of Midian. Of those slain were Evi, Rekem, Hur, and Reba. Their priest named Balaam was also slain."

"What of Chief Kaleb?"

"He and Zur escaped over the wall with some of their warriors. Our men followed them into the mountains but failed to overtake them."

"The land of Midian stretches the length of the gulf of Aqaba. If they link up with their southern tribes who live beyond the mountains, they may regroup and return."

"If they do, we will defeat them," Joshua said proudly. "Our God was with us during this battle."

"Is there word from Jacob regarding Jethro and his family?" Moses asked in a thick voice.

"Yes. When Jacob arrived at Jethro's compound, he found only Zipporah and your sons. She refused to leave with her family."

"What of Zipporah?" Moses asked, aware that all eyes were trained on him.

"Jacob reported she has answered to God," Joshua replied quietly. "Your sons are safe and being cared for."

"How much war booty have your men taken?" Eleazar asked.

Moses waved Eleazar away. "I am in no mood to hear of the spoils of war."

"We are now faced with a problem," Joshua said.

"What is it?" Moses asked.

"You issued orders that all Midianites be slain. Jacob and his battalion chiefs did not comply fully with your orders. They allowed thousands of women and children to escape. I captured many of them at a mountain pass."

"On whose authority did Jacob act?" Moses shouted, fearing the renewed wrath of God.

"Jacob issued the order by his own authority. He gave no reason. As for the Midian women and children, they are outside the city being held in the corrals where sheep were kept. What are your orders?"

"Have Jacob brought to me at once."

Eleazar smiled. He had no love for Jacob and saw this as an opportunity to eliminate another potential foe to his growing power and influence.

"Now that our army has conquered Midian, should we not also take possession of the land of Edom?" Eleazar said arrogantly. "King Zeeb should be punished for denying us passage to Midian."

"Are your ears deaf? Have you forgotten the words of God spoken to me? 'Meddle not with Edom; for I will not give you their land, no, not so much as a foot, because I gave Mount Seir unto Esau for a possession.' God does not want us to spill any more blood among those who are from the seed of Abraham. Let it be forever written in the sacred scrolls of our people."

Outside the city walls, several thousand Midianite women and children stood in overcrowded corrals peering through wooden fences. The cries of children, dehydrated by the blistering sun, went unheeded as guards stood watch over them. When Jacob arrived he became outraged at the conditions in the pens. He issued orders for guards to form assembly lines to some nearby wells. Soon clay jars of cool water passed through the fence into the waiting arms of the women. He had received word that one of his warriors had reported his decision not to kill women and children and was prepared to accept the consequences. He suspected it was the man he prevented from raping Zipporah.

Jacob caught sight of a tall young woman standing near the gate watching him. She remained still with her face covered. It was clear she did not want to attract the attention of the guards. When she slowly removed her shawl, Jacob's heart sank. He went to the fence and opened the gate.

"Zipporah, what are you doing here?" he whispered, his face pained. "Why didn't you go to the mountains as I told you?"

"I went searching for my family, only to find women and children hiding from your warriors. The women wept for their husbands and sons. The children were sick and dying for lack of food and water. I led them out of the mountains where we made contact with other refugees fleeing to southern Midian," she whispered. "When word came that you were sparing the women and children, I turned back and was taken prisoner with those you see here."

"Why?"

"Because I decided to share your fate."

"You precious fool. Don't you know what will happen if they find you here?" Jacob whispered tenderly as he glanced over his shoulder at the nearby guards.

"It does not matter to me now," Zipporah said, wearily. "You heard the voice of God and spared many of the women and children. Whatever happens, I want to be with you and share your fate."

"On that night in your father's temple your love boiled over and scalded my heart," Jacob said smiling.

"Is that why you turned your back without loving me?" she asked.

"I saw your compassion for your people and choked on my own deceit. Or maybe it was your God who placed his hand on my throat? Whatever it was, I could not take advantage of you."

Zipporah turned and covered her face when she saw Eleazar and Reuben standing outside the fence. Jacob placed his arms around her and escorted her to the gate.

"This woman is under my protective care," Jacob said. "Stand aside, father."

"Moses has commanded that you appear before him at once," Reuben shouted, enraged at the sight of them together. "Guards, remove that woman."

"Leave the whore to me," Eleazar hissed as he opened the gate and grabbed Zipporah's arm. Jacob slammed Eleazar against the fence and struck him in his face, knocking out several teeth. The guards quickly restrained Jacob and tied his hands.

"You will pay for this with your life," Eleazar screamed, wiping blood from his mouth. "Take this witch and place her in chains. Do not touch her for she is mine."

Jacob struggled to free himself, but could only watch helplessly as two guards dragged Zipporah through the arched city gate.

CHAPTER 34

And Moses was wroth with the officers of the host...And Moses said, "Why have you saved all the women alive? They caused the children of Israel,...to commit trespass against the Lord..., and there was a plague among the congregation...Now therefore kill every male child, and kill every woman who has known man by lying with him. But all girls and women who are virgins, save for yourselves."

Numbers 31:14-18

A heat wave, aggravated by the city's smoldering buildings, finally loosened its grip. Afternoon breezes flowed in from the gulf, but the stench of dead bodies still hung heavy over the area. Guards dragged Jacob in chains before the Council of Elders and Chiefs. He had been flogged twenty-five times for striking Eleazar. Despite the raw cuts across his back, he stood erect without a shred of fear. The members, meeting in the Hall of Chiefs, waited impatiently for Moses who was meditating in the palace garden. All rose when he entered the hall, took his seat at the council table and motioned for Jacob to approach.

"Jacob, you stand accused of not carrying out the orders of God," Moses said at the point of exhaustion. "Why did you countermand Joshua's order by sparing the Midian women and children?"

"It was not God's order I disobeyed. I defied orders issued by men sitting at your table, my lord," Jacob said. He turned and pointed at Reuben. "My father is among those who betrayed you and our God." Jacob's ears rang as elders and chiefs shouted demands that he be taken out and stoned.

"Let there be silence," Moses thundered, slamming his staff on the table. "Jacob stands accused of treason. I will judge him only after he has had a chance to defend himself."

Jacob lifted his head defiantly. "The elders and chiefs of the twelve tribes know of my devotion to God, and our people, Israel. Until this day I have never questioned any order given me. I have done God's will, even when I did not understand it." Jacob turned and faced the elders. "Our cousins, the Midianites, aided us in our hour of need. Moses' father-in-law taught us how to organize ourselves at Mount Sinai. He declared our God to be the universal God of heaven whom even the lesser gods worship. He spoke in this room before the kings of Edom, Moab and Ammon, pleading our cause. Where is justice when we steal the land of our cousins?" Jacob shouted, his voice quivering. "Where is mercy when we butcher and rape innocent women and children? Where is truth when our priest and elders place words in the mouth of our God to justify their blind ambitions?"

"Silence him!" Reuben shouted, frantically waving his arms. "This is no longer my son. See what witchcraft has done to him? At this very moment Zipporah has returned to spread her poisonous lies among us. She is now our prisoner."

Moses sprang to his feet, grabbed Jacob by the collar of his jacket and shook him. "Did you not tell Joshua that Zipporah died at your hands as I ordered?"

"I told Joshua that God has judged her," Jacob said calmly.

"What more evidence do you need? Jacob has betrayed you with his lies," Eleazar shouted as the chiefs rose to their feet demanding an end to the hearing.

Moses stared into Jacob's eyes and tried to restrain himself, knowing he could not let Zipporah live. He returned to his seat and slammed his staff on the table until order was restored. "No man will leave this hall until Jacob has finished speaking and judgment has been passed."

Jacob took a deep breath and said calmly, "When you ordered me to execute Jethro and his family, I went in haste to his compound. By the time we arrived, all had departed except Zipporah and your sons. After I placed the boys under the protective care of my men, I asked Zipporah why she did not flee with her family. She spoke of her devotion to you and her wish to remain at your side no matter what judgment might befall her. She stayed because she loves you." Jacob's voice rose passionately, "Just as Abraham prepared to sacrifice his son and God restrained him, I felt the hand of God on my throat restraining me."

Reuben pointed his staff at his son. "It was not the hand of God but the lips of Zipporah that restrained him," he shouted. "What did she offer you to spare the women and children of Midian?"

"She pleaded the cause of her people and would have sacrificed herself if necessary. What else would you expect from one so devoted to Midian and Israel," Jacob said, maintaining his calm.

"My sources tell me that Jacob and Zipporah are lovers," Eleazar screamed. "Both she and the Midianite woman, Cozbi, conspired against Israel and angered our God. The plague upon our heads was his punishment for allowing them to remain among us. Our people perished because of her."

"That is a lie and you know it," Jacob shouted, knowing he had nothing to lose. "You and your co-conspirators deliberately ordered the murder of Cozbi and had Rehob slain, knowing it would foment strife between Israel and Midian."

"Close your ears to his lies," Eleazar screamed, pounding his fist on the table. "He speaks treason against you and our God."

"You claimed God was vexed at Midian because their chiefs were outraged over these murders. Why shouldn't they be?" Jacob shouted, pointing his finger at Eleazar. "It was Phinehas who murdered the daughter of Chief Zur and you ordered it. One day these people will rise up and bring an unrelenting vengeance upon our heads."

In the melee that broke out, guards stepped back and allowed three of the chiefs to strike and kick Jacob, knocking him to the floor. Moses drove them back with his staff and ordered the attackers to leave the hall. The remaining chiefs and elders grumbled as they took their seats. Moses ordered Jacob to kneel, knowing he could show no sign of weakness at that critical hour.

"Jacob, you have spoken treason and have disobeyed the orders of God. Therefore, it is my judgment you be taken from this place and stoned," Moses said sadly. "The sentence will be carried out at dawn. Your head will be placed upon a stake outside the city gate for our God to see."

Shouts of approval echoed as guards dragged Jacob from the hall. Moses knew he could not allow himself to be swayed, even if Jacob had spoken the truth. It was all part of God's divine plan.

Reuben approached Moses and whispered, "What is your decision regarding the Midian women and children?"

Moses slumped in his seat and bowed his head. When he finally stood and faced the council, those nearest to him saw the agony on his haggard face.

"These are my instructions. Slay all male children and women who have had carnal knowledge of men. Spare those who are virgins and distribute them among the tribes along with the booty taken in war."

Jacob lay unconscious on the stone floor in a damp, narrow cell beneath the palace. Eleazar entered and instructed guards to throw water in his face to resuscitate him. When he opened his eyes, he saw Eleazar bending over him holding a torch. "At dawn you will be taken from this place and stoned. But not before you see Zipporah burned at the stake."

"What have you done with her?" Jacob whispered through swollen lips.

"You will know in time," Eleazar hissed. "I watched the clever way she gazed at men when Moses' back was turned. Admit you slept with her and betrayed your own people."

"Your words betray you, Eleazar," Jacob replied. "You hate her and all Midianites. It has made you sick."

"Not half as sick as she will be before this night is over." Eleazar rose and kicked Jacob in the pit of his stomach. He paused when he reached the gate. "I will return."

Jacob staggered to his feet and fumbled in the dark until he found a straw mat. His ears were ringing, but he thought he heard someone call his name.

"Who speaks?" he asked.

"Zipporah. I'm here in the cell next to you," she whispered.

200

His heart raced as he crawled to the wall and frantically ran his hands along the damp stones until he found a narrow window with bars. When he felt the tips of her fingers resting on the ledge, he held onto them as through they were precious stones.

"Did they hurt you?" he whispered. "Speak to me."

"The pounding in my head won't stop. Until I heard your voice I was sure they had thrown me into the circus pit."

Jacob massaged her fingers and listened to her labored breathing. He prayed for strength, knowing it was only a matter of time before Eleazar returned for her. The thought sickened him.

Moses ordered Joshua to bring in Hebrew women to cull out the Midian virgins. When Phinehas overheard the order, he leaked word that all married women and male children would be slain. Warriors rushed to the corral and broke through the barricades. Mothers screamed as their sons were snatched from their arms and slaughtered. After disposing of the old and sick, the women and girls were herded into abandoned buildings and stripped. The order of Moses was carried out when girls, twelve and younger, were sorted out and placed under protective care. Wild, shrieking screams excited the passions of men who gathered like clusters of jackals around their victims.

Joshua reported to Moses, "Our warriors act like wild animals in mating season. Nothing could be done to stop them. It is the madness that comes with war fever."

"All of your commanders could not put a stop to it?" Moses asked incredulously.

"I regret to report that most took choice women for themselves."

"And we wonder why God has forbidden this generation from entering the land promised us."

Moses retreated to a secluded room in the palace. When he opened the door to his sleeping chamber he heard muffled screams below his window. After drinking a cup of wine he fell into a troubled sleep. Turning restlessly, he dreamed he was walking along the beach at the Gulf of Aqaba. When he spotted Zipporah he called to her but she ran into the surf and swam away from him. Alarmed that she was out too far, he swam after her, repeatedly calling her name, but she kept swimming. He grew tired and could swim no further. Treading water, he watched as she disappeared beyond the horizon.

"Zipporah, why did you betray me?" Moses cried as he bolted from the bed.

When Joshua heard Moses' cries he ran into the room and found him standing beside the window holding a cloth over his mouth. The stench from burned flesh flowed through the open window.

201

"The elders and chiefs have assembled and are waiting to give their reports," Joshua said. Moses pulled himself up wearily and followed him to the council hall. All rose as he entered.

"Your orders have been carried out. Thirty-one thousand virgins were spared. All others have been put to the sword," Joshua announced.

Moses' hands shook uncontrollably as he lowered himself into his chair. "The lust of our warriors has stained the orders of God," he said.

"In the heat of battle men take their pleasure where they find it, knowing it may be their last," Reuben said, offering Moses a cup of wine.

Moses took the cup and threw it against the wall then turned and faced the chiefs. "Any man who has had carnal knowledge of a Midian woman must purify himself with water between the third and the seventh day. All gold, silver, brass and iron, taken from the dead must go through the fire to be cleansed. This is God's order of purification."

"The booty taken from this land is considerable," Joshua said.

"Give us your report."

"As of now we have rounded up seventy thousand oxen, six hundred-thousand sheep and sixty-thousand donkeys. In addition, there are vast quantities of gold, jewelry, bracelets, and necklaces taken from the dead," Joshua said, and held up a gold goblet. "How shall this booty be divided?"

"Take the sum of all the booty and divide it into two parts. Those who fought the battle are to receive one half. Distribute the rest among the twelve tribes. Warriors who took personal booty may keep most of it for themselves. Levy a two percent tribute unto God of all the prey taken. The tribute will be given to Eleazar and the Levites for the support of the temple."

"Does the tribute include the virgins?" Eleazar asked as the chiefs burst into raucous laughter.

"The order applies to all prey taken," Moses said, trying to control his rage. "Remember, you are the high priest of Israel. Never forget it."

"We face another problem," Joshua said. "Some at this table are whispering that we should remain in Midian, for the land is rich and good for sheep and cattle. They prefer to settle here and not in the wilderness of Zin as God has ordered. Will God be displeased if we remain here?"

"God has said this generation will not see the promised land." Moses replied. "In the fullness of time, our children will go forth and conquer Canaan. For now we will remain in Midian for God has delivered it into our hands." Cheers rang throughout the hall.

"There is another matter that only you can decide," Eleazar said. "You have ordered Jacob's execution. What is your judgment regarding your former wife?"

"There are no exceptions, only let her death be swift," Moses said without hesitation.

"It will be done as you ordered," Eleazar said. He whispered to a guard to summon Phinehas.

Zipporah leaned against the wall of the cell with her fingers extended through the narrow opening. The comfort of Jacob's touch eased the throbbing in her head, but the realization that death was only hours away terrified her.

"Although our earthly hours are few I must speak of what is happening to us," Jacob whispered.

"What more can be said? My husband condemned us to die."

"You are here only because the elders conspired against you. Their pride would not allow them to accept a woman of Midian as the wife of Moses."

"But Moses gave the final order. How could he do this to us?"

"He was deceived by men like my father who took advantage of his illness. He loved you as I now love you. May the angels of your better self find me in the afterlife."

"I once thought I could only love one man. You risked your life by sparing the women and children and you did not take advantage of me, even when I offered myself to you," Zipporah said, squeezing his fingers. "If we die, carry these words in your heart. I love you, Jacob."

The prison door clanged open, sending chills through Zipporah. At the sight of a flickering torch she backed against the wall. When she saw Eleazar peering through the iron bars, she clamped her hands over her mouth. Behind him stood Phinehas holding a torch.

"There is the woman who turned Moses against your grandfather," Eleazar said. "She is the reason God's wrath came down upon the heads of our people. Death at the stake is too good for her."

"Leave her alone. Punish me, but in the name of God let her die with dignity," Jacob shouted, testing his strength on the iron gate.

"To which of the gods do you pray, Jacob? Our God or the gods of Midian?" Eleazar replied sarcastically while unlocking the gate to Zipporah's cell.

Zipporah stood transfixed as Phinehas entered and unloosed his belt, allowing his loincloth to fall at his feet. She shivered when he came toward her flexing his muscular arms and torso. With sudden swiftness, he punched her face and grabbed the neck of her garment, ripping it.

"Stay away from me," she screamed, clutching the remains of the shredded cloth to her breast. She could taste the blood that gushed from her nose and mouth as his arms tightened around her waist like the coils of a python.

"Rehob pleased me the night before I stoned him," Phinehas whispered, saliva oozing from the corners of his lips. "Bow down and do likewise or I will cut out your tongue."

At the mention of Rehob, a blinding rage seized her. She broke his grip and clawed his face, leaving bloody scratches down his cheeks. "You will have to kill me first," Zipporah screamed. He seemed to revel in her resistance until she lifted her knee into his groin.

Phinehas grunted and backed away, massaging himself. With the vision in one eye blurred, he hesitated, then turned toward the cell door. "I will not kill you. If you do not obey me, I will cut out your lover's heart and eat it. The choice is yours."

Zipporah stared at his twisted face, making no reply. When he left her cell and opened Jacob's gate, she panicked, knowing that he was capable of committing such a heinous crime. Groans and choking sounds echoed through the narrow window. Where moments before she had determined to die before submitting to him, she now realized she had no choice if she wanted to prolong Jacob's life, if only for a short while.

"Leave him alone!" Zipporah screamed. "Come back." She dropped to her knees when she heard Jacob's cries of protest. In the brief moments that followed, she closed her eyes and muttered a prayer for deliverance. She could hear him now, breathing heavily.

"Look upon the rising of my god and worship him with your tongue," Phinehas demanded, his hands tightening around her head like a vice.

Zipporah's prayer ended abruptly, with her face pressed in the dark swamp of his underbrush. To maintain her sanity, she tried to visualize Jacob's face. The vision faded as fingers, like iron spikes, dug into her scalp. Images, like driftwood floating on a stream, passed before her eyes. The severed head of Amalek, the shattered and tortured faces of Rehob and Cozbi, all stared at her. Above her stood Phinehas holding a fish with a hook embedded in its throat, only she was the fish.

She gagged and retched in heaving motions, only to be pushed to the floor where her head rested in a pool of her own vomit.

"Didn't you like it?" Phinehas asked, stroking her hair. His face clouded when she refused to answer. "Now I will plant my seed so that you will bear my son in your afterlife." Her piercing scream convinced him that he had broken her defiant spirit forever.

Zipporah's fingers clawed at the stone floor while being dragged by her hair to a straw mat. Her hand became entangled in his discarded loincloth, striking a metal object which she instinctively seized. Sanity returned when she realized she was holding the handle of his knife. She calmed herself when he knelt between her legs and began licking her feet. Her silent rage boiled as the heat of his feverish tongue moved from her ankles up her legs. When he buried his face between her thighs, she gathered the locks of his hair in her hand, clamped her legs around his head and twisted, throwing him to one side.

Phinehas cursed and reached for her, only to discover the tip of his finger missing. He heard what sounded like a screeching bird of prey. Zipporah was now the hunter. When he slipped while backing away, she selected her target. He seemed oblivious to what had happened until she shoved his severed organ in his face. In shock, he opened his mouth but no sounds came from his lips. She watched as he crawled, frantically searching for his missing member.

Zipporah cleared her raw throat. "Is this what you are looking for?" She offered him his organ on the tip of the blade. A beastly howl echoed off the walls like the sound of a rabid wolf.

In the confusion, Eleazar raised the torch, unable to comprehend what was happening. Phinehas crawled toward him groaning hysterically. Eleazar threw the torch aside and helped him to his feet. With his arms locked around his son, he pulled him outside the prison door and slammed it shut.

Zipporah covered herself with the tattered remains of her garment and staggered to the narrow window. "Jacob, are you all right?" she cried, placing her fingers through the bars.

"Yes. Thank God you are still alive!" Jacob replied in disbelief. "What happened?"

"They're gone," Zipporah whispered, sliding the knife through the narrow opening.

"It is a miracle," Jacob cried. "I heard your sacrifice. How will I ever repay you?"

"You already have," she said, tightening her grip on his bruised fingers.

The gray haze of dawn lit Jacob's cell. He tensed when he heard footsteps echoing in the prison hall. He placed the knife to his side and waited. "Take courage, my love," Jacob whispered. "If we die, we will surely find each other in the afterlife."

Zipporah stepped through the pool of slippery blood and knelt in the corner with her eyes closed. She heard the gate to Jacob's cell opening, and covered her ears to shut out the sound of voices. She did not hear her cell door open and flinched when a hand touched her shoulder. She opened her eyes and saw Jacob's smiling face. Joshua was standing beside him holding a torch. After Joshua removed his cloak and covered her, Jacob gathered her in his arms and followed him outside the prison cell, down a long corridor and into the deserted streets. The stench of burned bodies still lingered as Joshua led them through the city gate to a secluded place where horses were hitched to a post.

"You are free to go," Joshua said.

"On whose orders?" Zipporah asked.

Joshua turned to Zipporah. "You are free on orders from the one man who will always love you."

"It would be far better if I had died," Zipporah replied bitterly.

"Why did Moses free us?" Jacob asked.

"When Eleazar came to Moses last night, his face was gray as ash. So great was his fear he fell to his knees and confessed that only God could have given Zipporah the power to overcome the strength of Phinehas. He begged Moses to forgive him for having wronged both of you," Joshua said, turning to Zipporah. "As for Phinehas, he will never be allowed to enter the Tabernacle again. You saw to that."

"What of my sons?" Zipporah asked.

"You and Jacob are free to go but your sons will remain with Moses."

Zipporah wept as she removed the lapis-eyed cobra ring from her finger and handed it to Joshua. "At the Gulf of Aqaba, Moses pledged his love and told me nothing would ever separate us," she said raspily. "Tell him I have not forgotten the confession that all spirits make to the gods in the Great Hall of Double Right and Truth. Say to him that the channels of running water have been broken; our cattle have been driven from their pastures; our orchards has been plundered; the men of Midian slain and our women raped, murdered and our young girls enslaved. Tell him the Gates of Sert have been broken and the stars of heaven have all burned out. When he meets the God of our ancestor, Abraham, I pray he will make his confession with a repentant heart."

Joshua and Jacob helped her mount the horse. With Jacob beside her, they galloped toward the eastern shore of the Gulf of Aqaba. Moses stepped out of the shadows and stood beside Joshua. Both men watched through blurred eyes as the last cloud of dust faded into the reddish mist of morning.

CHAPTER 35

"My God, my God, why hast thou forsaken me?"

Psalm 22:1

"...I, even I am the Lord; and beside me there is no savior."

Isaiah 43:11

Zipporah sat on a bluff located near the entrance of a mountain cave. From her vantage point she could see where the Gulf of Aqaba emptied into the Red Sea. She waved when she saw Jacob walking up the trail from the valley below. He sat beside her and, together, they watched as the evening sun sprinkled the bosom of the gulf waters with shimmering golden lights. In the valley were palm-dotted villages and verdant rows of crops tended by Midianite women and children. On every hillside, warriors stood guard over them. These were the Midian refugees who had escaped into the mountains to avoid the massacre. Four seasons had passed since Jethro and his family discovered the cave above the valley concealed by scrub bushes. It was dry, the perfect place to store his sacred scrolls.

Zipporah took Jacob's hand and kissed it. "I'm glad you've come. My father grows weaker and I fear his time on this earth is not long. He bids us come to him."

"I'm sorry I'm late. One of your father's sheep wandered from the flock."

"I'm certain it was one of Ga's children," Zipporah said, taking his hand. "Let us go to Father."

Jacob hesitated. "Do you think your family wants me to be present at such a time? Your sisters' husbands have been obliging, but I fear they have not forgiven me for my part in the war."

"I can only speak for father. He has never judged you. He treats you like a son," Zipporah said. She stiffened when he kissed her lips. "Be patient with me a little longer."

"I have been a shepherd to your father's flock this past year. Is there hope for us? Will the long shadow of that terrible night forever dim the light of your eyes?"

Zipporah placed her hand to his cheek. "I need more time. Until Phinehas attacked me, I never fully understood Naomi's pain. There are nights I wake up screaming," Zipporah whispered. "I so desperately want to return your love. But I would die slowly if I could not love you with all of the passion that is imprisoned within me."

"Trust me to blot out the memory of Phinehas."

"I do trust you, and it is not Phinehas that frightens me now."

"Then what stands between us?"

"To be honest, I'm afraid of losing you." She took his hand and held it tightly. "Your god turned my gentle husband into a murderer of innocent women and children, making a mockery of the commandment that we 'shall not kill one another.' What might he do to us if we marry? There is no way we can escape his wrath, even here in exile." In the stillness that followed, the wind ceased blowing and birds remained silent momentarily. He had taken her back into her memories, a dark place she wanted to avoid. She wondered if she would be forever lost in the void of that dreadful night.

Jacob placed his hand under her chin and turned her face to his. "Do you recall what I told you when we were held captive? My father and Eleazar tricked Moses and defamed the name of God. We do not have to fear the wrath of the God of Abraham, only men like my father."

"I no longer know what to believe or how to overcome my fear," she replied, her eyes filling with tears. "I weep when I remember Moses and my children. And I so miss Miriam."

"Your father has taught me that our God is not to be feared," Jacob said, placing his arms around her. "But I must ask one question that still haunts me. Do you still love Moses?"

Zipporah hesitated and squeezed his hand. "I love the memory of the man I married, the gentle husband who would risk his life, even for a lamb. But he was made a god unto Pharaoh, and from that moment he became a stranger to me. I have lost my faith and with it the courage to love."

Exasperated, Jacob stood, pulled Zipporah to her feet and stared into her eyes. "Listen to me, Zipporah. Among the many reasons I love you are your courage and fighting spirit. At that leper camp I saw you and Miriam care for the dying and feed the hungry. You taught me to be more than tolerant toward those who were different from us. You must not allow the horrors of that night to destroy the faith that has made you the incredible woman you are."

"But where was God that terrible night, and all those nights of destruction?" Zipporah asked, turning aside and looking out to the valley. "Why did He forsake us?"

"God is the fountain from which love flows," Jacob said fervently, placing his callused hands over hers. "He spoke to Jethro saying, 'You are my witnesses, and my servants whom I have chosen. I am the Lord, and beside me there is no savior.'"

"I don't understand," Zipporah said, puzzled. "If God is love, where is His power?"

"His power rests in the hearts of those who love Him and strive for justice and peace."

"If that is true, how do we protect ourselves from the fountains of lesser gods who flood the hearts of men with greed and hate?" she cried.

Jacob drew her hand to his chest. "Our love will be a shield against that hate. Trust these hands to lift that stone of pain that is breaking your spirit."

Zipporah softened, placed his hands to her lips and kissed them. "I love these hands," she whispered, locking her arms in his and resting her head on his shoulder. "The hour grows late. Let us go to father."

At the entrance of the cave, Ruth guided them to the place where Jethro lay. The six daughters, their husbands and seven grandchildren, encircled him. Clay lamps lit the area with soft flickering lights.

Zipporah fought back her tears at the sight of Jethro's weary face. It pained her to see him taking short breaths, knowing he was preparing for his final journey. She recalled the night Miriam died and could not contain her tears.

Jethro gestured for Zipporah and Jacob to stand on each side of his bed. He clasped their hands simultaneously. His bony fingers felt cold and clammy to the touch.

"Zipporah, Elohim has spoken to me this night," he whispered, his voice strained.

"What did our God say, Father?" she asked, massaging his hand.

"That you should walk beside the waters of Aqaba and meditate."

"I have listened but I heard no sound. There are only echoes in the chambers in my heart."

"That is because you are allowing your heart to drown in sorrow," Jethro whispered.

"I called to him from that pit but no voice answered me. Why did God forsake us?" Zipporah cried. She felt Jethro's hand quivering as his fingers began to warm. When they became feverishly hot, she felt panicky and tried to snatch her hand away, but could not break his grip. She glanced at Jacob. From his expression she knew he felt the same mysterious heat, only now it flowed, like an energy force, up her arm and through her body. When she looked into Jethro's eyes, she became mesmerized. He raised their hands and clasped them together, causing a spark that startled them.

"Go to Jacob, my child," Jethro said, his voice now strong and vibrant. "God's love shines through his eyes."

Zipporah recalled Jacob's words and suddenly realized what was happening. With her heart racing, she moved around the foot of the bed into his arms. She laughed joyously and kissed him when she saw the light in his eyes. Naomi left her husband's side and joined in their embrace. Zipporah knelt beside Jethro. "Thank you, Father," she whispered.

"Thank God, Zipporah." Jethro motioned for Jacob to lean closer. "Listen carefully my son. I see a vision," he said haltingly.

"Speak of your vision, Father," Jacob said.

"From the snow-capped mountain of God, seven streams flow into the valley and are joined to become a mighty river. It is the river of justice and mercy," Jethro whispered, pausing to catch his breath. "In my vision I saw it watering the dry places and making them bloom. One day a temple will stand on foundation stones of righteousness, and the children of Israel and Midian will sit at the table as equals. And peace, resting on the bedrock of compassion, will flower throughout the land. It will be called a 'House of Prayer for all peoples,' for God said to me, *'All Souls are Mine.'*"

"Your vision will be mine," Jacob said. Zipporah snuggled closer and squeezed his arm.

Jethro lifted his arms and motioned for his family to gather closer. "Come, my children and receive my blessing," he said, clearing his parched throat. When all had gathered closer he whispered, "Elohim, God of our father, Abraham. God of our mothers, Katurah and Sarah, hear our prayers. You have returned our daughter from the valley of death. You have sent us a son to replace the one lost to us. Bless these your children and make them fruitful. In this holy mountain I have placed your sacred scrolls for safe keeping. May future generations recover what is hidden here so that one day all peoples may know that you are the fountain from which the living waters of love flow eternally. Let there be-," Jethro gasped and took one final breath. As the sisters began wailing, Zipporah closed Jethro's eyes and kissed his forehead.

Jacob whispered, "Let there be peace with justice and mutual respect among all peoples and nations, Shalom."

Moses and Joshua stood at the summit of Mount Nebo and looked down on the plains of Moab. To the north they saw mountains that lay inside the border of Canaan. Joshua heard a weariness in Moses' voice when he asked, "Have the elders and chiefs assembled for the council meeting?"

"Yes, they await your final message," Joshua replied as he stared at Moses, his eyes questioning. "You look tired. Did you rest last night?"

Moses straightened his tired back and rubbed his eyes to shake off the effects of a sleepless night. "Forty years have passed and there has not been a night that I have not pleaded the cause of Israel. All who left Egypt with me have died, except you, Caleb and myself. God has ordered me to Mount Nebo so I could look over and see the promised land, but I will not be allowed to enter it with you. I have accepted his final judgment."

"Why has our God forbidden you to enter with us?"

"I have fallen short of his glory," Moses said. Thoughts of Zipporah burned in his brain like smoldering coals. "I asked the Lord to let me set my feet on that good land beyond the Jordan river. He became angry and said not to speak of it again. He sent me here that I might see it. Here on Mount Nebo I will die and be buried. You have been chosen to lead this next generation of our people, Israel, across the Jordan into that land."

Moses went to a hollow rock where rainwater had collected during the night. He washed his face and hands, then sat beside Joshua as they shared a meal of goat milk, bread and wild honey. Joshua knew that the destruction of Midian and the loss of Zipporah still weighed heavily on Moses' heart, even after all these years. From the morning Jacob had ridden away with Zipporah, he had watched Moses age rapidly.

After their meal, they joined the elders and tribal chiefs at the encampment. Moses looked at the distant mountains of Canaan, then turned to the assembled leaders and cleared his throat.

"Hear, O Israel. The Lord our God is one Lord. Love the Lord with all your heart, and with all your soul and with all your might. Keep his commandments." Moses pointed his staff at the sky then toward the distant horizon. "Behold, the heavens and the earth that were created by God. Circumcise therefore the foreskin of your heart, and do not turn your backs to him. The Lord our God is the God of gods and Lord of lords, who is mighty and terrible. He protects the fatherless, the widow, and he loves the stranger by providing him food and clothing. Therefore love the stranger, for we were made strangers in the land of Egypt. Those of you who brought slaves out of Egypt, if they escape, do not force them to return. Let them live among you in whatever town they shall choose. As for the Moabites and Ammonites, they may never enter the sanctuary, even after the tenth generation. The reason for this law is that these nations did not welcome us with food and water when we came out of Egypt. However, do not look down on the Edomites and the Egyptians; for the Edomites are your brothers and you lived among the Egyptians for four centuries. The grandchildren of the Egyptians may enter the sanctuary of the Lord. Always remember our God who has done great and terrible things for us, which our eyes have seen. Soon I will die, but you will go forth and possess that good land. Meditate upon all the laws I have given you, and pass them on to your children. These laws are not mere words. They are your life!"

At the close of Moses' message, the chiefs and elders shook their heads with astonishment. Did not the Edomites threaten Israel during the retreat to Midian? Did not the Egyptians force them from the land of their birth? What of the thousands of Egyptians who loved the God of Abraham, and had fled from Egypt with them? Why would only their grandchildren be allowed in the sanctuary? Out of respect for Moses' advanced age, no one spoke against the laws contained in his final message.

After the leaders disbursed, Moses returned to the edge of the cliff and looked southward toward Midian where he was once a stranger. He recalled how Jethro had given him sanctuary and had come to his aid at Mount Sinai. He wept when he remembered the beach on the Gulf of Aqaba where he had taken Zipporah and loved her for the first time.

Epilogue

Take away from me the noise of your songs; for I will not hear the melody of your viols. But let justice run down as waters, and righteousness as a mighty stream.

Amos 5:23-24

For forty years the Hebrew tribes occupied the fertile plains of Midian, not the wilderness of the Sinai. Following the death of Moses, Joshua led the armies of Israel east to begin the conquest of Canaan. Despite the admonitions of Moses that God did not want Israel to make war against the related kingdoms of Edom, Moab, and Ammon, Joshua conquered these nations and used them as stepping stones for the invasion of Canaan.

Before and during the conquest of Canaan, the book of Joshua records, *"All the spoils of these cities and the cattle, the children of Israel took as prey unto themselves: but every man they smote with the edge of the sword, until they had destroyed them, neither left them to breathe."*

Following the departure of the Hebrews, the Midianites slowly returned from their mountain strongholds and reclaimed their land. Decades later their tribal chiefs, Zebeh and Zalmunna, joined forces with the Canaanites and Moabites. Their united forces extracted revenge by conquering Israel and holding its people captive for seven years. During this period, the Hebrews were forced to live in caves and were hunted like animals. The Midianites and their allies were finally defeated and driven back to their homelands under the leadership of the Hebrew commander, Gideon.

Author's Bio:

Thomas B. Hargrave Jr., is President Emeritus of the YMCA of Metropolitan Washington, having served 19 years as President and C.E.O. After 41 years of distinguished service with six YMCAs, he retired in 1992 and has devoted his energy to his twin passions, biblical research and writing historical novels. Tom Hargrave has received numerous awards for his work in civil rights and was recently elected to the YMCA Hall of Fame. His accomplishments were highlighted by the Honorable Eleanor Holmes Norton, D.C., in the May 6, 1992 issue of the Congressional Record. He is the author of *Private Differences-General Good: A History of the YMCA of Metropolitan Washington* and *Songs from the Stresses of Life*, a book of poetry. He was educated in the public schools of Knoxville Tennessee and graduated from Knoxville College in 1951. Hargrave currently lives in Silver Spring, Maryland with his wife, Meredith and youngest daughter, Anna. He is completing work on a second historical novel on the early life of Anthony Bowen, the former slave who established the first YMCA for African Americans in 1853.

Printed in the United States
818700002B

9 780759 653658